THE
REAL JAZZ
PEDAGOGY BOOK

HOW TO BUILD A
SUPERIOR
JAZZ ENSEMBLE

RAY SMITH

Acknowledgements

Much appreciation to those who have helped to make this book possible!

• Steve Lindeman for helping to create Finale examples

• Mark Watkins for helping to create and format Finale examples

• Kristen Bromley for help with Finale examples for guitar

• Jory Woodis for helping to create Illustrator examples and help with InDesign

• Jeff Johnson for help with working with InDesign

• Josh Bendoski for help with video recording in the public schools

• Jay Lawrence, Matt Larson, Denson Angulo, Corey Christiansen, Kurt Reeder, Ron Brough, and Kristen Bromley for help with rhythm section chapters

• All the band directors and students who allowed me to film them

• BYU College of Fine Arts and the School of Music

• Tina and Colleen at Outskirts Press

• And most of all to my beautiful wife, Debbie, for support, encouragement, and patience

Dr. Ray Smith is the educator's educator. He is a master pedagogue and is respected as such by all of his peers. When he does clinics for educators, they flock to find out what they can learn. This book represents teaching ideas from forty years of directing jazz bands. The proof is in the pudding as they say. Smith's big band, Synthesis, has toured the world (Switzerland, France, Germany, Italy, Belgium, The Netherlands, Japan, China, Brazil, Russia, Siberia, Finland, Sweden, Norway, Denmark, Lithuania, Latvia, Estonia, England, Scotland, Spain, and Portugal); performed at numerous jazz festivals (Montreux, Umbria, North Sea, San Sabastian, Loule, Birmingham, Wigam, Marlboro, Edinburgh, Kongsberg, Pori, Lionel Hampton, IAJE, and JEN Jazz Festivals) and accolades repeatedly (*Downbeat* Top University Jazz Band, *Downbeat* Outstanding Performance, 1st Place Pacific Coast Collegiate Jazz Festival, 1st Place Lionel Hampton Jazz Festival, Musicfest USA Finals, NAJE-Epcot Festival Winner, and more); and recorded numerous CDs (*Downtime, A Kenton Celebration, The Day After Yesterday, Flyin' High, High Road, Original Compositions, Live at Nauvoo: Most Requested Tunes, Time Flies, Time After Time, Eye of the Hurricane, Distinctly Definitive, Shapin' Up, Live at the Montreux Jazz Festival 1988, Live at the Montreux Jazz Festival 1996, Synthesis '86-'87*), and has performed as the Harry James Big Band on the Queen Elizabeth II from New York to London. In 2019, the big band will tour Cuba, Puerto Rico, and Dominican Republic.

Dr. Smith's teaching is informed by his world class performance skills, and his performing credits are equally impressive as his teaching credits. As a performer, Smith is equally at home in either classical or jazz-related styles and is adept at all five of the woodwind instruments: flute, oboe, clarinet, bassoon, and saxophone. He also performs and records on the Yamaha WX7 Midi Electronic Wind Instrument and the AKAI E.W.I. and often plays recorders, pennywhistles, and other ethnic flutes in the recording studio. He has well over 200 CD credits and has recorded on many film scores and television themes and jingles such as *The Sandlot, Mi Familia, The Swan Princess, Good Morning America, The Today Show, The Ricky Lake Show*, Buick, Chevy, etc., and many Canadian and German television and radio themes. Dr. Smith performs periodically with the Utah Symphony and The Mormon Tabernacle Choir and is a regular with the Utah Saxophone Quartet and Q'd Up, a jazz quintet, as well as the jazz saxophone quartet, FOUR.

Smith also does clinics and performances at colleges and high schools and adjudicates at jazz festivals. His pedagogical credentials stem from learning from the masters: David Baker, Dominic Spera, Jamey Aebersold, Jerry Coker, and George Ross. In the summers, he teaches at various jazz workshops including the Birch Creek Jazz Camp in Wisconsin where he received the Woody Herman Award for musical excellence and professionalism. In 1998, he was given the Voice of Jazz Award for the State of Utah; and in 2008, he was recognized by the International Association for Jazz Education as the first Utah Jazz Master, a lifetime achievement award "for profound contributions and virtuoso performance in the field of jazz in Utah."

Education:

D.M., Woodwinds Performance, Indiana University, 1982.

M.M., Woodwinds Performance, Indiana University, 1976.

B.M., Music Education, Brigham Young University, 1975.

Introduction

My dear fellow jazz band directors and jazz vocal directors (and fellow private instructors),

My great desire with this book is to share ideas that I have developed over the last forty years of trying to figure out how best to teach the wonders of jazz in both private teaching and ensemble development. I feel that I have been blessed with many insights and approaches that are effective and have enabled me to consistently turn out a superior jazz ensemble year after year as well as excellent private students over the years. If I could help you do the same, no matter where you are in your career, I would feel that this effort is a success.

The book outlines so many good ideas and gives philosophical backing, but the video examples will be a most valuable help as you watch me work with real students having real problems out in the trenches and hear the before and after effects of various teaching strategies or see and hear me demonstrate various concepts. To receive maximum benefit, the book and the video clips should be used together. The video examples available will be referred to in the book, but you will have to go to my Youtube Channel or my website to view them. I will try to keep the verbiage as brief as possible so you can spend the time with the video examples. I am going to address the book primarily to school jazz band directors, but the principles and ideas will have application for vocal jazz directors and for the private jazz teacher as well. Except for Appendix C, I am going to leave the private teachers to take from this book what they will, and focus on the ensemble program. Except for Appendix D, I will also leave vocal jazz teachers to take what they find useful, but I can say that the general principles all apply to vocal jazz equally well. Help for working with your vocal soloist is found in Chapter 23.

I should say that it is not my intention to create *the* comprehensive jazz pedagogy guide. Others have tried to do this, and you may want to refer to some of them. I am addressing common, recurring problems that stand in the way of creating a superior jazz ensemble. These are issues that I see and hear every time I do a clinic in a school or adjudicate at a jazz festival (or go to my own rehearsals for that matter). You may run across a problem that I have not addressed in this book; but if your program is normal, I think you will find great value in the things that *are* included here.

There are many other good ideas out there, but give these a chance, and I believe you will improve both your teaching and the quality of your ensemble performances.

With all best wishes,

Ray

Ray Smith, 2018
Provo, Utah

ACCESSING THE VIDEO EXAMPLES THAT ACCOMPANY THIS BOOK:

Youtube Channel: http://www.youtube.com/user/charlesrsmith7

Website: http://www.smithstudio10.com

Contents

Section 1 In the Beginning: Let There Be Jazz

Section 2 Dealing With Basics: It Don't Mean a Thing if it Ain't Got That Sound

Section 3 Dealing with Style: It Don't Mean a Thzing if it Don't Swing

Section 4 The Rhythm Section: It Don't Mean a Thing if it Ain't Got That Time Feel

Section 5 The Soloists: It Don't Mean a Thing if There Ain't No Jazz

Section 6 Thoughts on Administrative Issues: Gives Meaning to Everything Else

Section 7 Appendices: Don't Have These Removed!

Section 1

. . . In the Beginning:
Let There Be Jazz!

Let's Begin . . .

Chapter 1   The Jazz Band Director: The Job Description or "What About Bob?"

No pressure, but your jazz program and your ensemble will be completely what you make it—no more, no less. We can blame demographics— small town, lower income area, non-existent parental support, no band booster support, lack of a strong feeder program—but ultimately, it is the band director that makes it or breaks it. Some schools may have much more support from parents than others, and students may come from affluent circumstances where better instruments and private lessons are available to them. These can certainly help us and make our jobs easier, but we have all seen examples of these great support systems where the quality of the school ensemble does not reflect it. We have also seen underprivileged areas where great things were happening in spite of the circumstances. It is the band director that makes the difference.

I am painfully aware that your college education has not prepared you for the jazz responsibilities that came with your job. This is not your fault. It is really an indictment on higher education that in our music education programs we have still never come to grips with what happened in the 20th century; and now we are in the 21st, and nothing has changed. The greatest advancement in music in the 20th century was jazz, and it is America's biggest contribution to music; but we still have not even included it in our college education programs. When I ask music educators out in service in what ways their college degree failed to prepare them for what they are doing now, I typically get the same three responses: 1) jazz, 2) marching band scoring, and 3) musical instrument repair. In fairness to the colleges, it is quite problematic today to fit anything more into an already overfull curriculum, and if something is added, something else has to be dropped; but it is certainly not fair to you nor your students for this to go unresolved. I hope this book and the videos will be a partial remedy.

I do have two axes to grind with you, though. As mentioned, I am very sympathetic that you have not been trained in jazz-style rhythm and articulation, rhythm section playing, nor in improvisation. This is a whole skill set and body of knowledge that is completely left to chance. I feel a lot of understanding for band directors who are out there trying to make it without these tools. I do have a hard time understanding, however, why we aren't seeing more evidence of the things we do know and have been trained to do. We should be prepared to teach tone production on each of the instruments, to teach intonation, balance, and blend—basic playing and section skills. These things should have been part of your college training, and they are the same issues in the jazz band as they are in the concert band. ***Capitalize on your strengths***!

Second, it is not necessary to remain in ignorance. Those who are conscientious can do a lot to overcome deficiencies over time. I am reminded of three true stories that illustrate this point. Many years ago now, my colleague, Dr. Don Peterson was teaching at American Fork High School in Utah. One morning he had a guest clinician come out to work with his band. After the rehearsal, the clinician took Don to task for not knowing more about the clarinet high note fingerings and offering the students the correct information. (Don is a trumpet player.) Don took the scotch blessing to heart; and for the next few months took a weekly clarinet lesson from the clarinet professor at Brigham Young University. Soon he was playing clarinet in the 23rd Army National Guard Band in Salt Lake City, which he did for many years until he retired from the Guard. Small wonder that while still at American Fork High School, he was recognized as the outstanding young high school band director of the western United States by the American School Band Director's Association. Today, he is the Director of Bands at Brigham Young University, and his weaknesses have become strengths.

I became aware of this second story when I was judging some years ago at the Northern Arizona University Jazz Festival in Flagstaff, Arizona. One of the bands that played for adjudication that day was from Thunderbird High School in Phoenix. I was blown away by the band—strong style, good sound and power, good time and rhythmic feel, strong soloists. It was a tour de force performance, and the band was easily named the winning big band of the day. Backstage, I learned the underlying story from Jeff Tower, one of the other adjudicators. As we discussed the performance, Jeff said, "Well, you know about Bob, don't you?" I said, "No, what about Bob?" Jeff proceeded to tell me that Bob, a few years earlier, had taken over the program with little or no previous jazz training or experience. At his first jazz festival, Bob and his band received very low ratings and received hard-to-hear comments from the adjudicators. Fortunately, Bob was also a humble and very conscientious soul, and over the next years availed himself of every possible learning experience in jazz. He invited in clinicians to his school and watched carefully and took notes. He went to summer jazz camps and was teachable enough to put himself into the experience as a student, playing in the ensembles, sitting next to high school students. He went to other clinics and workshops and watched other directors. And here, about five years later, he brought the winning band, a truly superior ensemble, to the NAU Jazz Festival. Later, I had the privilege of meeting Bob at an IAJE Convention. It is hard to adequately express my respect and admiration for Bob and the approach he took to improving himself. ***Take the steps to strengthen your weaknesses!***

I became aware of a similar story when I watched Janis Stockhouse of Bloomington Indiana North High School receive the John LaPorta Jazz Educator of the Year Award at the Jazz Education Network Conference in 2015. Janis told her story as she accepted the award. I have since talked with her personally to verify some details. Janis graduated from Indiana University with a Music Education degree having had zero jazz eduction. She had wanted to take an improvisation class but it always seemed to conflict with the required methods courses (woodwind methods, string methods, brass methods, etc.). In her senior year, she signed up with trepidation for the jazz ensemble auditions to play trumpet. When a peer saw her name on the list, he told her she had no business auditioning since she hadn't even had a jazz improvisation class or any previous jazz experience. She was even more intimidated and removed her name from the list.

Her first teaching job was in a very small school that had no jazz group. But the students were very anxious to have a band and gradually prevailed with her. She started a little jazz band, and she and the kids had fun with it, but it didn't operate at a very high level. When she landed the job at Bloomington North, she was blown away the first day by how accelerated the students were in the jazz bands (they had two of them) and knew that she was in deep trouble. Knowing she needed help, she called Dominic Spera at Indiana University. He was kind and came to the school on two different occasions and worked with the band. She watched and learned. He also helped Janis with things she needed to know, sitting down with her and showing her how to articulate scales in jazz and the like. She later brought other clinicians into the school to help the rhythm section during the rehearsals.

The next summer, she went to the Shell Lake Jazz Camp in Wisconsin. The following two summers she attended the Jamey Aebersold Jazz Camp as a student and played in the ensembles (next to her own students). She bought lots of jazz CDs (*Kind of Blue* by Miles Davis was the first) and started going to a lot of jazz concerts (particularly those at the university by David Baker's band). She immersed herself in jazz and became a real jazz fan. She took the band to every jazz festival she could and encouraged the students to get private jazz lessons from the college students in the area. She just kept working at it and working at it, and things kept getting better and better. The band started winning at the festivals, and they performed at the conferences of the International Association for Jazz Education and the Jazz Education Network.

In the 90's, she was able to partner with a friend to write a book on women in jazz and thus got to do some interviews with some of the great women in jazz in New York City, which was also a helpful learning experience.

It was gratifying when she received the first David Baker Award from the Indianapolis Jazz Coalition. Later she was named a Jazz Hero by the Jazz Journalists Association. And then in 2015, the very prestigious John LaPorta Jazz Educator of the Year was awarded to her jointly by the Berklee College of Music and the Jazz Education Network. Somewhat ironically, she now teaches four class sessions each semester for the jazz pedagogy class at Indiana University sharing insights from someone who is out in service in a public school program.

When I asked Janis what she would pass on to music educators who are starting the same way she did, she felt the most important thing she could say is, "Buy jazz CDs and listen to them all the time." She also felt that attending the summer jazz camps as a player was huge in her development. This is something YOU can also do. ***Take the steps to strengthen your weaknesses!***

In my mind, there are four areas in which we must be able to teach effectively in order to create a truly superior ensemble. The ensemble that successfully deals with these areas is the ensemble that honestly deserves a I Rating at the festival.

There must be evidence that we are successfully teaching the basics of playing the instruments and of ensemble and section playing—tone production, intonation, balance, blend, dynamics, precision, and the like. (This is covered in Section 2 of this book.)

There must be evidence that we are successfully teaching style, especially swing style as the beginning point in jazz ensemble performance. We must be teaching the basics of time feel, rhythm, and articulation, and the like as they apply to the style of each chart. (This is covered in section 3 of this book.)

There must be evidence that we are successfully dealing with the rhythm section—individually and collectively. (This is covered in section 4 of this book.)

There must be evidence that we are successfully dealing with the soloists, or in other words, with improvisation in the performance. Improvisation is the lifeblood of the music. (This is covered in section 5 of this book)

In addition, we do have to be able to deal with the basic administrative responsibilities of running an ensemble program. This extends from set up issues, to choosing appropriate literature and programming, to microphone technique, to inspiring the students and helping them deal with stage fright. (This is covered in section 6 of this book.)

So, here we go!!

Section 2

Dealing with Basics:
It Don't Mean a Thing if it Ain't Got That Sound

So Let's Sound This Thing . . .

Chapter 2 Helping Horns with Tone Production

Tone production is the beginning of developing an ensemble, and we are dealing with this issue for the horn players only (trumpet, trombone, and saxophone) in this chapter. Teaching tone production is something your college workshop or techniques classes should have prepared you to do, but let's review a few basic points. Tone production can be broken down to embouchure, oral cavity, breath support, and set up (reed, mouthpiece, instrument, etc.). See Appendix B for help with gear. Let's also include, in this chapter, issues auxiliary to tone production such as vibrato.

As mentioned in the preliminary material, I am not trying to make this *the* definitive source on wind tone production, but there are a number principles and problems that are constantly coming to the front in jazz rehearsals that I need to address here.

The First Main Horn Problem: The Air

First, the day I really began to grow on my instrument was the day I realized that 90% or more of playing a wind instrument is the WIND!!--Too obvious for most of us to think about it. The first really big challenge in the wind section is to get the air flowing. It takes energy into the horn to get energy out of the horn. There is a principle of physics, within the laws of thermodynamics, which tells us we cannot get more energy out of a system than we put into it. It is a constant challenge to get younger students to exert themselves and provide adequate personal energy to their instruments. I call it playing with professional solidness and authority. Professional players put a lot of air (and energy) into their instruments.

So, I think the first thing to do about this is to get the students to take a full breath each time they breathe. This maximizes the natural body weight or natural force of exhalation behind the airstream, and provides more energy into the instrument. I use an analogy of pulling back a swing. When we pull a child back in a swing, we generally pull the swing way back so it can achieve a good (therefore fun) momentum. What happens if we pull the swing back about four inches and just let go? (Big thrills?) It is the same when inhaling; we need to pull the swing back all the way, not just a tiny bit. It is surprising how much this starts to get the air going. I often tell the students that their instrument eats air, and they are starving the poor thing to death. "Feed it some air!!" The band director has to become a cheerleader to keep the air moving in the band. The typical syndrome is for the band to achieve a big sound by the end of the rehearsal (that is, if they are working on it and the band director is cheerleading); but by the next day, the sound has deflated, and we have to start over. This may go on for a while from day to day until the students finally realize that they can go ahead and blow without having to be coaxed to do so. Even then, the cheerleading role is not over for the director.

The Second Big Horn Problem: Embouchure and Support

When we start to use the air properly, a certain burden is lifted from the embouchure; and we can open the teeth and open the throat and "let" the air do the job. This increases brass endurance and solves a lot of tone and intonation issues. These issues are even more complicated in the upper register of the instruments where the students are usually pinching and straining. This causes choked sounds and sharp pitches and takes a toll on the embouchure muscles. I try to get the students to get the hang of letting the air do more of the work so the embouchure can relax and do less. My usual demonstration (see video examples for this chapter) is of the untrained vocalist trying to sing high in their range—choked off and strained—versus the trained vocalist who looks like he is more open and singing lower as he sings higher. Of course, all of this presupposes that we are teaching the basics of breath support and embouchure. (See chapter videos for ideas that will really help with tone production.)

The Third Big Horn Problem: Percussiveness

Except for some ballad playing, we need to play very percussively (unlike the concert band and orchestra where we usually work for more smoothness). This generally means that we need to help the students with how to attack the notes. In jazz, we attack louder than we sustain in order to create a strong percussive character in our playing. I usually have to help young players learn to pull the swing back, let the pressure build up behind the tongue momentarily, and then release the tongue so they get the percussive attack.

The Fourth Big Horn Problem: Decay in all the Wrong Places

It is also a very big problem for young musicians to decay every note right after they attack it. It is a substantial challenge to get them to sustain the note with consistency and no decay, even at the college level. But once they start doing this, their playing is far more professional in phrasing, legato, and power. I have them just play a note and hold it. As they do, I point out to them the decay that is happening. Then I ask them to sustain the note without decay. This can take several attempts; but once they actually sustain the note, then I have them move to the next note (with no lapse in air or tone intensity). Soon I can get them to keep the air moving through the notes with much more constancy and smoothness. (See video demo.)

An Effective Tone Production Ensemble Exercise

I have a blowing exercise that helps with all of the above problems immensely. I will have the students play a brief ensemble section where everyone is playing the same thing together. Then I have them sing the pitches with some emphasis on singing them in tune. Third, I have them blow it with the air stream alone (no horn) but pitched--akin to whistling but just with the velocity of the air. If they are hyperventilating, then I give them a short rest to regain equilibrium. (If they are not hyperventilating, they are not doing it right, so I will have them repeat it with deeper breathing and more air moving.) Then I will have them blow it with the air stream again, but this time with much more air—pull the swing back, take deep breaths, and blow, trying to project the correct pitch to the front wall of the room. Then I have them repeat it with the horns immediately. It is always like a magic trick. Bigness of sound, intonation, and tone quality are all fantastically improved, and there is a concept now of how to breath and how to blow. (See the video demonstration of this!)

The First Big Saxophone Problem: Jazz Mouthpieces

The saxophone section has a couple of its own very common tone problems. First, the whole section should be using jazz mouthpieces. The jazz mouthpiece is more open and usually has a little different internal chamber than the classical mouthpiece. This is helpful when trying to achieve power to balance the brass section. When the section plays on classical mouthpieces, the sound will be small and usually buried under the brass. Perhaps it is even more problematic, when one or two in a saxophone section are using jazz mouthpieces (often because they are the ones studying privately), and the rest are using their classical mouthpieces. This makes balance and blend next to impossible in trying to achieve a section sound. (See Appendix B for gear help.)

The Second Big Saxophone Problem: Mouthpiece Pitches

Another major problem in saxophone tone production is playing too high in the pitch. I have tested the mouthpiece pitch of literally hundreds of young players. Most of the alto players are playing an A# or a B, some are playing a C, and a few a C#. The correct pitch at a forte level is a concert A for the alto. This means that the player needs to learn to configure his oral cavity and tongue position so he is blowing down into the center part of the pitch (like the brass players). At this point, the tone really opens up, and the intonation of the instrument is much truer because the mouthpiece can be pushed in to where the instrument octaves will line up much better. See Appendix E for a more thorough treatment of this topic and for exercises that will help the student achieve this. For tenor saxophone, the pitch is Concert G (F# is possible, also); for baritone saxophone, concert D, and for soprano saxophone, concert C. For doublers, the clarinet mouthpiece pitch is Concert C (which will require blowing up to the top of the pitch instead of down into the middle), and the bass clarinet mouthpiece pitch is concert G. (See video demonstrations.)

The Third Big Saxophone Problem: Subtone

Another saxophone problem is understanding subtone and when to use it. The older players used subtone a lot; mainstream players still tend to use subtone from about low G on down to the bottom of the horn. The most contemporary players rarely use subtone. Subtone is accomplished by pulling the jaw back and loosening slightly in the embouchure and then not overblowing. It spreads the sound and allows a certain amount of air to come into the tone. Sometimes the whole saxophone section will appropriately attempt to play subtone together (such as in a unison background passage), and often it is very effective in solo playing, especially in the ballad; but for general section playing, I steer the section away from using very much subtone. This is especially true for the second tenor player who is often written low in the subtone range but will be unable to balance the section if he plays subtone.

The Fourth Big Saxophone Problem: Laser Edged Tone

Another issue in creating blend in the saxophone section occurs when we have some students playing with a laser-edged tone because they are using a very high-baffle mouthpiece. (The baffle is a build up inside the chamber near the tip.) It is very difficult to blend these edgy tones in a section situation. I ask each of the players to warm up their sound and play with more body. This is done mostly in the oral cavity. It is far easier to blend warmer, less edgy sounds. This is even more necessary in the older, classic swing era sound.

A General Trombone Problem: Bore Sizes and Mouthpieces

The best blend and balance in a trombone section will be created when all of the tenor trombones use a small bore instrument such as the King 2B. Of course, the bass trombone will be using a much larger bore instrument. In a school, it is difficult to get this consistency with horns; and often the players will be using large orchestral bore sizes that make it difficult to get the necessary range and tighter focus in the sound. A mixture of bore sizes really makes it difficult to get a good section sound. Some schools have a set of small bore trombones to be checked out by the jazz band students.

It also helps if the all the players are using a jazz-type mouthpiece--especially the lead player who often needs to play quite high in his range. (See Appendix B for gear help for horns.)

A General Trumpet Problem: Horns and Especially Mouthpieces

The trumpets will also profit from having horns that are not a huge orchestral bore size. This is especially important for your lead and second players who will often be playing very high in range. However, with young players, it is not practical to have more than one instrument.

A bigger issue would be the mouthpieces. Jazz mouthpieces generally have smaller backbores and probably a little shallower cup that makes it easier to get a more focused sound and to play higher. Your lead trumpet player will be dying (and probably doing damage to himself) if he does not have the right equipment. (See Appendix B for good suggestions to help your players with equipment.)

Another General Ensemble Issue: Vibrato

Vibrato usage is another thing we must deal with in creating the ensemble sound. The majority of charts we will program for the ensemble will require very little vibrato. When we do use the vibrato, it will be only on a longer note value, usually the last note of the phrase, and then only near the end of the note. Some call it terminal vibrato—vibrato only on the termination of the note. The exception to this would be the old swing era sound where we may color with vibrato across more of the value of the note. The lead player has the prerogative to set the pace for how the vibrato will be used. In older tunes, the section will follow the lead on style and use of vibrato. Sometimes in more modern charts, only the lead will do vibrato.

It is imperative that there be no vibrato in unison playing. This rule fits all style periods. Use of vibrato in unison is heard as intonation problems.

Chapter 3   Helping Horns with Intonation

So much of intonation depends first on solid tone production. At a certain level, it is possible to separate tone and intonation, but at the higher level they are largely one and the same. In other words, by manipulating the system (tuning slide, mouthpiece), I may bring a note to the correct pitch without finding the correct tone; but normally I will find the correct tone and the correct pitch at one and the same moment. I call this being in tune and being in tone. By correct tone, I mean a tone that is centered and therefore vibrating at its optimal level. In physics (acoustics), this is called maximum resonance or natural frequency. Each note has an ideal speed where it physically wants to vibrate; and when our blowing (embouchure, air, and oral cavity) is aligned with the ideal, the tone is full, free, and solid. It feels like the note "locks" into its own slot. I can push it hard at this point without "popping" it or overblowing it.

I compare this to tuning in a radio station. (This analogy is beginning to be lost on the kids who have only had experience with a digital tuner, but I think you will still identify with this.) When we tune in a radio station, we have to get the dial in just the right spot for clear tone reception. If we are off just slightly either way, we introduce fuzz or static or other noise into the sound. Tone production is much this same way. We have to zero in each note. When we do, we will find a great tone (what I am calling the correct tone), and the pitch will be right at the same time (may have to be fine-tuned only slightly). I don't know that we can really make headway with intonation problems without working on it as a function of how we are blowing the instrument in the first place.

A great practical example of this is found in the saxophone section. If the players are blowing the wrong mouthpiece pitches, no amount of pulling or pushing the mouthpiece will solve all the pitch problems. In fact, it makes things worse to keep pulling out the mouthpiece to try to solve the problem of playing too high in the mouthpiece pitch. The low notes go flat, and the high notes are still sharp, and the relative pitch of one octave to another gets bizarre. Now multiply that by five as we try to tune the section. No wonder so many band directors are pulling their hair out when they try to work with the saxophone section for pitch. (Please see my article in Appendix E that was published in the NAJE Journal in 1987.) So what do we do?

Use the Band Warm Up

Warm up the band with tone and pitch issues in mind. Check mouthpiece pitches in the saxophone section daily. Have the band play unison scales and tune each note. I will have them play two or three notes up the scale, and stop them and ask them to sing the next pitch up. Can they pre-hear the correct pitch? We do it until they can. Or if one pitch is not getting quickly tuned, I will have them stop and sing that pitch until we can hear it in the right place. I do believe the key to fixing pitch issues is to help the students learn to pre-hear the correct pitches in their mind's ear. If they are fingering one pitch and hearing a different pitch in their heads, they will not center the tone or play the pitch in tune. Often, the section player is hearing the lead player's pitches instead of his own which will, of course, create tone/pitch problems.

The band can go from holding unison notes together to holding harmonies together. These chords can come from a section of one of the charts the band is rehearsing, or could be from chord warm up pages such as Greg Yasinitsky's tuning warm up sheets. (See Appendix F.) Tuning complex harmonies is a tall task for those who have tuned mostly triads in the past. So, it takes some help from the band director to understand how they should sound. Teach that the narrow intervals such as half and whole steps are typically too narrow and usually need to be spread a little more. The wider intervals are normally too wide and have to be contracted.

On the saxophone, notes above the break (middle D and up) are usually sharp and need to be blown down, while the notes below the break (C# and below) tend to be on the flat side. (This is exacerbated by the students playing too high in the mouthpiece pitch and then pulling the mouthpiece out too far in an attempt to fix the sharpness of the higher register.) On the trumpet, it is essential to be aware of how sharp the low C# and D are and that the third valve slide must be pushed out to help with the tuning. Every instrument has it's own idiosyncrasies.

When the chord is successfully tuned by the band, it will ring when the note is cut off. If there is no ring, the pitch for that note is not happening. When the chord is sustained in tune, it will have a clarity and sparkle. When the chord is not yet happening, it will have a certain "clutter" in the sound. After a while, the students will begin to catalog the tendencies of each note on their instrument and what they usually need to do if they are not locking in the note to the correct pitch.

Here is a parenthetical thought on teaching the concept of intonation. The old idea of having two persons sustain a note and then "get the beats out" is actually not a bad idea for first teaching the notion of what it means to play in tune. Unfortunately, it virtually has no practical application. We rarely have time to hold a note and then listen for beats and try to tune the beats out. (The rhythm section is on the next tune by now.) Rather, we must become proactive about tuning. Meaning, that we cannot just push buttons or move the slide and let the note go wherever it wants to go and then react to it—"Let's see. Is it sharp or flat? I think it is flat. (adjust) Oh, no! I guess it was sharp. Too late now!" No, this is not how it is done in the real world! We have to hear the note coming, pre-hear it just before we play it, and then simply place the note on that pitch in the first place. This is the only way we will ever have a fighting chance of playing in tune.

A Band Tuning Procedure

After some warm air has gone through the horns, then it would be appropriate to give the band a chance to tune to the tuning note. This is usually not very successful because the students don't really know what they are tuning to. They cannot hear the piano anymore after everyone starts to tune, so they figure they are tuning to each other; but that is like the blind tuning to the blind (or the deaf to the deaf—just kidding!). I teach them that they are tuning to the note they have internalized in their heads. So the first step is to hear the piano note (which I always have the pianist give in octaves--especially lower octaves--for more accurate hearing) and then sing it (so it becomes internalized).

Then when the band begins to tune, they should deliberately play a little flat to the pitch and then bring it up to the pitch that is in their heads. Why? Psychologists of music have shown by experiments that musicians and non-musicians alike prefer to hear sharpness to flatness. Given two pitches slightly out of tune, the higher pitch will always be selected as the correct pitch, even if the lower pitch is the correct one. If we start tuning sharp, we may never get all the way down to the correct pitch before we have decided we like it where it is (sharp). So I have the students start below so they can hear more accurately when they have actually arrived at the pitch of the pitch standard.

Then when they have arrived at the correct pitch, I ask them if they like the way they are blowing. If it feels like they are blowing too loose, then the pitch must be sharp because they are blowing in a way to bring the pitch down. If they feel too pinched, then they are trying to blow a flat pitch up. Then they can make the appropriate adjustment with the mouthpiece or tuning slide positions so they can blow where it is comfortable. (Of course, they would pull if sharp or push in if flat.) This will yield much better tuning results. (Refer to video examples for this chapter.)

Summary: 1) Sound the tuning note and sing it to internalize it.

2) Begin playing too flat and bring the pitch up to the tuning note.

3) Make the adjustments necessary with the tuning apparatus of the instrument.

Working on Tuning While Rehearsing

Most of the above strategies are happening in the first few minutes of rehearsal. As we go on into the rehearsal, we still need to keep worrying about intonation. Don't let out-of-tune unisons or out-of-tune chords go unchecked. For fixing unison problems, it usually works to sustain each note of the line together and tune to each other and find out where the problems are. If this is between two (or three) people, maybe lead alto and trumpet, I may give them a moment away from the band to solve their issues. If it involves more people, especially across sections, then I need to do it in the rehearsal.

If the problems are in harmonies and go across sections, I sometimes dissect the chord by having all the 5th players play their notes, then all the 4th players, then the 3rd, then the 2nd, and finally the lead players. Sometimes, it is useful to have the lead trumpet and the bass trombone player sustain their notes together (or lead alto and bari). It is often useful to have baritone saxophone and bass trombone (and sometimes the bass in the rhythm section) sustain and tune notes. It could be the two altos and the top two trumpets or the tenor trombones and tenor saxophones (and/or sometimes bari) that need to sustain notes.

When I have a full band chord that is not resolving itself quickly, I may have to build it from the bottom up. I will have the trombone section tune it, then the saxophone section. Then have the bones and saxes play it together. Then have the trumpet section tune it. Now start with the bones and saxes and then add the trumpets. Somehow, we have to become aware of where the problem is and what it sounds like and feels like when we get it.

It is very common for the lead trumpet player who is often playing high in his range to be sharp. I find myself often coaching the lead trumpet player about bringing his note down to pitch. This has yielded huge dividends in pitch for the whole ensemble. (It is important that the lead trumpet be playing on the air stream and not on his chops so much, as discussed in Chapter 2.) Of course, the same could be true of the lead alto or the lead trombone. If the low root people, baritone saxophone or bass trombone, are playing sharp, it causes serious repercussions as we go up the range through the band and can really cause trauma by the time it gets to the lead trumpet. I try to ride herd on the pitch from the bottom up.

Using the Tuner and Smart Music

Using the tuner as a tool can be a great help if it is used correctly. The tuner will not make anybody play in tune, but it can make us very aware of where our problems or tendencies are so we can deal with them more successfully. The first place the tuner is very helpful is at home in the individual practice session. I use birthdays and Christmas and the like to try to help students get a tuner (and metronome or mouthpiece or CD's or whatever). It is important that the tuner be used to strengthen ears (not eyeballs). When we stare at the tuner and try to get the needle to stay in the middle, we are making it an exercise for the eyes. If we work by listening to the note and then playing the instrument until we feel that we have a good tone and pitch for the note and then looking at the tuner, this can be a very good exercise for the ears. The tuner is used for confirmation (yes, I got it!) or for correction (man, I am still hearing that note too sharp!). But exercise the ears first!

The tuner can also be used while playing with a CD for confirmation or correction. First, calibrate the tuner to the tuning note on the CD; then put the CD in headphones so the tuner can only hear you. Or, use a tuning cable to the tuner so it still only hears you. I am talking about something like the Korg CM-100L Clip On Contact Microphone for tuners, which is particularly well conceived (about $10). This clip on contact mic is also wonderfully helpful in rehearsals (and even concerts) because it only hears the instrument that it is attached to. I let my lead trumpet player use mine during a rehearsal, and he became convinced that I was right—he was often too sharp. Life in the band has been better since then.

SmartMusic by Make Music (the makers of Finale) contains a phenomenally valuable tuner. (I think it is $40 a year for a subscription that includes the use of a huge accompaniment library with lots of tools including the metronome and the tuner.) The student clips a small mic on the bell, and the program hears the notes he is playing and plays them right back but exactly in tune. It is like a cow touching an electrified fence. Soon you don't go there (to that really out-of-tune "E" for example). It is one of the greatest awareness tools I have ever seen. Get your featured ballad soloist to spend a little time with this tool.

Thoughts on Dynamics Versus Intonation

Just a word about dynamics in the horn sections—every time we change volume, we also change pitch, unless we compensate for it properly. The bad news is that the effects of dynamic change are not uniform across the horns. The saxes get sharper when they get softer, and the brass get flatter when they get softer. The saxes will naturally get flatter as they crescendo, and the brass will naturally get sharper as they crescendo. Of course, we do not want this to happen, but naturally it will, and we have to make compensations to even this out.

I like to use a warm up exercise to help the students become aware of this issue. I have the band play a five-note scale pattern, 123454321. At first, I have them play it in eighth notes with swing rhythm and articulation and then repeat it three times before coming to rest on the root. The first time is loud, the second is soft, and the third is loud again. Then we take the whole thing up by half steps. (Later, we may do it in sixteenth notes.) The challenge is to play the same pitch level and be just as in tune with each other on the soft repetition as on the loud repetitions. This requires that we make the appropriate embouchure and oral cavity adjustments to maintain the proper air speed for the loud versus the soft. In the natural world, the volume of air controls the volume of sound. The speed of the air controls the tone center and pitch of the note. Unfortunately, the speed of the air is linked to the volume of the air and will ride up and down with it unless we take control. So the tendency is for the air speed to slow down on the soft pass when we decrease the air volume. It is difficult to keep the air moving the same speed when we are changing the volume of air to change the dynamic; but logically, if "A" vibrates at 440 cycles per second, it should be at 440 whether loud or soft. So our biggest challenge becomes one of keeping the speed of air (or speed of reed) constant across varying dynamics (as air volume changes), which is why the compensations are necessary. The above 5-note exercise really helps develop this skill and sensitivity.

I would also encourage the students to practice with their tuner and/or SmartMusic at varying dynamic levels. Another tried and proven method to work on this dynamics versus pitch issue is long tones with crescendo and diminuendo. This is effective with a group tuning with each other, but should also be practiced individually with a tuner to keep the pitch constant across the dynamic changes.

Intonation Summary

It is impossible to have a superior sounding product without caring and worrying about intonation. So much of this chapter may seem self-evident; and if it does to you, that is great! If it is self-evident to everybody, I sure don't hear the evidence of that when I am out and about. Hopefully, these ideas will be helpful; but either way, I have found that the biggest secret to helping intonation is just to get bothered about it. Get the students bothered about it. There is something about the collective effort that goes down when everyone is bothering about it that works wonders. You'll be disappointed (or someone will) if you just leave intonation to chance.

Chapter 4 Horn Balance, Blend, and Dynamics

Balance and blend depend so much on solid tone production and good intonation. All of these issues are interdependent and do not stand alone, so you'll notice that elements of each are interspersed into the chapters of the other elements. As has been previously mentioned, it is easier to blend warmer sounds than laser-edged sounds. I also previously mentioned the problem of mouthpieces in the saxophone section. To balance each other, it is essential that the saxophonists are all using jazz mouthpieces—not a mixture of jazz and classical mouthpieces. This is also important in the brass sections. The brass sections should be using mouthpieces that allow for a more focused jazz sound and not so much the very dark and broad classical brass sound. The upper players need to be using mouthpieces that make it more reasonable to get the higher range demanded of them. When possible, instruments should also be the correct instruments for the style. This is particularly important in the trombone section where all the tenor trombones, especially the 1st and 2nd players, should be playing small bore horns. The bass trombone player can be using a large-bore bass trombone. I realize that these horn choices are not always possible in a high school setting, but often these issues can be addressed in college situations; and some schools have small bore instruments that can be checked out by the jazz band students.

Thoughts on Balance and Blend

I think the most typical balance issue that I often hear when adjudicating is the lead players sound very strong compared to the lower section players who mostly disappear. This top-heavy balance sounds more like a glorified combo than a big band. The beauty of the big band is all those horns and thick harmonies. I want to hear them! My concept of balance is not like the rooftop where there is a pinnacle and then a sharp drop-off. I think of the balance as more flat across the section with the lead just a little above but strongly supported by all the parts. I have developed a capacity to close my eyes and listen to the section and hear where the holes are. Is there a hole where the second alto should be? Or where the third trombone should be? Or where the 4th trumpet should be? Most lead players really like the feeling of just riding on top of a section that is really supporting them.

Many years ago, the first time I played with Ernie Northway, I was asked to play second alto. Ernie was the contractor on the gig and played lead alto. After about half of the night, he turned to me and said, "I'm sure glad I hired you. I knew you would play like this. You are pushing me hard." It felt good to him that I was right there underneath supporting him. I have found over the years that the second alto is often the hole in the sax section. I have to encourage the second alto to play up to the lead. My tenor players tend to be strong, often too strong on the lead tenor, but usually not on the second tenor. The fullness of the sax section depends a lot on the strength of that second tenor player. I have had situations where I asked my most powerful tenor player to play the second part, even though he deserved the lead tenor part, because it just brought the section to life to have that power on the second tenor part. (Of course, I made it up to him with the solos that I gave him.) I can rarely get too much bari. I am usually pushing for more and more. I tell him that if I ever get too much, I'll let him know. Until then, keep pumping!

I usually tell the trombone section the same thing—if I get too much, I'll let you know. I can go a whole day at a high school jazz festival and never notice the trombone section. Their range just doesn't naturally project as much as the saxophones and trumpets. Also in the trombone section, I want the bass trombone to be like the bari—strong!! Sometimes I have to push for that, other times the player just has that concept. Some years ago, we won the first place at the Lionel Hampton Jazz Festival. In the clinic after the performance, the adjudicator talked to the bass trombone player and told him he was too powerful when the trombone section was playing. He threw in arm up in the air in a triumphant gesture and shouted, "YES!" That is what Karl lived for—Karl Johnson now in the Marine Band. But a good point was made that day—the bass trombonist needs to be aware of who he is playing with and what he is trying to accomplish musically. Is he playing bass to the trombone section or to the whole ensemble? Or is he playing in a trio with the bari and the contrabass? The bari player has to be similarly aware—is he playing bass to the saxophone section or to the whole band, or is he playing as a quasi trombone player balancing into the trombone section, or is he playing in a trio with the bass trombone and the contrabass?

The biggest problem in the trombone section by far is the hole left by the third trombone player. It is in a range (like the second tenor saxophone) where it is more difficult to project naturally. It takes a strong player on third to really make the trombone section work. I find myself constantly driving for more third trombone (and 4th if there is one in a five man section). At one time, Professor Will Kimball played third trombone in my band (later lead), and he tells the story of being a bit put out with me for always pushing him to blow out more. Some years later, he won an audition to play third trombone in a professional jazz band in Chicago. After being given the chair, the other players told him that he was the only one that could play strong enough on the third part at the audition. Similar to the second alto, the second trombone needs to strongly support the lead trombone without competing with him for the top.

In the trumpet section, the most difficult thing is to get the third and fourth trumpet parts to balance the first and second. The upper parts are typically playing in a higher range where they more naturally cut through. I tell the lower players that they have to dig in and play twice as hard as the upper players. The lower range just does not cut through as easily. This is why I also often have a problem with the whole trumpet section being too soft when they are all playing low. Trumpet players tend to get this feeling of power that they can always overpower if they desire. This mentality makes them think they are naturally loud enough in the low register when in reality they have got to work a lot harder to project. When the fourth trumpet (and fifth when there is one) play with a huge sound and in tune with the lead trumpet, it truly makes the trumpet section come to life and makes the lead trumpet player sound like a million bucks. (This is especially true for the fifth player when written in octaves with the lead trumpet.)

To achieve the thick, blending section sound it is imperative to work on intonation. If the players in a section are not in tune with each other, they are cancelling out each other to a certain degree. When we are in tune, there is more power and blend. In fact, when we are in tune, difference tones—tones we are not even playing—come into the picture to help beef up the sound. It is like angels are helping us out, and we are stronger than we really are on our own. That thick sax section unison sound—and that two tenor and bari unison sound—is truly a function of intonation. When we work on tone production, intonation, and balance, the blend tends to work itself out.

A Thought About Dynamics

I find myself mostly working with young bands to get them blowing and putting some air in the horns. I talk a lot about personal investment and playing with professional strength and solidness. But as the big sound is achieved, we do need to realize that dynamic contrasts are vital to making music. I find when I am adjudicating that few bands use dynamics. Many are just loud all the time while others are just wimpy all the time. Often, the charts themselves are lacking much information about dynamics. We always have to be thinking about how we can bring more dynamic nuance to the lines and dynamic contrasts between sections of the chart.

When Shelley Berg worked with my band a few years back, he talked about the band finding their "mezzo". I thought that was a great way to phrase it. The band needs to find its mezzo or medium (the base) volume level and then work to broaden the contrasts from mezzo down to whisper soft and then from mezzo on up to blazingly loud. The wider the dynamic range of the band, the more expressive levels that are available to make more interesting and effective music.

It is a real challenge to maintain balance and blend (and intonation) while working on wider dynamics. For example, it is typical for the more advanced players to try to make up for the weaker players in a crescendo. This obviously leads to a distortion in the balance. During dynamic contrasts, pay special attention to what is happening with the balance and shape the process as necessary.

Chapter 5 Helping the Horns Work as a Section

There are few things as exciting as a section that has really captured playing together. Many years ago, my band shared the Big Band Night at the Montreux International Jazz Festival in Switzerland with the great Gerry Mulligan New York Big Band. Gerry's band had trouble on the road and arrived just before they had to play. It was imperative to have a good sound check because the concert was being recorded in 24 tracks and videotaped. Gerry very artfully orchestrated the sound check in front of the audience as a "Meet the Band" kind of thing—now meet the saxophone section! The section played a soli that just knocked me out. It was so tight in every small nuance. It was the highlight for me of that whole musical month in Europe. Gerry Niewood was playing lead alto to die for, and people like Seldon Powell, and of course, Gerry Mulligan, were in the section. I remember it to this day.

In the process of developing such a section, there are at least three issues we need to deal with and teach. First, the lead players need to really function as leaders in the section. Second, the section players need to learn what it means to be a section player. And third, the section needs to learn how to really become unified and function as a true team.

How the Section Functions

The traditional section is set up very similar to a president with four counselors or cabinet members, so to speak. The counselors should feel the responsibility to give counsel when asked for, or in a sectional rehearsal. The wise counselor will voice his opinions and feelings freely; but when the president makes a decision after gathering the counsel, then the counselor will fall into line and support the president in his decision, even if it is counter to the counselor's previous recommendation. The wise president will invite counsel when appropriate and will listen respectfully, then weigh the ideas on the table and make a decision. The counselors then support him unanimously, and unity is established in the section.

I learned about being a lead player in the school of soft knocks. Thank heaven it was a kind man who sat next to me in the section and tutored me. (It could have been hard knocks.) Just a short time before I left high school, I was hired to play in the Valley Music Hall Orchestra on the baritone saxophone and bass clarinet. I think the first two gigs were John Davidson and Jimmy Dean. After those first two gigs, I was moved over to lead alto because Murray Williams retired. (Murray was a seasoned lead alto player who had played with the likes of Harry James and Woody Herman and had even recorded with Bird.) I was barely 18, and any of the other guys in the section could have easily been my dad. Sitting next to me on tenor was Don LeFevre. We would be playing along, and I would choose to play a particular quarter note long. When we repeated it, I played it short. Don would lean over and kindly say, "You know, Murray would always make a decision about the length of the quarter note on the first time through, and then he would be very consistent to play it the same way every time. That way I would always know how he would play it, and I could invest myself into that note with him. If you play it long one time and short another time, then I don't know what you are going to do the third time; and I have to hang back and withhold, so I don't embarrass myself. This makes the section sound loose and very tentative!" "Oh! I get it." Then we would be playing along, and I would add some little high-schoolish turn. Don would lean over and say, "Murray would never do those kinds of surprises because I wouldn't know how to follow him." "Oh!" And this went on with one issue after another.

I gradually learned to make decisions quickly and be very consistent with implementing them. I had to discipline myself not to suddenly surprise the section with something they couldn't follow. If I felt I had to make a change in my first decision, then I would say, "Guys, I'm going to play that quarter note in bar 5 short instead. Sorry!" This is the reason why it never works to double the lead part. Doubling the lead destroys the concept of having a lead and prevents the lead player from properly styling the melody. Of course, I also learned about the lead player prerogatives that it takes to style in a vocal manner, but I also learned to provide solid leadership for my section. (Those lead player prerogatives are best learned by listening to great lead players on recordings with the great big bands.)

If I am playing in the section, then I feel the responsibility to listen very closely to my lead player and follow him in the direction he points. I try to support him in volume, match him in pitch, match his articulations and inflections and vibrato, and be unified with him in every way. If I really disagree with something, I will voice my idea (if it is in a rehearsal—never on a gig), but then I follow whatever the lead player decides (despite how I may feel about it).

A few years back, I was playing for Frank Sinatra Jr. and sitting next to Mike Smith for the first time. Mike is, of course, the legendary lead alto player of Sinatra Sr. and Jr., Buddy Rich, Harry Connick, Jr. and on and on. It was a great thing to sit next to him! However, he has a very unusual scoop style compared to what I am used to, and at first I couldn't quite capture it. Gradually, I psyched it out. When he got up to leave the rehearsal, I said, "Mike, tonight I am going to be on every one of your scoops." He smiled. But that night, I nailed him on every scoop; and I felt really good about achieving that unity with him. (Incidentally, I was blowing my guts out to try to balance with him, and I am not a weak player.)

I always have one ear on my lead player, and respond as quickly as possible to anything I hear. I was playing tenor on a gig with Tevis Laukat (owner of the Cannonball Saxophone Company) who was playing lead alto. We played the same show six nights a week for a month. In the third week of the show, a particularly dull passage of straight half notes became too much of a temptation, and Tevis put a little turn in between two of the half notes. On the very next set of half notes, I duplicated the turn. Afterwards, Tevis looked at me, and I said, "Hey, do I follow my lead player or what?"

Many years ago, I had Jon Faddis play with my band. Afterward, Jon said, "You've got to get your trumpet section listening to the lead. I tried several little things, and there was no response. The section did not hear one note I played!" Ouch!

Holding Sectionals is the Key

A large key to establishing really functioning sections is to have them hold sectionals. I require the sections in my band to hold a weekly section rehearsal outside of the full ensemble rehearsals. When I played lead alto in high school, I required my section to come to my home on Saturday mornings for sectionals. Somehow, we have to do this if we are striving to become a superior ensemble. This is where we can learn to behave as a section and become unified as a team.

You may ask, "What exactly are we trying to unify?" Unity includes sound quality, balance, blend, intonation, articulation, scooping style, vibrato style, and the like. We have to truly play together. Here are some things I would suggest for the sectional.

Sectional Ideas

Hold unison notes together and find the pitch with each other.

Hold harmony notes together and find the pitch with each other.

Dissect chords and build from the bottom up when necessary. Use a tuner or piano or some pitch standard for reference when working on pitch issues.

Decide which notes are long and which notes are "Dot" (the "short notes") and mark them. Also, decide how long or short the short notes are depending on tempo and style.

Decide which notes are scooped and mark them. Decide how wide and how long the scoop will be and exactly when to arrive at the full pitch. In more modern charts, it may need to be decided if everyone is scooping or only the lead. Do the same with other dramatic devices like falls and doits and turns and the like. "When will we begin the fall? How long is it?" "How long will we hold the note before the turn starts?"

Decide vibrato style and whether all will vibrato or only the lead player. Mark "NV" when there is "no vibrato" (such as unison passages).

Unify breathing places, dynamic changes, cut-off's on long notes, and mark them with a pencil.

One on One Sectional Technique

Use the one-on-one section rehearsal technique to unify each player to the lead player. Have the lead alto and the second alto play together while the other section players share what they are hearing. For example, "The second alto is a little behind the lead alto in bar 7." "The lead alto is not being consistent from bar 4 to bar 8 with what's short." "The intonation is not happening in bar 10." " In bar 9, the lead alto is playing the quarter note short, and the second alto is playing the same note long." "On the scoop in bar 12, the lead alto is taking longer to get to the pitch than the second alto." And so on and so forth. Work until the two altos are really unified. Then go through the same process with the lead alto and the lead tenor, the lead alto and the second tenor, and finally the lead alto and the bari. This goes a long way toward making the section a team. And, of course, precisely the same process should be used with the trumpet and trombone sections. The section players take turns listening objectively and offering help. This could also happen when the whole section is playing, and individual section members could take turns listening out front of the section.

Unifying Accents

I have found another huge unifying factor is simply to unify the accents. In bebop type lines, the top notes of contours should be accented. In unison, this is easier. In harmony, the third trumpet player might be at a low point in his line at the same time that the lead player is at the top of his contour. It is essential that everyone accent at precisely the same places. This will be very unnatural for the third trumpet player to accent at a low point, but it must be done. The third trumpet may have a high point in his line when it is not so in the lead. He must restrain himself from accenting where it would be natural to do so, but detrimental to the section sound. So in a sectional, the lead player may say, "Guys, take out your pencil and let's mark in the accents. In bar 1, mark an accent on the downbeat of 3. In bar 2, mark an accent on the upbeat of

2 and the downbeat of 4. In bar 3, the accent is on the upbeat of 3, and so on. Let's try not to accent any place we haven't marked to accent. Okay, let's try it a little down tempo."

Use of the Metronome

It is great if the section can pipe a metronome through a speaker loudly so all can hear while playing. (EQ out the lows, so it can be cranked.) The metronome will make the section more aware of discrepancies and more aware of spots where there is rushing or dragging. In the section, we do all have to play with a similar time feel, but time is the area where the section players do not "follow" the lead. "Follow" implies that we are following from behind. Instead, we all play the time independently with the rhythm section, and if we are successful, then we will line up with each other better than if we are trying to follow each other. Rhythmic feel must also be unified with the lead player. For example, "Just how hard are we swinging?"

Of course, when all three sections are playing together, these same issues must be unified, and similar rehearsal techniques can be used across the whole ensemble.

It is a wonderful thing when the section discusses and sets goals together and then supports and helps each other as they strive for unity and greatness!

I know this seems like a lot of detail, but it is in the detail that the battle for excellence is won. Some years back, my band won first place at the Pacific Coast Collegiate Jazz Festival in Berkeley, California. That evening all of the bands were invited to a reception. My people reported that students from other university bands were coming up to them and saying things like, "Wow, it seemed like your band had decided exactly how to play every single note in every single measure!" Well, SURPRISE!! That's exactly what we did. That's what it takes.

Chapter 6   Mutes and Doubling for Horns

Often in an attempt to utilize new colors the brass are called upon to use various kinds of mutes—straight, cup, harmon, bucket, etc. The brass players may also be asked to use a plunger (preferably, not previously used). Trumpet players usually double on the flugelhorn, and the bass trombone player may occasionally be asked to play tuba. The woodwind players are expected to play clarinets and flutes and sometimes other woodwind or ethnic instruments. It is most common to see the lead alto doubling on soprano saxophone, clarinet, flute and piccolo. The second alto will usually have flute and clarinet. The tenor players often have clarinet and may also have flute. If there is oboe or english horn, it will often be on the second tenor book, but may also be on one of the alto books. The baritone player will often have bass clarinet and sometimes clarinet or flute. If there is bassoon, it is usually on the bari part. These extra instruments and mutes create a whole new set of problems to deal with in the rehearsal.

Brass Mutes

A common misunderstanding about mutes is that they are used to make the brass sections softer, and so the brass sections are asked to play softer. In reality, the mutes are only to change color, and the player must blow even louder and work harder to make sure he is projecting. I am usually asking for more from the brass when they are in mutes, not less. I want those harmon mutes in the trumpet section to really buzz.

It is important that brass players be coached to get the proper mutes and be prepared for whatever is required in the part. I often use birthdays, Christmas, and the like to help students get these things that they need. Each brass player should have a straight mute, a cup mute, a harmon mute, a bucket mute (or hat), and a plunger. At least one of the trombone soloists should have a pixie mute for that older Ellington solo sound. The pixie mute is used with a plunger to get that sound.

It is important to know that the harmon mute in not used with the stem. Take that out! And most players dent up the harmon mute a little bit, intentionally, to give it the right sound and response.

The biggest problem when playing with mutes is intonation, and special attention will need to be given to this issue in the ensemble and section rehearsals. It helps to know some of the tendencies. For example, when using the straight mute and the harmon mute, the pitch will go sharper; and the player must make compensation. This may mean pulling the tuning slide for a longer passage if there is time. The cup mute and especially the bucket mute will make the pitch go flat; and, again, compensation must be made.

For the trombones, the bucket mute must be sized to the bell and may vary between small and large bore horns and bass trombone. If the player is serious (especially at the college level), he should have this equipment, even though it is a bit expensive. It is possible, of course, for the school to own an array of mutes so they can be checked out by jazz band students.

Doubling

Doubling, whether brass or woodwind, causes pitch issues to deal with. As you know, the temperature of the instrument is a huge factor in intonation. When the player has been playing one instrument for some time and then picks up a different instrument, it will be cold and, therefore, flat. I try to get the students to anticipate when the new instrument is coming up soon, and start blowing warm air into it when there is a moment here and there, so they can try to have it warm by the time they need it. They may need to be pushed in a little when they switch over to the new instrument. The clarinet warms up much more slowly; and in cold situations, it will really help to have a shorter barrel (63 or 64 millimeters instead of the standard 65). It can also be a huge problem to have a dried out and/or warped reed when picking up the clarinet or soprano saxophone. I try to get the students to keep wetting the reed periodically, and to keep a mouthpiece cap on it to keep it from drying out so fast. This is obviously a much bigger issue in the dry West, and here I even have the students tape up the holes in their mouthpiece cap to keep the moisture inside. Warped reeds can cause squeaking that is ugly in your ensemble sound.

Both brass and woodwind doublers can be aided in their intonation by using the Korg CM-100L Clip On Contact Microphone with their tuner in the rehearsals and even in concerts.

Woodwind Doubling

Saxophonists have a tall order to become proficient on the clarinet and the flute. These are not just automatically easy for the saxophonist and require a real commitment and lots of work. I highly recommend the doubler take private lessons on these secondary instruments and study the standard classical repertory. With the exception of playing an improvised solo on the clarinet or flute (or a Dixieland approach on the clarinet) which, of course, is going to be jazz-oriented; when the clarinet and flute come up in a written ensemble part, the performance approach to those instruments will be classical, even in the middle of a full-on jazz chart. So classical study is a real necessity. I even try to get my doubling students to play a piece on their secondary instrument(s) for the solo and ensemble festival.

I also try to get my doublers to play one of their secondary instruments in the concert band or orchestra. When I was in my senior year of high school, I played lead alto in the jazz band, first clarinet in the concert band, and first flute in the orchestra. I continued similar patterns into college. Doing this, I gained proficiency, but also confidence, that I could sight read on my doubles and sit in a section and play them in tune.

One other thought! I would suggest that the doubler actually practice doubling. Play the saxophone for 10 minutes, switch to flute for the next 10 minutes, then clarinet for 10, back to flute for 10, then saxophone for 10, then back to flute for 10, etc. If needed, throw the piccolo or soprano saxophone into the rotation. Then when the chart only gives the doubler four measures to switch to the new instrument, at least he has a fighting chance to make the embouchure and fingering changes required. This is not so simple as some of us make it look. It takes some serious practice. Dabbling will not do it!

This doubling rotation idea can also be valuable for the brass—ten minutes of trumpet, ten minutes of flugelhorn, ten minutes of trumpet with harmon mute, ten minutes of flugelhorn, and so on.

Section 3

Dealing with Style:
It Don't Mean a Thing if it Don't Swing

So Let's Swing Into this Section . . .

Chapter 7   Working on Time Feel

The development of personal and ensemble time feel is a huge issue for the jazz educator. NOTHING is more important than time feel. This is NUMBER ONE in making an ensemble superior. No matter what other good things are happening in the ensemble; if it *feels* bad, the ensemble will not get full credit for the other good things that are happening.

As with intonation, the most important thing in the development of time feel is to get everyone bothered about it and focusing on it. Left to chance, time will be a disaster. We simply need to ask for it…and ask for it….and ask for it…! If we don't ask, we will never get it. We ask the rhythm section to play time together. We ask the horns to play time with the rhythm section and with each other. I usually hear a lot of time schisms when I am adjudicating. I will never forget, when I was adjudicating with Jeff Tower some years ago, glancing over to see him rapping the pulse of the chart with his pencil on his tape recorder (the one he was using for comments to the band), and then yelling into the tape recorder, "Time, Folks! Time!!" I have often felt like I needed to do the same.

So time feel is a difficult thing to get a handle on, especially with young kids, but let me suggest a few things that I have found helpful.

Thinking in the Long Meter

I have found that learning to think and feel in the longer meter really helps to shore up the time. In other words, in 4/4 I think in 2 instead of 4. When I think in cut time, my pulse becomes more stable and much more relaxed; so I always think in the longer meter when the tempo of the tune is medium and faster. Although when thinking in quarter notes it is easy to add a beat or drop a beat without realizing it, I don't typically have this problem when I think in half notes. Of course, this is not practical or necessary with a slow ballad tempo.

For long meter thinking to work, however, I need to think in 2 on beats 1 and 3, not 2 and 4. I realize this sounds like heresy; and for a long time after I started thinking this way, I was afraid to say it out loud for fear of censure—that is until I heard Hal Galper talk about it at an IAJE Conference. When somebody as heavy as Hal Galper (Phil Woods, Chet Baker, Michael Brecker, and everybody else) was willing to talk this way, it validated me and gave me some confidence to teach it more publicly. Hal demonstrated how thinking in 4 was very nervous and frantic feeling. Then he demonstrated how thinking in 2 on 2 & 4 created the same nervous feeling in the time; because to think on 2 & 4, you also have to think 1 & 3 which makes it like thinking in 4 with all four quarters. But thinking in 2 on 1 & 3 was much more relaxed. He pointed out that he was basically thinking in slow mode all of the time. On the ballad, he was thinking 1-**2**-**3**-**4**; and on the up-tempo tune, he was thinking **1**-2-**3**-4 with the pulse moving at a similar speed for both. I have felt exactly the same way about this issue, and I believe it really helps young people develop a more solid and relaxed-feeling pulse.

Now before you close the book, let me say that I fully understand the need for jazz players to practice with thinking the pulse on 2 & 4. I have my students do this; and at a more advanced level, it also helps to strengthen time feel. I also have them practice with the metronome on just 4 or just 2 or just on the upbeat of 2 or just on the upbeat of 4 and the like. These are great exercises, and yes we need to be able to play with the metronome on 2 and 4 as if it were the hi-hat. But for training a younger player and a younger band, I feel that thinking the pulse in the long meter on 1 & 3 is much more helpful for a while. And I have found this is not wasted on the more advanced players either.

Use of the Metronome or Drum Machine

I also like to use the metronome as an awareness tool in rehearsals and lessons. I'll turn on the metronome (this might be pumped through large speakers in a full ensemble rehearsal), and establish a tempo and then kick off the tune. Then I turn the metronome off. After 12 or 16 bars, I will cut off the band while maintaining the prevailing tempo and then turn back on the metronome. Then we can see if we are still at the tempo or we have rushed it or dragged it. Then we repeat it. Is the tendency the same? Then I will go longer, maybe 24 or 32 bars, before checking the tempo. This is very revealing and helps the band gain a sense of what needs to be done. We have also used a drum machine so we could have a hit every four bars. It's amazing how far the time can stray in 4 bars. Again, it is the awareness that is incredibly helpful.

The Stick

I can accomplish something similar by using a heavy-duty drum stick on a cowbell. It is amazing what it does just to unify the concept of where the pulse is for the group. If the ensemble is having trouble unifying where the pulse is, just pick up your stick, and soon the time will straighten itself out. I used to bang my stick on a music stand, but it didn't do much good for the stand—or the stick. I've found the cowbell can be heard over the whole band.

It is not uncommon for a young band to get the time turned around between the rhythm section and the horns. What the rhythm section is playing as 1 & 3 has become 2 & 4 in the horns. It can also be a problem within the rhythm section when the drummer's 2 & 4 has become the bass player's 1 & 3. In this case, give accents on 1 & 3 with the stick to unify for everyone where 1 is. When everyone in the band knows precisely where 1 is, the difference is "striking". (Sorry!)

Quarter Note Feel: Locking in the Time

The last few years, I have found great success in teaching what I call quarter note feel (versus eighth note feel). What I mean by this is that horn players can play a line of eighth notes in such a way that it feels more like quarter notes (with incidental, in-between notes) than like eighth notes. When the quarter notes of the horns line up exactly with the quarter notes of the rhythm section, great time feel is born. In other words, the quarter notes of the bass player and the quarter notes of the drummer line up perfectly, and then the quarter notes of the horn players line up with that perfectly (as perfectly as possible). This is called locking up the time within the rhythm section *and* locking up the time between the horns and the rhythm section. I have included some examples of this in the videos that accompany this book. Let me go deeper now into what I am calling quarter note feel for the horn players who are actually playing eighth notes. This is next to impossible to explain in writing and is far easier to demonstrate, but I'll give it a try. This explanation will fall woefully short, however, if you don't take the time to hear the examples in the videos.

When I first passed out the Basie chart, *Corner Pocket*, to my band back in 1990, I had to say to the saxophone section playing the melody line, "There's just one problem with that line saxes—it's not swingin'!" "What do you mean it's not swingin'? We're not playing it straight." No, they were not playing it straight; they were playing the eighth notes unevenly. But I told them they were only giving lip service to swing. To truly swing, they needed to play the downbeat notes much longer and the upbeat notes much later in the beat. This makes the line sound more like quarter notes. The eighth notes written on the upbeats become more like the incidental notes played in between the downbeats by the drummer on the ride cymbal or the bass player in the walking bass line. You can try to imagine this; but, really, stop reading and take a moment to listen to the video examples for this chapter. The first printed example below is a phrase from *Corner Pocket* by the Basie Band, and the second example is a phrase from *Sig Ep* by the Woody Herman Band. I am using the tenuto markings to indicate the extra long downbeats that bring out the quarter note feel in the lines of these examples.

This last example is an exerpt from *There Will Never Be Another You* also demonstrating quarter note feel—especially on the second line where the arrows indicate the quarter note line that is inherent in the melody even though there are eighth notes in the line as well.

Again, please take the time to refer to the videos demonstrations for this concept.

Chapter 8   Swing Rhythm

The "quarter note feel" concept is critical to the way I am going to now approach rhythm and swinging, so please don't go on if you haven't taken the time to first listen to the examples for Chapter 7.

The Effect of Quarter Note Feel on Swing Rhythm

We often hear people say of a swing chart, "Get that laid back feel." What is laying back? If we lay back the downbeat, that is called *dragging*. But if we lay the upbeat material very deep in the beat, that creates the *laid back feel*. If the downbeat quarter note is predominantly long, and the in between eighth note is laid back very late in the beat, then nothing is happening in the traditional "upbeat" space. In fact, there is no such thing as an upbeat in swing rhythm. Yes, there are many eighth notes written on the upbeat, but they are not played on the upbeat in actuality. There is no such thing as an upbeat! This has led me to develop a new terminology intended to create a different attitude about rhythm with the students.

Where do I play those eighth notes that are written on the upbeat? I play them almost on the next downbeat. How long, then, is the downbeat note? It is almost the whole beat long. The "upbeat" note is played as a downbeat gesture, almost on the following beat. It is not played as an "upbeat" gesture as it looks on the page. It has nothing to do with the non-existent "upbeat". This issue is at the root of most of the loose rhythms in the band and is a real deterrent to the ensemble precision we are seeking. We were all programmed as young students to view these notes written on upbeats as upbeats. It is so hard to overcome this past conditioning; but if we view them as nearly downbeats, it makes all the difference in tightening up the rhythms in the ensemble and getting the swing feel happening. The written "upbeats" are like grace notes to the coming beat, or the relationship of the upbeat to the downbeat is like a flam in drum language.

A while back, when I was teaching this concept at a local high school, I asked the band, "If the upbeat note is almost on the next downbeat, how long is the first downbeat note?" One of the trumpet players blurted out, "15/16's". I said, "I never thought of it quite that way before, but I'll take it." Playing the upbeat is like playing chicken, "How close can I get that upbeat note to the next downbeat without actually putting it on the downbeat?" Of course, if I wait too long and put the upbeat on the next downbeat, then I've gone too far—the rhythm is distorted now; but how close can I get without falling over the edge onto the downbeat?

But What About Triplet Subdivision?

Now, of course, the tempo does play a part in the actual ratio of the downbeat to the upbeat, and you may be asking yourself, "What about the old triplet subdivision idea?" When the tempo is slower, especially if it is swing ballad tempo, the triplet subdivision has real merit. I also think the triplets are a great way to introduce swing rhythm to a young student. I have the young student physically subdivide triplets with his/her tongue on every etude for quite some time (similar to subdividing 16th's with the tongue on dotted eighth-sixteenth rhythms to understand the correct ratio). I would also suggest having the young ensemble regularly subdivide triplets with the tongue.

The mature ensemble will also profit from the rehearsal technique of tonguing the triplet subdivisions on a swing ballad or medium slow tune. For example, when I was trying to tighten the ensemble on the intro to *You Don't Know What Love Is*, I had my college band tongue the triplet subdivisions to create a unity of mindset for playing those figures. (Please refer to video examples.) *Georgia on My Mind* would be another example where triplet subdivision will pay big dividends.

But when the tempo moves up, thinking the triplets becomes impractical. Of course, we hope for some effect from the conditioning we have done with triplet subdivisions at slower tempos, but using triplets as a rehearsal technique to try to tighten the ensemble on the rhythms is not useful any longer at fast speeds. However using the eighth note line to subdivide in our minds for longer notes, such as a dotted quarter, can be very helpful. (See Example 2 on the next page.)

At the faster tempos, I would have the students learn that there are four places a note can start: right on the beat, almost on the beat, ricochet off the downbeat, or right on the upbeat. "Wait a minute, right on the upbeat? I thought there was no upbeat!" That is true at the quarter note level, but remember at the faster tempo, we are now thinking in the longer meter or at the half note level; and at the half note level, the upbeat is either beat 2 or beat 4 in the bar. In other words, everything is about the downbeat): either it is right on the beat, or almost on the beat, or right after the beat (ricochet). The only exception is if the note is written on beat 2 or beat 4, then it is right on the direct upbeat. I think the next examples will make it clear what I am trying to verbalize. I realize this is a whole new terminology, but I have found it very effective in rehearsing the band for rhythmic precision. Think in 2 on each example.

Some Examples of a Different Way to Think About Swing Rhythms

Example 1

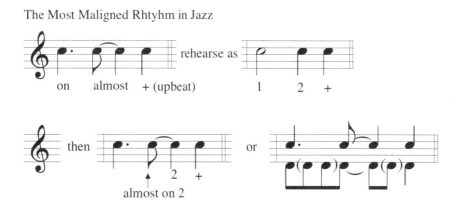

An effective rehearsal technique for the above rhythm would be to have the band play a half note and two quarter notes (since we're in cut time, this will be like a quarter and two even eighths). When this is solid, then reintroduce the slight anticipation to the second note, (like a grace note to the second note). This makes the second note a downbeat gesture, *almost on the beat*. When it is conceived as it looks, an upbeat gesture, it will always be played too early and will yield a loose ensemble sound and not swing.

Another effective rehearsal technique is to have the band subdivide, with the tongue, the eighth note line that runs through the dotted quarter note (duh ga du gah du gat) as shown in the last measure above.

Example 2

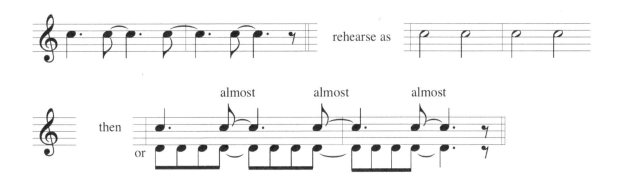

An effective rehearsal technique for this rhythm would be to have the band play half note, half note, half note, half note (with a breath following). It could be repeated and cycled until accurate. Then reintroduce the slight anticipation to the 2nd, 3rd, and 4th notes as a downbeat gesture (grace note or flam to each beat).

Again, a second effective rehearsal technique would be to subdivide with the tongue the eighth note line that runs through the whole figure (duh ga du gah, guh du gah, guh du gah, guh du gah). It is important that the eighth note subdivisions are swinging, not straight.

At faster tempos, the first dotted quarter note is usually late or sluggish (Example 3). We have to bounce off the beat or ricochet. So I call it a ricochet note. Of course at a slow tempo, this same dotted quarter note would not be a ricochet note at all, but would be an *almost on the beat* note, almost on 2.

Example 3

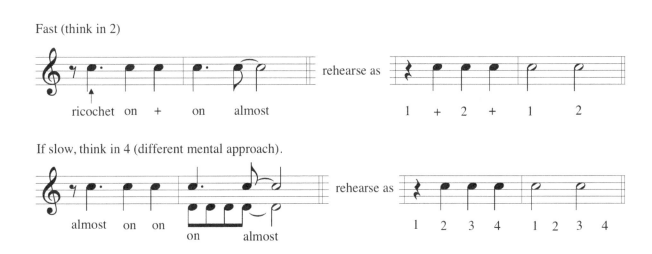

The second problem in this figure will be the last note being played too soon as an upbeat gesture (as it looks). Again for a rehearsal technique, have the band play it right on the beat a few times. Then reintroduce the slight anticipation, grace note to the beat idea. Also, it would be good here to tongue the swinging eighth note subdivisions on the dotted quarter note in bar two.

on   almost   +   ricochet   +   on

Example 4 (above) is obviously a particularly difficult rhythm to play precisely with the whole band. This is even a difficult figure to subdivide eighth note lines through because of the speed and complexity. (Subdividing might help on the first note to the second note, but then becomes more difficult than it is worth.) This is an example of where my new terminology really works well to establish a mental approach and a unity of concept. A good practice technique would be to play this figure much slower, but still in 2 (long meter), emphasizing On the Beat, Almost on the Beat, Ricochet off the Beat, On the Upbeat, and On the Beat. Then gradually speed up.

Example 5 (below) is a similar problem but more extended and would lend itself well to the technique described for Example 4. Example 5 also illustrates that the ricochet approach not only applies to the dotted quarter note, but can be the approach for getting started with a line of eighth notes written on the upbeat.

(Thinking in 2)

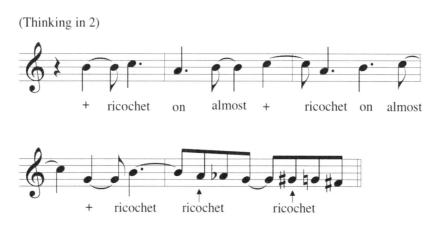

+   ricochet   on   almost   +   ricochet   on   almost

+   ricochet   ricochet   ricochet

(Thinking in 2)

ricochet   on   almost   on   +   ricochet   on   on

Example 6 (above) illustrates a good point in the second bar that the little note written on the upbeat of two is also played almost on the beat even though it goes to a different note instead of being tied. I have found that there is much more rhythmic vitality and accuracy when these little notes are snapped tight to the beat instead of how they are often played (a little early gives an almost arhythmic feeling). Also, note that in the third bar the tied eighths that are functioning as a syncopated quarter note must be articulated short (DOT) or the ricochet is difficult to play correctly.

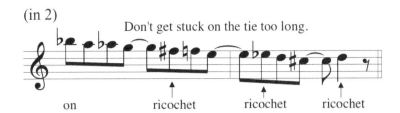

Don't get stuck on the tie too long.

on   ricochet   ricochet   ricochet

Example 7 (above) points up another very common problem of getting stuck on ties too long. The tie in reality is miniscule (since the upbeat note that starts the tie is almost on the beat—only a gnat's eyebrow before the beat, then it is very little different than just playing the second note of the tie, the downbeat, normally. This is another example of conditioning that we all experience from the time we are young—we want the tied note to be longer than it really is. (This is also an issue in the last bar of #5 above.) Also note that the last note of the figure (Example 7) is a ricochet note.

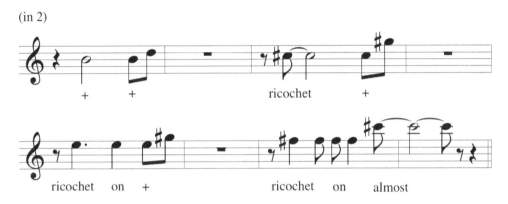

Example 8 (above) helps to illustrate making the difference between playing a note on the + (and or upbeat) and playing it as a ricochet note.

Example 9 (below) is an example combining most of the issues above all in one phrase. Here again, don't get stuck on the tie in the last measure.

Example 10 (next pagre) is another summary-type line, but also illustrates how to decide if a note is almost on the beat or if it is a ricochet note. The difference is the tempo. Since line 10 is much slower than the previous lines, the upbeat of 1 in bar 2 is almost on the next beat. At a faster tempo, it would be a ricochet note.

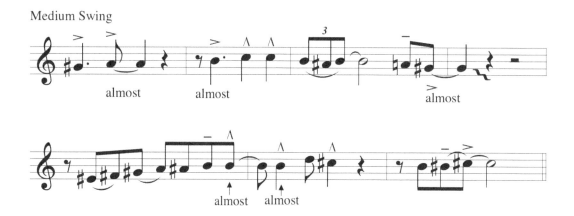

Springboard Notes

There are certain notes in a rhythmic figure which if held long enough springboard the whole figure to swing. If not held long enough, they springboard the whole figure to failure. These notes I call "Springboard Notes". I discovered a dramatic example of this when I was still in high school and transcribed Cannonball Adderly's solo on *So What* off the *Kind of Blue* album of Miles Davis. Here is the part of Cannon's solo that I am referring to:

I tried to figure out how to notate the rhythm on the last bar, and I realized that there was no other way than eighth, quarter, eighth—standard syncopation. But oh how instructive is Cannon's length on the first eighth note! That is a "Springboard Note" at its finest. Check out the length on the first eighth notes of the syncopations preceding that one as well.

I have found great success if I can help the ensemble define and mark into the parts where the springboard notes are. I have them use a standard tenuto marking over the springboard notes. By defining just a few notes that the band really has to lay on, everything else starts to fall into place.

So here are some examples of springboard notes. They tend to fall regularly in certain predictable places: (I am using the tenuto marking to indicate where the springboard notes are.)

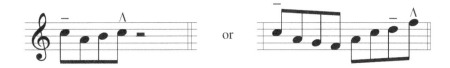

or

Du Wah

Here are a couple of examples of how I would help the ensemble define springboard notes in a particular passage of a chart. (Again springboard notes are indicated with the tenuto marking.)

Does Swing Rhythm Change When the Tempo is Fast?

I have heard some very good jazz players, that I respect otherwise, teach that we cannot swing when the tempo is fast—the faster the tempo, the straighter the eighth notes. It reminds me of a student who came into my office many years ago for a lesson and had done an impressive transcription of an up-tempo Phil Woods solo. I asked him to play it. I could tell immediately that he was playing the eighth-note lines very straight. I said to him, "That is an impressive transcription of <u>a lot</u> of notes, but you are not swinging." He quickly responded, "Oh, you can't swing when it is this fast! Phil Woods doesn't swing it." "Really," I said, "Have you got the tape?" This was long enough ago that he pulled out a cassette tape of Phil's solo.

We put it into my Marantz two speed tape recorder and began to listen to the solo at full speed. I could tell that Phil was swinging, but it would have been difficult to determine that with an untrained ear. I said, "Let's see what it sounds like at half speed." I popped the switch on the tape recorder down to half speed. Why, Phil was swingin' his tail off!

I grant you that you will find variations on the degree of swing out there between various players; but I think in the big band, especially if we are playing standard swing stuff such as an up-tempo Nestico chart, we make a big mistake if we suppose that it does not swing because it is fast. A great way to help the band keep swingin' at fast tempos is to carefully define the springboard notes and hang onto those notes a little extra, even if it feels like we'll never get the next notes played in time. Don't worry, you will!

Another good rehearsal technique for working on an up-tempo chart is to play the chart down tempo for a while and get the band really swinging it nicely. Then gradually speed it up over several rehearsals until it is burnin' but still swingin'.

Math or Feel?

One more thought on swing rhythm. It is critical that the students be listening all the time to swing music if they hope to swing. We can teach a lot of important concepts about swing rhythm as outlined above, but it will fall short if the students are not experiencing the swing feel regularly. There are intangibles that we cannot teach that can only be acquired experientially.

Is swing rhythm a math problem, or can it only be truly conceived at a feeling level? We can teach the math part of it, but ultimately swing rhythms have to be felt as figures that feel good with the rhythm section. Sometimes when a rhythm has become very "studied" and therefore stiff, I ask the band to sing the figure with me without looking at it a few times. I ask them to conceive of the rhythm as a figure instead of a math problem and to make it feel good with the rhythm section. There is usually a dramatic difference in the feel and the precision of that figure.

I often talk about time feel being vertical or horizontal. Swing rhythm tends to be more horizontal as it is conceived in forward moving lines. Latin and Rock rhythms have to be conceived more vertically in how they relate to the even subdivision of the beat. We will get into that more in Chapter 10.

Using These Rhythmic Approaches in Non-Swing Music

These same rhythmic mental approaches also work just as well in other styles of music. This includes Latin or funk or rock styles. For example:

Mambo (Thinking in 2)

Mambo (Thinking in 2)

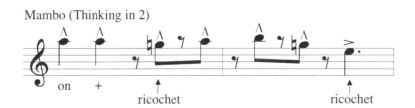

In funk style playing where the rhythms are written in sixteenth notes, the same mental approaches can be applied, but now we are thinking in quarter notes instead of half notes and applying the idea of almost on the beat or richocheting off the beat or on the upbeat to sixteenth notes. Of course, we can also subdivide both mentally and with the tongue—the tongue for practice only to aid with mental subdivision. The labels refer to the note just underneath or just above. Start from below, then dodge above, back to underneath, etc.

Funk (Thinking in 4)

A little practice thinking this way will really help to solidify rhythmic thinking and will truly help with sight-reading. When I get a group thinking this way, the precision really tightens up!

Chapter 9   Swing Style Articulation

By now you can tell that I think it is very important to start with the Swing Style. This is the point of departure for understanding all the related contemporary styles. We have already talked about time and rhythm and experiencing feel. The third part of this triad is the articulation. It takes all of the above to really get an ensemble swinging.

When I am adjudicating, I often find myself saying on the tape something like this, "To someone who speaks the jazz language, it doesn't sound like you'all do." We often hear a jazz band trying to speak jazz with a concert band accent. We must become bilingual, ultimately polylingual these days. And I want to be true or pure to whatever it is that I am speaking at the moment. Articulation is a huge part of defining style and must not be left to chance.

How Do We Define the Correct Articulations?

I have heard, while observing in classrooms, the jazz band director say, "Play the articulation the way it is written there! Do you see that slur?" This is usually a large mistake to insist on getting what is written. Unfortunately, what is written is not dependable and is rarely what you really want the band to do. So the first critical principle of articulation to understand is that we articulate according to principle, not according to what is written. On the written part, slurring is almost always wrong. Sometimes the Dot notes are indicated correctly, but sometimes not. Many things are not indicated at all such as DuWah's and Ghosted Notes. By learning the principles of swing articulation and their application, the student can become independent in problem solving. This is preferable to making them dependent on you by just telling them what to do without teaching the principle behind it. The following principles have been codified over many years of listening, playing, and teaching experience. So what are the principles of swing articulation? Let's get started!

Swing Articulation and Phrasing Principles

I am going to give the extended, educator version first, and then I will give a student, abbreviated version second. I will even include a basic beginners version third. I would not give the students this first extended version. It would be like giving them a drink out of the fire hydrant. In the extended version, I will give the principle and then make comments in brackets. It will be critical in this section to refer to the video examples to hear the application of the principles.

1. Running Eighth-Note Principle:

•Running (consecutive) eighth notes should be swung in tripletized fashion (2/3 + 1/3) and should be played with a very legato approach, articulating <u>every</u> upbeat note with a "Dah" tongue and slurring to the downbeat notes. (The basic slurring from the upbeat to the downbeat eighth note concept is what I call "default mode," but every other principle takes precedence over it; although, we normally return to default mode as soon as the reason for departure has gone by.)

•Exception (reason for departure from default mode): <u>Top notes of contours are always tongued and accented.</u> (If we draw a line that follows the up and down contours of the notes, there will be periodic notes that sit in the peaks of those contours. Every time the line changes direction, there will be a new top note.) This does not change our slurring pattern when the top note is an upbeat—we were already going to tongue it anyway. But when the top note is a downbeat, at least 3 notes in a row will be tongued—the upbeat that precedes the top note, the top note that is the downbeat, and the next upbeat note to get the default mode pattern going again. (See Notes #1, #2, and #3.)

Here is a simple scale example that I often use to teach this principle:

In the first scale, the top note of the contour is the upbeat, so the articulation pattern does not need to change, but in the second example the top note is a downbeat which changes the articulation pattern.

Here is a more sophistocated running eighth note example transcribed from Charlie Parker:

The example above is correctly edited, but often in a published chart it may look like the next example (too much slurring and some of the accents are in the wrong places):

•Accents in the line should fall asymmetrically, never in a methodic or predictable fashion. The beginning note and sometimes the ending note and the top notes of contours define the only notes we typically accent in a phrase. Extra, unwanted accenting will seriously hurt the line. DO NOT accent *every* upbeat!! That is a sure recipe to destroy swing!!! When it is tempting to accent every upbeat in a line, crescendo through the line instead. Here is a non-example of accenting every upbeat:

It is just as much a problem to accent all of the downbeats as shown in the next example:

Accents are performed with an extra surge of air above the basic playing level but do not drop below that basic level. In other words, we do not decay below the basic level as we might in classical accenting as seen in the following drawings. (See Note #4.)

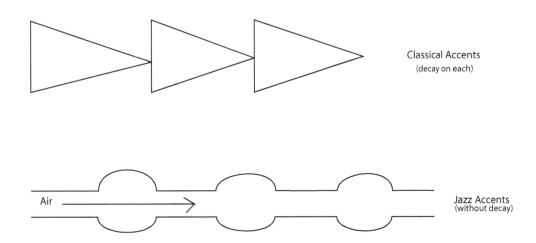

• In a section, everyone should accent where the lead part naturally accents (i.e. top notes of contours) even though in the harmony parts it may be unnatural to accent in those places. (Refer to Chapter 5 for a more expanded discussion of unifying accents in the section.)

• If we are reading sixteenth notes, then we have to determine if the sixteenths are actually acting as if they are triplets in the line (usually the case if there is just one set of sixteenths in a line of eighths) in which case the triplet slurring principles in #2 apply, or if the sixteenths are actually double time (usually the case if there are multiple sets of running sixteenths) in which case all of the eighth note slurring and accenting principles from above apply—just twice as fast. (See Note #5.)

NOTE #1: There are some corollaries that come from the principle above that I would like to underscore:

1) EVERY UPBEAT MUST BE TONGUED IN EIGHTH NOTE LINES! (The only slurs to upbeats we can allow will come into the line when we introduce DuWah's or Triplets.)

2) WE NEVER SLUR MORE THAN TWO NOTES IN A ROW, but many notes in a ro w may be tongued—even up to every note. (Refer to Note #2.)

3) NO T OR TAH ATTACKS HAPPEN IN JAZZ ARTICULATION; EVERYTHING IS D OR DAH OR N OR NAH. T or Tah does not fit into swing, and two T's or Tuh-Tuh is anti-swing. The only place we use the T in swing is to end a note, never to start it (except if we need to be deliberately corny which does happen occasionally.)

Young players often have a problem of tonguing with Tah instead of Dah. I find I am always struggling with players to get them to play both articulate and legato at the same time. The trick is to keep the air moving between the notes and tongue with a legato, Dah, tongue. The tongue must make contact for a minimal time in the attack and withdraw quickly, like touching a hot stove. Players who begin to master the legato default mode may still have the problem of Tuh-Tuh slipping in when they have to tongue two or more notes in a row, such as in a top-note-of-contour situation. I will sometimes have those players tongue every note for a little while until they can do it legato. Then when they go back to the usual slurring patterns but need to tongue multiple notes in a row, they can still be legato when doing it.

NOTE #2: Please note that in principle 1 we are defining the maximum amount of slurring, not the maximum amount of tonguing. Clifford Brown always tongued every note. Sometimes, Cannonball or Dexter or Brecker for example, tongue every note, but always still legato. However, most of the time, professional players will be using the slurring principles stated above.

I find that my trumpet players will try to slur too much, so sometimes I will say to my brass section, "Everything is tongued until further notice." Or "If in doubt, tongue more." Of course, trombone players are already tonguing every note all of the time, but they need to learn to do it so it is very legato and imitates the sound of the saxophones and trumpets tonguing upbeats and slurring to downbeats.

With young players, it is a real problem to keep the eighth notes legato; and I usually find either the air or the tongue at fault. The air may not be constant and may not be going through (between) the notes. Often the air is decaying instead of maintaining on each of the downbeat notes. Or the tongue is staying on the reed or the teeth too long when tonguing and causes a space between the notes.

NOTE #3: It is also common for young players to miss the tonguing at the top of the contour or to let the top-of-contour tonguing lead to backward slurring—tonguing the downbeats and slurring to the upbeats (which will always sound like the rhythm has straightened out and swing has stopped). Always correct these details whenever they are wrong! Never let these things slide in rehearsals.

NOTE #4: Many years ago after a performance, a young man came up to me and said, "How do you get that 3D effect in your playing?" 3D effect? Is this kid on drugs? I didn't get it until about four days later, when it suddenly hit me—"3D Effect! Yeah, some notes are in your face and some notes are in the background. It creates a third dimension in our playing." As I thought about it, I realized that this is a very apt description of the accenting patterns that should happen in Bebop lines to bring the primary melodic notes forward and keep the accompanying notes in the background. It describes Bird's playing very well. I have used the 3D Effect for teaching Bebop accents ever since.

――――――――――――――――――――――――

NOTE #5: The best way to help the band with double time figures is to rehearse the sixteenths as eighths half as fast. Really get things swinging and articulated properly, and then gradually speed up until everything is still there when it is back up to double time speed. It would have to be ridiculously fast, faster than I think I have ever seen written for a whole big band, for me to discard any of the principles of articulation or accenting that we have talked about. It is possible for a soloist to play a double or quadruple time that is so fast that it is not possible to continue the normal articulation patterns. In that case, there may be more slurring than usual, but the accents on the top notes would be articulated, and the general effect would still seem the same.

――――――――――――――――――――――――

NOTE #6: Why isn't the second note of the triplet the top note? It is only a decoration or embellishment to the true top note, which is the first note of the triplet.

――――――――――――――――――――――――

NOTE #7: **Remember** that all of the principles, including this one, are helping to define the maximum amount of slurring, not tonguing. One may always tongue more; and if in doubt, tongue more, not less--always keeping legato, of course.

――――――――――――――――――――――――

NOTE #8: Sometimes, I ghost or half-tongue a note or two just before the top note of the contour. Then the top note really pops out front.

――――――――――――――――――――――――

NOTE #9: Sometimes the traditional staccato marking is used instead, but technically, that is incorrect. I use that marking only for when I want something deliberately corny. Of course, I still interpret the staccato marking as a "Dot" under normal circumstances, realizing the inconsistencies of published sheet music.

――――――――――――――――――――――――

NOTE #10: In the Dot (or Daht) articulation, the D means it is tongued, the o (ah) means it is fat, and the T means it is squared off with the tongue on the note ending while the air pressure is still fully up. This requires that the air pressure follow through without attenuation past the time the tongue stops the sound.

functioning as if it were a triplet   functionaing like a gliss or a plop

functioning in double time

•If a note is a blue note, bend or inflect it. (Playing a blue note plain or straight takes the soul out of our playing.)

blue note

2. Triplet Principles:

•When triplets are introduced in the eighth note line, then one may do more slurring. It is possible to slur as much as from the pick up note before the triplet all across the triplet to the note after the triplet (five notes) to then start the eighth note default mode slurring pattern again.

•If the note after the triplet is the top note of the contour, it will normally need to be tongued—hence only four notes will be slurred.

•If the first note of the triplet is acting as the top note of the contour, it will need to be tongued—again only four notes are slurred. (See Note #6.)

•Multiple running triplets may be all slurred or legato tongued on the first of some of the triplets according to personal taste. (See Note #7.)

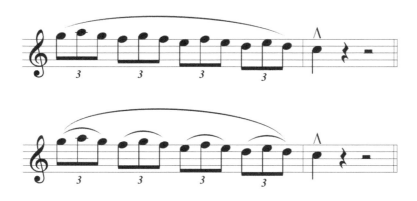

3. Ghosting Principles:

•Ghosted notes may be notated with "x" note heads or in parentheses, or they may not be notated at all (but we would still play them ghosted).

•Generally, the lowest note of the line contour will be ghosted, which simply means it is played softer (less important) than the notes around it. (See next example on next page.)

Sometimes, I will ghost more than one bottom note of the contour such as in this example:

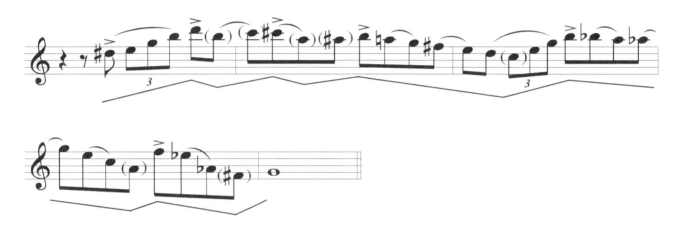

• The ghosted note does <u>not</u> disappear, nor is it eliminated altogether. It is fingered; it does have a pitched tone; and because it is normally an upbeat, it is also tongued, although it may be a softer "N" type tongue—what is sometimes called a half-tongue. It is the tongue that muffles it, not the air changing--air is constant. On trumpet, ghosting may at times be accomplished with half-valving, too. (See Note #8.)

4. Longer Note Principle:

•All notes longer than an eighth note are always tongued, except in a DuWah.

•An exception may come in slurring a long-note background line.

5. Dot Note Principles

In general, the Dot notes are square-shaped notes that are cut off with the tongue. Where do they occur?

•Eighth notes on an upbeat before a rest <u>and</u> all quarter notes should be articulated "Dot" (symbol is ^). This is especially important when quarter notes are syncopated. (See Note #9.)

For example:

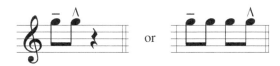

Or,

•However, a single downbeat quarter note may be either long or short depending on taste and context.

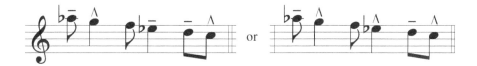

•"Dot" is fat (not necessarily that short), and it is square-shaped (i.e. no tapered or resonant ending), which is accomplished with a tongue cut-off.

•"Dot" does not necessarily imply an accent, unless the line would be accented in that spot for other reasons.

•The very nature of the "Dot" articulation does not permit slurring into these notes even if a slur is written on the part such as in the first bar of the example below. Fix to be like the second bar. (See Note #10.)

•"Dot" is "Dot" whether written on an eighth note or a quarter note or two eighths tied, etc.—there is no difference in length. Length is determined by the tempo and style of the tune-- slower=fatter, faster=shorter! In swing, the length is roughly 2/3 the value of a quarter note. In funk, it is much shorter, crisper—often changing the articulation syllable to "Dit".

•The tongue cut-off is the very thing that causes line to happen (surprise), not the other way around. When tongue cut-off's are incorrectly omitted, the sense of line is severely undermined.

•"Dot" may not be written on any rhythm with an accumulated value longer than a quarter note. (See Note #11.)

•Chains of syncopated quarter notes can either be played all long "Doo" or all "Dot", depending on taste and context, but be consistent with yourself.

•Chains of downbeat quarter notes are usually played as "Dot's" with accents implied on 2 & 4. (See Note #12.)

6. Preceding the Dot Principles:

•The note preceding the "Dot" should be played long and articulated "Doo". In other words, don't slur into the note preceding the "Dot."

•When the note preceding the "Dot" is a dotted or tied note value, it should be slightly decayed just before the "Dot" note.

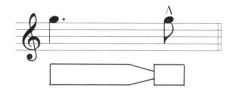

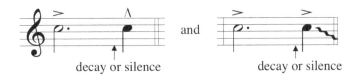

decay or silence   decay or silence

•In big band playing, there may be times when the note preceding the "Dot" is cut off with the tongue on the rhythmic dot or tie.

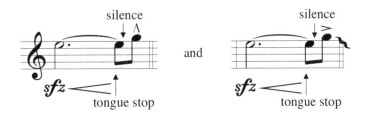

tongue stop   tongue stop

•The "Doo-Dot" punctuation is the transliteration of "Be Bop" which is the punctuation that gave the language its name. Pronunciation of B's and P's requires lip involvement; so with a horn on the face, we have to change the B's to D's and the P's to T's to get the articulation on the horn—Doo Dot to sound like Be Bop.

7. The DuWah Principles:

•Generally, when an eighth note on the upbeat is tied to a longer note value than itself, it is a "Wah" note (the rhythm may also be written with a dot instead of a tie). The downbeat preceding the "Wah" note is articulated "Du", which then produces the "DuWah".

•The "DuWah" articulation is a dynamic effect, **not** a pitch-bending effect. "Du" is soft or closed (muffled) and "Wah" is suddenly loud or open. (See Note #13.)

•"Wah" is normally slurred, but can be tongued very lightly (such as when it helps to tongue in performing a high range thing in a lead trumpet part—as long as the dynamic change is there and legato, it will still sound like DuWah).

•The pitch bending sound of the "Wah is an automatic by-product of the sudden dynamic shift from the soft "Du" to the loud "Wah" and is not accomplished by lipping. Lipping or bending into the "Wah" results in an immature-sounding inflection (what I call "high school scooping" or "junior high school scooping").

•All of the above describes the classic "DuWah" where the "Du" is a lower note than the "Wah". (See the next example, "classic".) Sometimes the "Du" is higher than the "Wah" and is functioning in an upper-note-of-contour-type position. When this is the case, both notes may be accented and the "Du" is not able to be softer or more muffled, although I would put a slight decay between the notes so the "Wah" will sound more accented. (See the example labeled "top note".)

The brass notation + means Du or closed and O means Wah or open.

•Sometimes the "Du" and the "Wah" are the same exact pitch. When this is the case, then there *is* a little pitch dip between the notes that can be done by lipping or fingers or a combination of the two. It is very important that the dip be timed late so that we also arrive at the upbeat material appropriately late for swing rhythm. Starting the dip too soon will force the upbeat note to come too soon, and swing rhythm is destroyed. (See Note #14.) This is how it may be written, but the little "u" may or may not be written.

But this is how I would think of it:

•Another issue worth noting is exemplified in this example repeated from #7 in the Chapter 8 rhythm examples.

The tied notes look like they should be treated as syncopated quarter notes and therefore articulated DOT, but somehow we sense that the tied notes are really disguised DuWahs and should be treated as DuWah with an after thought--DuWah, Oh! And by the way...Doo DuWah....(refer to the videos). However, the last tied set of eighth notes is functioning as a syncopated quarter and should be tongued DOT.

Closely related to the DuWah notes are the Bwah notes. I treat most upbeat dotted quarter notes as Bwah (accented and a quick rise to full pitch--a vocal effect): (For consistency, should be Dwah?)

Repeated Pitch Principles:

•Four or more notes of the same pitch repeated in a row always imply a crescendo and require clear articulation.

•Sometimes repeated notes will also require accenting the upbeat notes or deciding on what the hippest accenting pattern will be for that context. Whatever the decision, it does need to be unified.

9. Long Note Values Principle:

•There is usually an implied sfz-crescendo or forte-piano with crescendo on whole notes and other long note values, whether written or not. In up-tempo charts, the note would usually be cut off with the tongue at full value. This may need to be quite exaggerated in big band playing. (See Note #15.)

10. Percussiveness Principles:

•With the exception of some ballad playing, attacks in jazz are very percussive!! We always attack louder than we sustain. In classical playing, we usually attack softer than we sustain to keep a very smooth, non-accented approach.

•In big band playing, we want the accented approach, and we _exaggerate_ attacks, accents, dynamics, etc. even beyond what we would do in the combo setting. If we fail to do this, the ensemble sound will be limp and lack definition. I always ask the students for a lot of punch on the attacks and a lot of muscle under all of the notes. This makes a huge difference to the overall clarity and excitement of the band.

•In ballads, the long notes will be shaped according to phrasing and given a resonant ending more like concert band or orchestra—not cut-off with the tongue. It is important to note, however, that the long notes do not die. Typically, a note goes up before it comes down. In other words, crescendo a little through the long note and decay only right on the end of the note for the resonant ending.

NOTE #11: I sometimes, for example, see a Dot written on a dotted quarter note. This must be attributed to a notational error and must be corrected accordingly (not Dot).

_____

NOTE #12: I have been known to go down the line in the sections and make sure every individual understands the concept of tongue release. I have even spent up to 45-50 minutes of a rehearsal on this concept. If the concept is not in evidence, it will surely sound like an attempt to speak jazz with the wrong accent. I have had trombone players (I'm not sure why it is always trombone players) argue with me that they can't cut with the tongue. Some years ago, I had John Fedchock (lead trombone Woody Herman, etc.) elaborate on trombone tongue release; and for him it was very simple, "Just keep blowin' and stick your tongue in the way." I have found with all players that violating this idea is the biggest problem with the Dot articulation. They may be bringing their tongue back up to cut off the note, but the air already ended the note before the tongue got there. I always have to coach young players to follow through with the air pressure past the time the tongue has stopped the note. I am sure you can sense the importance that I feel about this issue.

_____

NOTE #13: I often write DuWah's in the part with brass notation using the + to mean soft for the Du and O to mean open for the Wah. For saxophonists, I suggest performing the DuWah by pulling the jaw back to muffle the sound for the Du and then thrusting the jaw forward for full sound for the Wah. This works to an extent for brass players, too.

_____

NOTE #14: This may be a good time to note that the same exact principle applies when inserting a turn or other jazz dramatic device between eighth notes: Wait and play the turn late so it does not force the upbeat material to come too early and undermine our effort to play swing rhythm.

_____

NOTE #15: I would recommend on longer note values delaying the crescendo so as not to peak too soon. Most young bands tend to crescendo too soon and peak too early, and it minimizes the effect.

_____

Be sure to refer to the Swing Articulation Handouts! These are placed on separate pages at the end of this chapter so you can copy them and use them with your students as you see fit. One is intended for college or high school students. The other is simplified and is intended for junior high school or middle school students.

Using the Daily Warm Up to Teach Articulation Principles

The daily warm up can provide a good way to teach these principles to the band. Then the application will come as the rehearsal progresses to the charts for the day.

Scales and Chords in Warm Up

In the warm up, I would start with scales and chords to teach the basic default mode for eighth notes, tonguing the upbeats and slurring to the downbeats in a legato fashion. This is also a good time to recognize that even the scales and chords have a top note of the contour, and if we are going to the 9th of the scale or the chord as we ought, then it will be a top note on the downbeat and will require three notes tongued in a row over the top. I also like to do five note scales (the first five notes of the scale up and down). The five note scale also has a top note of the contour on the downbeat and should be articulated accordingly. This can be combined with one of the dynamics-intonation exercises mentioned in Chapter 3.

Rhythm and Articulation Warm Ups

Next, I would have the band play up and down scales doing certain standard jazz rhythms with the correct rhythmic feel and the correct articulation. (This is also a good time to work on intonation as you go and, of course, precision and unity.)

Here are some examples:

Warm Ups

tongue cut on 4   tongue cut on 4

This fourth exercise takes care of three ideas at the same time: 1) the DuWah, and 2) treating long notes with an accent and a crescendo, and 3) cutting off the note just before the fall or accent.

You can come up with other similar ideas for warm up exercises that drill the band on common rhythms and articulations. I always use different scales each day and work on tuning at the same time.

Rehearsing the Charts

During the rehearsal of the tunes, it is important to pay attention to the articulations and rhythms and correct them as necessary or provide to the band the way you would like them to standardize the approach. Everybody in the ensemble needs to be on the same page with these issues.

Since in many cases your approach will be different than the way the chart is written, it is imperative that the band members pencil in the articulations the way they are decided in the rehearsal so they can practice them the same way each time and make them conditioned.

To aid the students, I do a lot of verbalizing of the syllables for articulation during rehearsals (like language training), and I have the band sing them as well. The following would be an example of that:

Doo Du--ooh   Du-ooh Day Doo Dot   Bwah   Du Wah
                                    (Dwah)

Here is another example:

Doo Du-ooh Day-u Du-ooh Du-ooh   Du Day Du-u Du-ooh Du-ooh   Du Day Du Day Du   Du Wah

Yet another example:

Doo Du-ooh N Doo Dot   Dot   Dot   N Doo N Du Wah

These examples show syllables that we want to sound from the horn and that communicate to the tongue what actually happens physically on the instrument. Other syllables can be used that would be more like what you would do to scat sing or like you might verbalize the phrasing as you are hearing it on a recording. We are teaching the language of jazz, and anything you can do to help the students' awareness and concept of pronunciation (on the horn) is valuable.

Note for the Rhythm Section Players

The pronunciation of jazz syllables and phrasing was developed on the the wind instruments, and every player owes a debt to Charlie Parker no what what the instrument.   When working with students who are playing piano or guitar or even drum set for that matter, you must help them try to imitate in the best way possible how it would sound on the saxophone. I have had former drum students who were studying at New England Conservatory or Berklee School of Music who were working with the Charlie Parker Omnibook (transcriptions) in private lessons.   I have taught a number of private violin students working on jazz style and improvisation, and we worked out of the Charlie Parker Omnibook and struggled with how to make violin articulation sound like Bird.   What does it take to make a note on the violin (or guitar, or bass, or piano) sound like a square-shaped tongue cut-off? That is the kind of challenge we face.

Articulation and Rhythm in Improvisation

Maybe this is obvious, but I don't want to be guilty of assuming anything. The concepts and principles we have talked about for time, rhythm, and articulation are the same whether reading a part in the ensemble or stepping out front to improvise a solo. We want the correct articulations *so* conditioned that when we call up a certain set of materials during the heat of battle in a solo, it comes with the articulation already attached. We don't have time to analyze it and think about it at that critical moment.

_____

The next pages are set up as handouts that you may freely copy for your students as you desire.

_____

Swing Articulation

(High School/College Version)

Dr. Ray Smith, Professor of Music

Brigham Young University

1. Running Eighth Notes

•Running eighth notes should be swung in a tripletized fashion (2/3 + 1/3) and should be played with a very legato approach, articulating every upbeat note with a "Dah" tongue and slurring to the downbeat notes. Exception: top notes of contours are always tongued and accented; when the top note is a downbeat, at least 3 notes in a row will be tongued. We never slur more than two notes in a row, but many notes in a row may be tongued if legato.

2. Longer Note Principle:

•All notes longer than an eighth note are always tongued, except in a DuWah.

•An exception may come in slurring a long-note background line.

3. DOT Notes

•Eighth notes on an upbeat before a rest and all quarter notes should be articulated "Dot" (symbol is ^). This is especially important when quarter notes are syncopated.

•However, a single *downbeat* quarter note may be either long or short depending on taste and context.

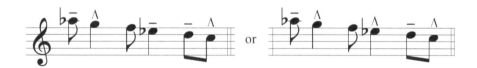

•"Dot" is fat (not necessarily that short), and it is square-shaped (i.e. no tapered or resonant ending) which is accomplished with a tongue cut-off.

•"Dot" does not necessarily imply an accent, unless the line would be accented in that spot for other reasons.

•The very nature of the "Dot" articulation does not permit slurring into these notes even if a slur is written on the part.

•"Dot" is "Dot" whether written on an eighth note or a quarter note or two eighths tied, etc.—there is no difference in length. Length is determined by the tempo and style of the tune, slower=fatter, faster=shorter! In swing, the length is roughly 2/3 the value of the note. In funk, it is much shorter, crisper—often changing the articulation syllable to "Dit".

4. Preceding the DOT Note

•The note preceding the "Dot" should be played long and articulated "Doo". In other words, don't slur into the note preceding the "Dot."

•When the note preceding the "Dot" is a dotted or tied note value, it should be slightly decayed just before the "Dot" note.

5. Du Wah's

•Generally, when an eighth note on the upbeat is tied to a longer note value than itself, it is a "Wah" note (the rhythm may also be written with a dot instead of a tie). The downbeat preceding the "Wah" note is articulated "Du". The brass notation + means Du or closed and O means Wah or open.

which then produces the "DuWah". The "DuWah" articulation is a dynamic effect, **not** a pitch-bending effect. "Du" is soft or closed (muffled) and "Wah" is suddenly loud or open. "Wah" is normally slurred, but can be tongued very lightly (such as in a lead trumpet part).

•The pitch bending sound of the "Wah is an automatic by-product of the sudden dynamic shift from the soft "Du" to the loud "Wah" and is not accomplished by lipping. Lipping or bending into the "Wah" results in an immature-sounding inflection ("junior high school scooping").

6. The Blue Notes

•When you can tell a note is a blue note, give it an inflection, usually bending it. This gives your playing more soul.

blue note

©Ray Smith, 2018

Swing Articulation

(Junior High/Middle School Version)

Dr. Ray Smith, Professor of Music

Brigham Young University

1. Running Eighth Note Principle

When playing many eighth notes in a row, such as a scale, the eighth notes should be swung (uneven or tripletized) and played very legato. The tonguing must be done with a Dah tongue, not Tah, and <u>every</u> upbeat is tongued. Then we slur to the downbeat notes unless one is the top note of a contour in the line, in which case it must be tongued and accented. We never slur more than two notes in a row, but many notes in a row may be tongued if legato.

2. Longer Note Principle:

- •All notes longer than an eighth note are always tongued, except in a DuWah.

- •An exception may come in slurring a long-note background line.

3. The DOT Notes

If an eighth note is on an upbeat just before a rest, then we tongue it DOT. The same is true of most quarter notes, especially if syncopated. An exception can be made when there is one single quarter note on a downbeat; then it can be either long or short depending on what sounds best to you. We cannot slur into a DOT even if a slur is written; it must always be tongued and cut off with the tongue to create a square-shaped note. DOTs are fat, but square notes.

4. The Note Before the DOT

The note before the DOT also has to be tongued, but it is long and sounds like DOO. So the punctuation of the line is often DOO-DOT. (This can be seen in the examples above.)

5. The DuWah Notes

We have to learn to recognize when the notes should sound like DuWah. When an upbeat eighth note is tied to a longer note value than itself, it sounds like WAH, while the note before it on the downbeat should sound like DOO or DU. Put them together, and they sound like DuWah. The brass notation + means Du or closed (soft or muffled) and O means Wah or open (loud and full).

(classic)

6. The Blue Notes

When you can tell a note is a blue note, give it an inflection, usually bending it. This gives your playing more soul.

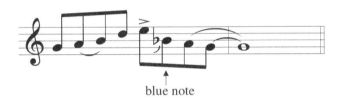

blue note

©Ray Smith, 2018

Chapter 10   Applying the Principles to Styles Other than Swing: Latin/Rock/Funk/Waltz, etc.

I feel it is important in training a band to emphasize Swing Style; but, of course, the band is going to play other styles as well. So we need to address how things change (or remain the same) when we move to playing something different than a 4/4 straight ahead swing style, which is what we have been addressing up to this point.

It is not my intention to repeat what other sources can offer on the plethora of styles we deal with as jazz players, especially the enormous number of variations in the Latin styles. Rather, I will pass on a few observations that will help you get started and help you in rehearsals.

Let me make another general observation about moving into other styles. As with swing and every other style, the critical key to learning a new style is to do some listening and playing along with the recordings. Get the students to do this, but this is also the key for the jazz band director who is not certain what should be happening in a given style.

There are several written style indications you will see, such as Shuffle, Jazz Waltz, and Swing Ballad, that still swing and receive basically the same articulation and rhythmic style that we have been talking about.

Other Styles That Still Swing

Shuffle

A shuffle is still a swing chart. What the rhythm section does changes a bit, and we'll deal with that in a later chapter; but what the horns do does not change from what they would do in straight ahead swing. The exception to that would be if we use a certain stylized articulation effect that is sometimes used in a shuffle. The following would be examples of this stylized idea. I would slur to the Dot in this case.

Listen to the video examples to learn how these should sound.

Jazz Waltz

The jazz waltz (3/4) still swings, but tends to be fast enough that we think in 1 count per measure. Again, the rhythm section will change what they do, but the horns really don't change anything to swing in 3/4. However, The American Dance Waltz (*Moon River* for example) will be slower in 3 counts per bar, and the eighth notes will be straight.

Swing Ballad

Many ballads are straight eighth notes, but some ballads still swing. A good example of a ballad that still swings would be *Georgia on My Mind.* As mentioned previously, the triplet subdivision tends to work well to help the rhythmic development on swing ballads. Swing articulation doesn't change when playing a swing ballad. Sometimes, it is effective in a swing (tripletized) ballad to make a few notes straight. Note the following example:

The straight eighths just before the double bar will each be pushed or accented such as a vocalist might do to stylize this type of figure. (Listen to the video example.)

Half-Time Funk or Shuffle Funk

This is a style of funk where the horns swing at the sixteenth note level (double-time feel) while the rhythm section plays more of a half-time rock feel with snare accents on 2 and 4 but with some underlying swung sixteenth note feel in the subdivisions. There is a version of this style known as the *Purdie Shuffle*, named for drummer Bernard Purdie of Aretha Franklin's band. In this style of funk there is a constant triplet undercurrent for everybody in the band with a backbeat on 3 (snare) ghosting the middle notes of the triplet. Examples are Steely Dan *Babylon Sisters* and *Home at Last*, and Toto *Rosanna*.

Afro Cuban, Bembe, and Other Triple Meter Styles

Styles that are in a 12/8 feel, counted in 4 with 4 triplets per measure, have a swing effect, and horn players tend to perform them with a feel and articulation similar to swing. Although, there are certain articulations that can be used in these styles that would not normally be used in swing. Again, it is the rhythm section that changes for these styles more than the horns.

Straight Eighth-Note Styles

Many jazz-related styles do use straight eighth notes, but the articulation may or may not be the same as swing. Although, the rhythms are evenly subdivided in these styles, let me be quick to point out that most of these styles were adopted and perfected by jazz players who could swing. Even though the eighth notes don't swing in these styles, there is still a hint in the recordings that the players are able to swing, even if they don't choose to do so at the moment. The performance of the eighths is rarely ultra straight, but has hints of swing in the way the first note will be a little longer and in the totally legato approach to the line. This may change in some rock examples.

Bossa Nova

In the bossa nova, the rhythm does straighten out, and the horns play straight rhythm; but they articulate the same as in swing. However, there are some things that can be done in Latin styles that we would typically not do in Swing. Here is an example on the next page:

Bossa / Samba

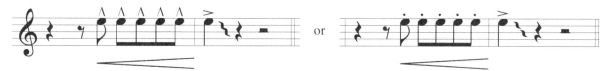

Samba

For the horn players, the Samba is really just a sped up bossa. The rhythms are straight, but the articulation is like swing except for the effects that can be added in this style that don't usually fit in swing (as just noted above).

Other Latin Styles

There are myriads of other Latin Jazz styles, and it would be impossible in this format to explore their complexities in much depth. For the purposes of horn rhythm and articulation in the big band, most of these other Latin styles such as Songo, Salsa, and the like are straight-eighth based rhythms; and for the jazz player who has been raised on swing, it is very easy to get the articulations for these styles with a little listening and playing along with the recordings. We will get to more of the changes the rhythm section has to make for these styles in Section 4 of this book.

Latin Dance Band Styles

Latin styles such as Cha Cha, Tango, Cumbia, Guaguanco, Mambo, Meringue, Bolero, and Son Montuno are straight-eighth-rhythm tunes. There are differences in articulation between them. For example, a Cha-Cha is very crisp staccato, but the Tango tends to be more smooth and legato. A Bolero is a Latin ballad, so it is slower and smoother. Again, the way to pin down the subtle differences is to listen to them and play along with them on CDs.

The Jazz Ballad

Probably, far more of the jazz ballads are straight-eighth based than are triplet based, but that is the first thing to determine when playing a ballad. We tend to use less tongue cut-offs in ballads favoring the tapered note ends. At the double time level, the lines may still swing even though the basis is straight at the half time. Ballads are dealt with in more detail in the next chapter. But here is an important point: <u>even in a straight-eighth-note ballad, I still always swing the DuWah's.</u> Note the following examples:

straight   swung

Rock and Funk (Tower of Power Type)

The rock styles use straight eighth notes with the exception of the Shuffle Funk mentioned above. The articulation, however, can be quite different from swing. There are some things we would do in rock that we would not do in swing. For example:

Du Dit Du Dit Du Dit Du Wah (sfz-crescendo, Du Wow
although not written)

The standard swing syncopation articulation, shown first in the next example, is completely reversed in some rock charts (especially from the 1960s) as shown in the second line of the example.

In funk charts, we often tongue multiple stacatto notes in a row with a long note inserted at some point.

We may also do mixed slurring and stacatto combinations that are much like classical articulation patterns and may include the concept of cutting off the last note of the slur that precedes the stacatto note.

clip this note short, too

The most important point in funk playing is that the articulation is ultra short and crisp. Successive staccato eighths will be super short as in "Dit". I have gone out of a three hour funk gig with blood on my reed from cutting my tongue playing so many incredibly short notes over such a long period of time.

The above example is going along in 2, and the short notes are brittle short—would never work this way in swing. The example below is in 4, and again, the short notes are brittle short—Dit.

The other important point about funk is that all of the longer notes crescendo up to a square tongue cut off. Rarely can anything tapered be of use in funk styles. (Refer to video examples.) This can be seen in the next example below. Some crescendos are marked; others are not, but we still put them in.

The half note in bar 5 above will be crescendoed even though it it not written, as will the long notes in bar 6. The long note in the last bar has a written crescendo, but we would still do it if it were not written.

The Rock Ballad

The rock ballad is always straight-eighth based rhythm and is pretty straight forward otherwise. The articulations will match rock style articulation.

Fusion

Fusion articulations may depend on what it is that we are fusing. We can fuse jazz with classical (Third Stream), jazz with Latin, jazz with many other ethnicities, jazz with rock, jazz with pop, etc. In jazz, we tend to accept and adopt anything that is good and substantial and fuse ourselves with it. I even had a student who has gone on to be very successful in Nashville that was trying to fuse bebop with country. So articulations and note shapes will depend to a certain extent on what we are borrowing from. LISTENING IS THE ONLY WAY to get a handle on the variety possible in fusion tunes!!!

A Word About Swing Versus Straight Time Feel

I have found it very useful in rehearsing the band to differentiate between a horizontal and a vertical time feel. Swing styles tend to be horizontal in time feel, while straight eighth styles tend to be a vertical time feel. Because the eighths are straight, they go straight up and down which gives a vertical feel to the time. I try to get the students to subdivide internally in the straight up and down feel and to lock their rhythms onto those subdivisions. The triple subdivision basis of swing gives it a more relaxed horizontal time feel. These terms, with a little demonstration, seem to really help the ensemble get on the same page for time feel.

A Word About Teaching Musical Style

What are the elements that go into differentiating between styles? This will be a little over-simplified, but I think we can reduce this issue to teaching in three areas.

1) Time Feel and Rhythmic Basis

Is it a horizontal time feel or a vertical time feel? Does it have a triple basis or a duple basis?" (Is it swing-oriented or straight-eighth based?) Do the eighth notes feel like eighths or like quarters with incidental upbeats? Etc.!

2) Articulation and Note Shape

Is the articulation basically legato or staccato? Are the attacks percussive in general or smooth, non-percussive? Do the notes have square shapes or tapered, rounded shapes? How short is short? Etc.!

3) Vibrato and Other Dramatic Devices

What kind of vibrato use is there? Is it all across the note or only toward the end of the note. Is it on nearly every note or only on some notes? How wide and how fast is the vibrato? Which notes are scooped, if any? How wide are the scoops? How long does it take the scoop to get to full pitch? What other dramatic devices help create this style?

As you listen to jazz and related styles, and as you play along with recordings in these styles; try to catalog the differences between the styles in terms of the above three categories. Your sense of style and how to teach it will grow rapidly.

Chapter 11   Teaching Ballad Playing

There is a reason that a ballad is required in your festival set and should be part of every program—the ballad separates the men from the boys and forces the band to come face to face with important musical concepts. There are two primary issues in getting the ballad in your set working, helping the soloist and helping the ensemble. We will deal with helping the ballad soloist in Chapter 22. But in this chapter, we are dealing with helping the ensemble succeed and specifically with what is different about playing a ballad from a straight-ahead swing chart.

Straight or Swung Eighths?

The first thing that must be determined when approaching a ballad is whether it is a swing or tripletized ballad or whether it is a straight-eighth note ballad. Examples of a swing ballad would be *Georgia on My Mind* or *Unforgettable*. In this case, the rhythm tends to be pretty close to the triplet subdivisions, and the articulation is basically all the same as if it were a medium swing or an up-tempo swing chart. Of course, the slow tempo does have an impact on the length of the DOT notes, which will be fatter, and the length of effects like falls, which will be longer. But generally, nothing really changes. In swing ballads, sometimes I do like to create an effect (it's more of a vocal effect) by straightening out a set (sometimes more) of eighth notes. For example:

The next two examples are both swing (tripletized) ballads where it makes sense to straighten out a set or more of eighth notes.

There are far more straight eighth ballads such as *Over the Rainbow* or *Misty*. The straight-eighth ballad involves a number of different performance practices besides straightening out the rhythm. And let me say before we tackle that, the straight rhythms still involve a little more weight or length on the downbeat notes, particularly the one that starts the phrase; but then, I would do that in classical playing as well.

So many of the differences in the straight-eighth ballad might be summed up under the idea that we shape notes more like we would in concert band playing (or orchestral playing). We usually don't cut off with the tongue on long notes or ends of phrases; but rather, we can use the tapered (resonant) note endings. The playing of the long notes, though, is usually a problem for young players who let the long notes taper (or die) across most of the note value. The long notes should at least maintain, usually crescendo, before any taper—which would only come at the end of the note. I give my students the watch phrase, "Go up before you go down on the long notes." However, we also have to be on guard against bulging or milking the long notes. As usual, listening is the key to understanding the shapes of these notes.

When the whole ensemble has to play several straight eighth notes in a row, they would often need to be individually "pushed" or accented—though legato with line direction—similar to the way jazz singers would do it. Also, as previously mentioned, even in straight-eighth note ballads, I would still swing the DuWah's. In addition, for straight-eighth ballads, we may yet swing certain figures or parts (similar to straightening something in the swing ballad). For example, the last bars of the bridge on *Skylark* are swung and then back to straight at the return of the A section:

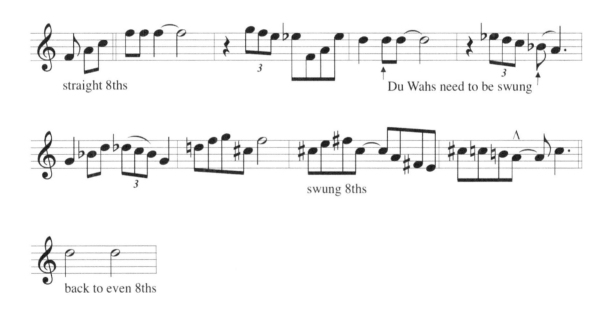

Of course, there are other styles of ballads. All rock ballads are even eighth note ballads. Some ballads are 12/8 feel (in four, but with continuous triplet feel). An example of this would be Carubia's arrangement of *At Last*. A Bolero is a Latin ballad that is based on straight eighth notes, such as Mintzer's *Carla*.

Double Time in Ballads

It is typical to have some double time figures or to actually move into double time in a ballad. Even in the straight ballads, the double time usually swings, but I cannot make that statement as a concrete rule because sometimes it doesn't swing. How does one know if it should swing or not? Listening and experience are the only way to really know; but if in doubt, it is probably safer to swing it.

Some ballads make use of what I would call "implied double time". This is where the band does not move into double time as an entire ensemble, but parts of the band may move into double time while other parts do not. For example, the horns may have a double time figure, but the rhythm section does not go into double time with them. Or, the drummer helps a double time figure in the horns, but the bass player continues to play at the half-time.

When figures are in double time, then all of the usual swing rules of articulation and rhythm apply. If the whole ensemble moves into double time, then everyone will play the same as if the whole chart were that medium to medium fast swing tempo—same rhythmic and same articulation principles.

Dynamics in the Ballad

There may be parts of the ballad that are softer than we usually play in other charts. It is often appropriate to use subtone in the saxophone section to get very soft, but it is usually necessary to work on maintaining tone and pitch at the soft levels. (See Chapters 2 and 3 for ideas on this.) However, the dynamics may vary widely in the same ballad, and the shout section should normally be a wall of sound. Sometimes the notion that the ballad is supposed to be pretty (and pretty is soft and gentle) may get in the way of asking for the kind of big band power that should be in force at the shout section. Listen to some Stan Kenton ballads, and you will know what I am talking about.

Motion Versus Emotion

It is the motion in the lines that makes music happen. The slow tempo of the ballad does not provide much natural motion, and the challenge is to create motion without the aid of the tempo—obviously, rushing is not an option. If there is no motion, then there is also NO e-motion, and the tune fails. This is a particular challenge with young bands. How do we help them create motion?

Another way of talking about this motion versus music issue is to talk about tension and release in the music. Stravinsky said it well when he said music has to have respiration. What did he mean? Respiration includes inhalation (tension) and exhalation (release or relaxation). It is the respiration, or tension and release, that breathes the breath of life into all those otherwise dead notes. That life in the lines creates the motion, which brings about the emotion in the music.

Psychologists of music have long theorized that the tension and release patterns in the music are what give music the power to touch our emotions. These tension and release patterns capture symbolically the rhythms of our own emotional life. Then when we listen to the music, we identify (normally subconsciously) with those emotional expressions and the emotions we have experienced in the past in our own lives. Of course, this concept applies to all western music at whatever tempo; but it is particularly a challenge to make it happen at the slow tempo of a ballad, and the ballad makes a great vehicle for teaching the concept to the band.

This brings up the necessity of each musician creating for himself a catalog of tension-producing devices and release devices. Here is a beginning list to help start the development of the catalog.

Tension-Producing Musical Devices

•Playing louder or making a crescendo

•Playing higher in the tessitura of the instrument(s)

•Playing faster or busier

•Playing more complex rhythmically

•Creating greater harmonic complexity or dissonance

•Using dramatic devices such as shakes, doits, growls, and the like

•Repetition of an idea over and over

•Silence—but only when it is set up properly so that it creates a tension

Musical Release Devices

•Playing softer or making a diminuendo

•Coming down in the range of notes

•Slowing down or simplifying the rhythms

•Harmonic resolution

•Silence—when set up for release

•Falls

Again, these lists are to prime the pump, and the musician should listen for examples of these devices and add to the lists as other ideas are discovered while listening and experiencing music. (This list is also essential for the improviser who must control tension levels during his solo—more in Chapter 22.)

When I am working on a ballad with the band, I usually start with the rhythm section to help them create the tension and release in the accompaniment. As they begin to see that the tension-release patterns are built into the harmonic chord changes and typically occur every two measures, every four measures, and even more every eight measures, they can apply the devices listed above as they make up their parts to bring the music out of the chord changes. When the band hears the accumulations of tension and releases the rhythm section is creating, then I can guide them to also use the devices listed above as they interpret their written lines to match the tension-release places of the rhythm section. This creates the life, the motion, the emotion we have been talking about. (Refer to the video examples for this chapter to see and hear demonstrations of this concept.) The soloist must also be guided both in interpreting his written lines and in his improvised lines to (usually) match the tension and release patterns inherent in the changes and in the rhythm section.

Chapter 12   Rehearsing the Big Band: Philosophies, Techniques, and Ideas

Rehearsal Philosophies

The following is a list of general philosophies that I believe are critical to becoming more effective in rehearsing the big band.

1) The success of the ensemble depends completely on the educator up front!! No amount of rehearsal technique or discipline or affluent demographics can make up for the educator's personal musical deficiencies. So, it is critical that the educator be in a constant program of personal improvement. It is also critical that the educator be prepared on the specific music for each rehearsal. Do some listening and analysis on the score, and anticipate the issues that you need to be ready for. You might even take out your instrument and play along with the recording by ear and feel out the style and approach for the tune. Also, play along with the recording from a couple of the printed parts and get some insight into concepts that will need to be taught.

Your personal capacity to model what you are teaching is your biggest asset! It is worth some extra effort to make your self a worthy model.

2) Take the time to teach principles in the rehearsals rather than just giving directions. The student who understands guiding principles can begin to think for himself and solve problems without you. This ultimately makes your job easier and prepares the student to become an independent musician. When I studied with Eugene Rousseau, he would often say, "My job is to become useless as soon as possible." In other words, we are not trying to reinforce the students' dependence on us, but rather, we want them to become independent, functioning musicians. This can only happen if principles are taught. An effective daily warm up period is a great time to teach principles and concepts in a methodical way.

*3) A huge key to developing a superior ensemble is working on **DETAIL**!!!* A little detail work really pays off!! When the band knows that you hear *everything* and that you are serious about the detail of the chart, they sit up and dig in; and things really start coming together. If you make a comment, follow it through to a meaningful change. If there is no change after your initial comment, then stick with it until you get the change you need. Sometimes, I feel that I cannot go on until I get the change I am asking for; but other times, the change I need is too big to expect in one day. I may give an assignment with a check up date built into it.

We cannot assume we have done our duty when we have made an astute comment, but nothing changes. Every detail of articulation, dramatic device, dynamics, phrasing, rhythm, time feel, and ensemble precision must be dealt with. You cannot afford to leave any of these things to chance.

4) We will ultimately get what we ask for from the students! If we don't ask for it, we will never get it. We may have to ask often, but we need to persist until we get what we ask for in the rehearsals. I think we make a mistake to assume that young students cannot do or understand a certain difficult thing. I believe we can acheive astonishing results with even very young students if we are not afraid to go into it and ask them for it. With the younger students, we do have to teach smaller amounts more gradually over a longer period of time; but they can grasp most things. Young students can play with a good sound and in tune. Young students can deal with style. Young students can improvise!

5) *Achieving excellence is the ultimate ensemble morale builder!* Sometimes it seems more fun just to read through one chart after another. It may seem like we will lose the kids if we start working on too much detail and slow down the rehearsal. This approach will seem fun for the students at first, but it will gradually sap the morale out of the band when they realize they are not part of anything special—in fact, part of something that is somewhere between poor and mediocre. But the rehearsal approach that demands excellence and does the nitty-gritty detail work will ultimately build the morale of the ensemble when the students realize they are part of something really great.

6) *Sight-reading regularly is a key to developing a great ensemble!* The bands that sight-read often become faster, and rehearsals go better—not to mention the students develop one of their most important professional skills. I always think of my friend, Jeff Tower at Hemet High School, when I think of sight-reading often. Jeff had one of the greatest high school jazz bands in the country for a long run. Jeff would have the students sight-read every rehearsal from the beginning of school until about Thanksgiving. He would keep notes on the charts he liked and then go back to those charts when he began rehearsing the band. By that time, the students were such good readers that the rehearsals went fast and less rehearsal was needed.

Rehearsal Ideas and Techniques

One of the great challenges educators have is to create a tight, precise ensemble. Although, we have already discussed many ideas that will help us accomplish this; in the rest of this chapter, I will try to give a summary of as many rehearsal techniques and ideas as possible for creating a clean, precise, great-sounding ensemble.

I. Tightening the Time Feel

Tightening the time was discussed in Chapter 7, but here are some additional teaching ideas that will help. (The rhythm section concepts will be elaborated more in Section 4 on the rhythm section.)

Typical Time Issues

1) Locking In the Time Between Bass and Drums: I teach the 12 o'clock analogy. The pulse hits at 12 o'clock and each player must hit right at 12. Sometimes individual concepts are different, and one player will play at 11:55 while the other player plays consistently at 12:05. Each may be playing good time and neither rushing nor dragging, but they are not playing together. This creates an uncomfortable time schism that will hurt band unity. Getting the bass player and the drummer to focus on each other and strike perfectly together on the quarter notes is the key—not mysterious, but still challenging. Give them some time alone with each other to work on this, and give them frequent feedback during rehearsals.

2) Getting Energy in the Time Feel (personal energy vs. electronic energy): Bass players tend to rely too much on the electricity to provide the energy and volume. Have the bass player turn down the amp, but play just as loudly by investing more personal energy. This produces a different time feel that has more energy and drive. The bass player needs to be coached to provide a strong attack and a good sustain for every note in the bass line. This will provide clarity to the pulse and aid the whole ensemble.

3) Working with Comping: The piano and guitar or any other comping instruments must also play good time with the bass and drums. If the guitarist is using a Freddie Green quarter note style of comping,

then he must hit exactly at 12 o'clock with the bass and drums. The comping instruments that are creating syncopations to the quarter-note feel must match the same rhythmic concepts that the horns are using—for example, upbeat material is almost on the following downbeat, downbeats are exactly on the downbeat, etc.

4) Getting the Horns to Play Time with the Rhythm Section: The horns should be playing with quarter-note feel, and the quarter notes must hit right at 12 o'clock with the bass and drums. All the horns need to individually lock their personal time in with the rhythm section—NOT following each other, which by definition puts them behind.

5) Often, the time hassles in the rhythm section are caused by players trying to play with too much complexity. When time feel is a fight, get the rhythm section players to simplify what they are doing. Then get the horn players to simplify by thinking in the long meter and relaxing. Trying *too* hard is often an enemy.

Techniques and Ideas for Time Work

1) As previously mentioned, use the metronome or drum machine. Turn it on and get the tempo, then turn it off and start the tune. After 16 or 32 bars, stop and turn it on again. See what has happened to the time and make adjustments, then try again. With a drum machine, program it to hit more sparsely such as every four bars. This is very revealing. The awareness is the big thrust of this technique.

2) Use "the STICK" to line up the time. Bang a heavy drum stick on a cowbell and provide a pulse that everyone can hear for a section of the chart in question, and amazing changes will take place. This could also be done with a metronome piped through a speaker for volume. Again, creating awareness is a large part of the director's role. Only through awareness will change be possible.

3) Have the ensemble sing the figures with the rhythm section playing. The horn players can hear and feel more how they are aligning when they are not struggling at the same time with the technique of the horn. They can also hear better when their personal volume is not overshadowing the things they need to hear in the rhythm section. It is also easier for you, as the director, when they are not powering through the horns to talk over them to give them instant feedback.

4) It is really enlightening and creates great awareness to have the band go back and forth between half time and double time while a metronome is blaring through a speaker. I would do this with both swing moving to double time swing and bossa nova moving to double time, which ends up being basically a samba. The normal problem is moving a little faster than double time when moving up and moving to a little slower than half time when moving back down.

5) It is possible to create clapping exercises that may be helpful. Have the rhythm section play and the horns clap in various patterns. Have them clap on 2 & 4 and on 1 & 3. Then have them clap only on 2 or only on 4, then maybe 4 in one measure and 2 in the following measure, etc. How tight is the clapping? Can you get them to be really accurate and really together?

6) Fixing rhythms in the horns or comping instuments will also help a lot to solidify time feel. Ideas for this are outlined in Chapters 7 and 8 and in the next section of this chapter.

II. Tightening the Rhythms

A lot of ideas for tightening rhythms have already been outlined in Chapter 8. Be sure to read that first if you haven't. So much of what we need to do is get every individual in the band on the same wavelength in their rhythmic approach.

Typical Rhythmic Issues in Swing

1) The most constant challenge we have in swing rhythm is getting the upbeat material to be played late enough in the beat to swing. I used to teach, "Don't play the upbeat material so early in the beat." Now I find myself teaching, "Play the downbeat a lot longer—almost the whole beat long." Then the upbeat note cannot come too soon. I teach, "The note written on the upbeat is played like a grace note to the next downbeat—'almost on the beat'." Problems with this concept may be the biggest deterrent to rhythmic tightness in the school band.

There is a lot of pre-conditioning (from very early) to treat written upbeat material as an upbeat gesture—played in the upbeat subdivision of the beat. This affects virtually every rhythm we have to play. I think of the written upbeat material as having nothing whatsoever to do with the upbeat, but rather is part of the downbeat gesture and nearly on the next downbeat. All written upbeat material is conceived of in relation to the next downbeat, not conceived of in relation to the upbeat in which it is written.

2) This idea, of course, leads to what I am calling quarter note feel as discussed earlier in Chapters 7 and 8. The eighth-note lines feel more like quarter notes (that lock in with the rhythm section quarter notes) with incidental notes in between. When there is no evidence of this concept in the band, then there is another major issue—lip service to swing. Most of the swing that I hear at junior high school and senior high school jazz festivals is in the category of giving lip service to swing, and there is no evidence of true swing concept. Just playing the eighth notes unevenly does not ensure that we will be swinging.

3) Most all of the students that I get at the university know that eighth notes are not played straight, and most of them know that they should be subdivided into triplets; but very few of them seem to know that _every_ other rhythm also needs to swing, and if we are subdividing in triplets, then _every_ other rhythm also needs to be played with triplet subdivisions.

4) Another rhythmic issue we seem to encounter often, is the students wanting the rhythm to be something other than what it actually is. When we look at a chain of dotted quarter notes, for example, we want all of the notes to be equidistant and coequal. This is not the case at all, and the upbeat dotted quarters are a different value than the downbeat dotted quarters. It is a challenge to see accurately how to interpret the notation that we are looking at.

5) I find another conditioning issue is wanting all of the tied notes to be longer than they really are, just because they look longer and we have become conditioned to think of them as longer. In swing, because of the lateness of the upbeat material, the tied notes end up being hardly any longer than the note would be without the tie.

6) Introducing turns, dips, or other embellishments into the eighth note line frequently causes the swing feel to be lost. The embellishment is played too soon, forcing the upbeat material to come too early, thus negating the swing feel. Delaying the effect or embellishment will delay the upbeat and help preserve swing feel.

Rhythmic Rehearsal Ideas

1) I would suggest the use of scales and chords (and patterns) as eighth note material for the band warm up. Then help the band to achieve good rhythmic feel on eighth note lines. This exercise can and should be combined with the correct articulation—legato tonguing and slurring, correct accents, etc.

2) For initially teaching the swing concept and when working on a swing ballad, I would have the band warm up on scales, chords, chart passages, and the like while actually subdividing triplets with the tongue and accenting where the real notes are. In other words, there are twelve triplet notes in every measure, and the band needs to be able to apportion the notes in the measure to exactly the right triplet on which they should occur. With a young band, a dose of this every day would really pay off over a period of time.

3) I would also use the warm up period to play certain standard jazz rhythms and unify them. (This is outlined in Chapter 8.) Use this opportunity to help the band learn to attack the notes percussively—each note is attacked louder than it is sustained.

4) When working to shore up a rhythm that involves written upbeat material, I would suggest, only as a rehearsal technique, getting rid of the upbeat and having the note hit right on the downbeat. Then put the upbeat back in, but help them perform it as a note nearly on that downbeat, like a grace note or flam to that downbeat. As stated above, most students will play that upbeat material too early, and this is a way to get them to play it later. I often tell them that performing the upbeat is like playing chicken, "How close can I put that note to the downbeat without actually putting it on the downbeat? How close can I get to the edge without actually falling over the edge onto the downbeat?" Think in 2 for these exercises:

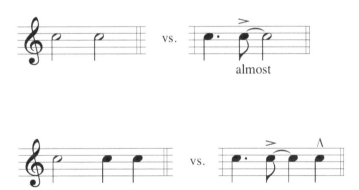

5) Springboard notes—certain notes when held long enough springboard the figure to swing or when not held long enough springboard the figure to failure (See Chapter 8)—are a huge key to getting the band to swing together and especially helpful to preserve swing feel at faster tempos. It is worth the time in the rehearsal to define which notes are the springboard notes in a passage so the whole band knows exactly which ones they are. This means every player marks his part with a pencil. The marking to use would be the standard tenuto line above the note (maybe especially wide in some cases).

6) In a conducting class of many years ago, my instructor was trying to illustrate how to get the musicians to enter on an upbeat. He showed us that if we would provide the downbeat in what he called a "gesture of syncopation", then the performers could bounce off that downbeat to make their upbeat entrance. In effect this is what the drummer is doing when he provides what we call "set-ups" for the band. He does

a set up that lands before the band entrance in such a way that the performers can bounce off of it for their entrance.

When the drummer does a good set up, the rhythmic figure in the band will be a lot tighter. This is one of those things that we often have to ask for with younger drummers. We may also need to provide an example of a fill rhythm they could play that will end up in the right place to spur the band to play the rhythm correctly. Then give them a chance to repeat (drill) it several times to establish the coordination needed.

When I am rehearsing a young band, I find I have to pay special and constant attention to this issue; and I am often singing drum setups to the drummer. (Even better if you can sit down and show him or have someone come in who can.) Listening to CDs for this concept is key—both for the drummer and the director.

See Chapter 16 for a more extensive discussion of the role of the drummer in setups and kicking the band.

III. Tightening the Articulation

Articulation principles have been discussed fairly comprehensively in Chapters 9 and 10. Be sure to review those chapters in the context of this discussion.

Typical Swing Articulation Issues

1) Most young bands have large issues with staying legato in the lines. They often use T or Tah tonguing when all of the attacks should be done with a D or Dah or Doo tongue. When tonguing multiple notes in a row, Tuh-Tuh is often a big problem. It happens when young students decay most of the longer note values (down-beat notes), creating a choppy, non-legato sound, then use T's for tonguing. Blowing continuously through the notes is a difficult thing to get from students, and sometimes getting consistent D articulations can present a challenge. Both are critical to swing articulation.

2) Accenting all the upbeats in an eighth note line is one of the surest ways to prevent it from ever swinging. (YES! I said that, and I mean it!!) I have often heard this actually taught, but listen to the music: it is not validated! It would be very rare to find anything like accenting every upbeat or accenting every downbeat. The "real" players accent in asymmetrical, unpredictable places, rarely methodically—neither all upbeats nor all downbeats—but rather top notes of contours. When predictable accents are a problem, substitute a crescendo through the line to help avoid it.

3) It is typically a problem for students to let the top note of a contour go without a tongue or an accent. We just have to correct this when it happens. When we do get them to do it, then it often turns into a Tuh-Tuh problem, and we have to work on making it legato, but still tongued with Doo.

4) Most bands have huge problems with tongue cut-off's—the square-shaped DOT notes. They are either not using the tongue cut-off's, or they are too short for the tempo or style. There is also often a lack of unity on which notes should be the DOT notes and how long or short they should be. (There are demonstrations of these problems and fixing them in the videos.)

5) Most bands have a problem with creating consistent percussive attacks, and the result is a limp ensemble effect.

6) It is another common problem for long notes to crescendo too soon and then peak too early. We have to get the band to delay the crescendo until later in the note, so the peak is at the end of the note.

7) Sustaining longer note values without decay is another common issue. Most young players begin the decay as soon as they hit the note. Keeping the note up will bring about a much more mature sound in the band.

8) There is also often a lack of unity on which notes should receive accents. This is particularly problematic for harmony players who need to accent the same notes as the lead player.

9) Most bands have the problem that the note cut-off points are not unified. In orchestral and band playing, the notes taper off to nothing and there is a lot of crossfading of the parts; so cut-off points are usually not an issue. This is just the opposite in the jazz band (except for some ballad playing). We square off the notes, and therefore, they must end just as precisely together as they started. We often define with a pencil on the parts where those cut-off's will be. For example, I may write over the top of a dotted half note -4, which means I will cut off the note on beat 4 with the tongue (and with everyone else). We also have to unify lengths of even a quarter note DOT since it is going off square without a taper. Those lengths are defined by tempo, but we have to talk about it and unify thought.

10) Notes before falls or punches are often not clean, and the fall or punch loses its impact. There should be daylight before the fall or decay just before the punch. If the fall or punch is on the off-beat, the previous note is cut off with the tongue on the downbeat. This approach must also be unified.

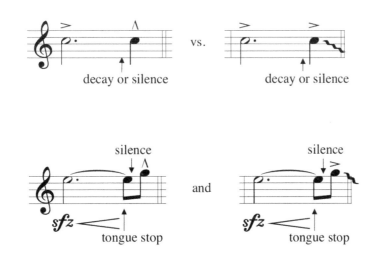

Typical Funk and Rock Articulation Issues

1) In funk, the single biggest issue is that the short notes are not DOT's; they are DIT's. In other words, the "short" notes are much shorter—in fact, brittle-crisp short. Most bands are not even in the ballpark for how short these notes should be.

2) In the older rock, it is important to note that the typical syncopation figure, eighth-quarter-eighth, is not only straight rhythm but the articulation actually turns around from swing with the eighth short and the quarter long.

Rehearsal Ideas for Articulation

1) Take the time to unify (with a pencil) in every player's part exactly which notes are short and long, which notes are accented, where the cut-off's are for longer notes, where the springboard notes are, which notes may be slurred, where the dynamic nuances are, where the dynamics changes are, where the DuWah's are, etc. etc.

2) When making a general request to the band for any of the above issues, and the band does not respond with the needed change or the needed unity; I do one or both of at least two things.

(a) Go down the line of each section and have individuals complete the request. Coaching and repetition will probably be needed. Sometimes, having one or two players from each section play alone will send a message to everyone else; and you can just have the ensemble play it again, and it will be fixed. Sometimes, it is necessary to hear every individual in the band play it alone to get it fixed.

(b) Have two or more individuals play at a time (even from different sections) and unify. This is really the same as point (a) except you can have more individuals play at once, and it may save time and be adequate to fix the problem.

3) In conjunction with the use of scales and chords (and patterns) as eighth note material in the band warm up, help the band to achieve true legato lines with correct accents and tonguing, DuWah's, etc.

4) Also use the warm up period to teach all of the articulation principles and then consistently follow up during the rehearsal of the charts. I like to have the band play unison heads or unison exercises during the warm up where we are all working on the same concept on the same material at the same time. This is most often not the case in the charts we are working on.

5) Constantly ask the band to be more articulate and more percussive in attacks while maintaining the legato.

6) Few things are more effective than the band director bringing out his instrument and modeling exactly how he would like a particular passage to sound. Model what you want and what you don't want. Show the difference and why you need it a certain way. If you do not have an instrument that lends itself to this (or in either case), sing it to the band the way you need it and even have them sing it back before trying to play it again.

7) It is imperative that the band director be very consistent in asking the band to play passages

based on the same principles that have been taught and the same decisions that have been made in previous rehearsals. It is the band director's responsibility to establish a unified mental approach to every aspect of performing the music—rhythmic concept and feel, accuracy of rhythms, springboard notes, accents, dynamics, etc. Absolute consistency and never letting things slide is very important in training a band to be an ensemble.

IV. Tightening the Section Sound of Each Section

Rehearsal Ideas to Help Each Section

1) First, fix the notes. I find I can save a lot of rehearsal time by using the 60 second noodle idea—give the band one or two minutes just to noodle the challenging passage in their part and solve personal note issues on the figure being rehearsed.

I also often use the holding notes idea—have those who play the questionable notes sustain the notes together one note at a time. Problems will be immediately apparent and can be corrected.

2) Use the one-on-one technique to tighten each person in the section to the lead—lead player with second, lead player with third, lead with fourth, etc. This will really point out what each player must do to fix his part for the good of the section. This incredibly valuable rehearsal idea is described in great detail in Chapter 5.

3) Be sure in the parts of the chart that are unique to the section that you have taken the time to unify accents (especially important in a soli), unify dynamic nuances, cut-off's and other articulations just as you would with the whole ensemble. Be sure the section has marked these things in their parts with a pencil.

4) Also, be sure to unify breathing places—mark in breathing places so phrasing will be the same. In a few cases this may mean marking in how the breathing places will be staggered to avoid breathing together.

5) It is at the section level where we can best solve issues involving tone production, intonation, balance and blend. Teach the individual players to listen to themselves and correct poor tone quality or fix balance and blend issues. If brass bells are not up over the stand and aimed out, balance is severely affected.

I teach my players to put their music stands in a much lower position and then flatten the tray so they can still see the music. Then they can hold their bells over the stand more easily. I ask them not to use the music stand as a mute.

The saxes will have problems balancing and blending if some are using jazz mouthpieces and some are not. (See Chapter 2.)

6) Intonation problems can best be solved if we use the idea of holding out notes one at a time. The source of problems become more apparent and can be fixed. Use of a chromatic tuner down the line can help solve problems quickly by bringing an awareness of where the problems are. (See Chapter 3 for more ideas.)

7) It is imperative that all required mutes or woodwind doubles be at every rehearsal so the resultant pitch and balance issues can be properly addressed.

V. Tightening Across the Horn Sections

Ideas for Rehearsing Figures that Go Across Sections

1) I like to use cross-section checking of parts. For example, have the lead trumpet and the bass trombone play together perhaps with the rhythm section, or the baritone sax and the bass trombone and the upright bass.

2) Similarly, I like to hear the leads of each section play together. This gives us a chance to unify all of the issues mentioned above across the leads. Then I like to hear the 2nds of each section, then the 3rds of each section, then the 4ths, then the 5ths. Hearing a set of players at a time can really help pinpoint intonation, articulation, balance, and rhythmic problems.

3) It can be very helpful when lining up figures that need to be coordinated between sections to simply make the affected players aware of how things are supposed to fit. For example, the brass punches have to fit at certain points in the sax eighth-note line. Show them how this is supposed to work by first describing it and then having a representative from each section (probably leads) play it slowed down so all can hear how it should fit.

4) In an effort to bring about the consistency of note cut-off's, I teach that cutting off together on long notes is like articulating the rest. In other words, when I am holding a dotted half note that should cut on 4, the cut-off on 4 is the same as articulating the rest that starts on 4. When these cut-off's are defined and tight, the next entrance will be much tighter because of it.

5) Intonation across sections will be greatly benefited, again, by holding notes and chords just like in the sections. This may be a matter of holding notes between the baritone saxophone and the bass trombone, or the lead trumpet and the bass trombone, or 2nds or 3rds, or with the whole ensemble. (Again, refer to Chapter 3.)

6) I find it very important to teach the difference between primary musical material and secondary musical material. The students have to be coached to recognize whether they have secondary material that must not compete with the primary material or whether they have primary material that must be projected to be more out front.

7) I often sing phrases for the band to help unify conceptual approach and have them imitate it by singing it back. This singing is an important rehearsal idea that not only helps unify the approach but also saves chops. We can drill a figure many times while singing, but if we played it that many times, it would be wearing down chops, especially for the brass. Often, the phrasing will require seeing when a rest is really not a rest, but rather a way of writing articulation as shown in the following example.

not really a rest,
just articulation

Could have been written:
(no difference at all)

8) A lot of things are solved simultaneously in the ensemble if I can get the air going through the horns. Tone production issues, intonation issues, balance and blend issues, chops endurance issues, range issues, even articulation issues are more quickly solved when the air is doing more of the work.

I teach that taking a full breath is like pulling back a swing when we are swinging someone on a swing set—it gets more natural momentum going in the air stream and takes a certain amount of the burden off the chops. If we pull the swing back only 6 inches and let it go, we are not going to have any big thrills. Similarly, if we barely inhale when we breath, there will be little momentum behind the air stream, so the embouchure will have to get more involved, and pinching will kill tone, intonation, and endurance.

Have the whole ensemble blow the line you are working on with just the air stream, but pitched (a little like a half-whistle). Insist on correct articulation at the same time. This is a great time to also work on tongue cut-off's, crispness, etc. Sometimes, I use this technique just to work on the articulation in the first place. I'll have the band blow the passage with the air first for accuracy of pitch. Then when the pitch is secure, I'll ask them to put a lot more air into the exercise. Immediately afterward, we play it with the horns, and it is always amazing to hear the difference when the air is working more as it should. (Refer to Chapter 2 for more detail on this idea and refer to video examples.)

9) Falls, doits, bends, blue note inflections, shakes, and all such dramatic devices must also be unified across the ensemble. Certain questions must be answered in each player's mind about any given effect—how long will it last? How wide will it be? How much will we do? How fast will we do it? And are the answers to these questions affected by style and tempo differences? All of these things need to come from a unified mental approach created by the band director.

Also, questions about vibrato cannot be left to chance. We need to define the vibrato approach appropriate to the style. And remember, we don't use vibrato in unison. (Refer to Chapter 2 for more detail on vibrato.)

10) It is also important that we define, especially for ourselves as directors, how long the last note of the piece will be. Most of the last notes of pieces I hear when I am adjudicating are played too short for finality, sounding abrupt. I always hold out long last notes, and I warn the players to be sure they get a breath that will be adequate for a long final note. Even when the chart ends on a short note such as a quarter note or an eighth note, I will have the band hold it very fat for finality.

Samba

Could be played as:

11) The old adage, "A picture is worth a thousand words" is really true when working with a big band. Give the band a sound picture. As much as possible, work on tunes for which you have a recording. Provide to the band a way of listening to the things you are working on, and inspire them to listen and play along with the recording—both with their parts and also with improvising. This really can save a lot of words and a lot of rehearsing.

As far as copyright concerns, we can copy up to 10% of a work for educational purposes. You should stay within that limit, but there is much you can do to help the students within those limits. It may also be possible to have the students purchase recordings or stream on Spotify or a similar service. You could also make purchases from the band account to develop a more extensive listening repertory.

A Word on Rehearsal Strategy

When I begin the rehearsal, I usually like to do some band warm up exercises. These can be aimed at tone production, intonation, articulation, rhythm, and the like; or they may be aimed at theory, technique, and improvising, and the like. This needs to be determined by the needs of the band and where we are at in the ensemble training process.

The next decision is what chart do I start with? I try to start with a chart that lets the band feel comfortable with time but that also lets the brass chops warm up before placing greater demands on them.

During the rehearsal I try to vary the tempo and style of successive charts to maintain interest (not unlike programming for a concert). Along the way, I try to use the teaching of concepts and the singing of lines and passages to spell off brass chops.

I try to end the rehearsal on an up note to send the band out excited about what is going on and excited about practicing. If we are in the middle of the chart when it is time to quit. I will have the band skip to the last letter of the chart so we can end the chart and have some finality to the rehearsal.

Chapter 13   Sight-Reading Development

Each year I do summer jazz camps where I work for one week with high school students in a big band setting. We start rehearsing Monday and do a concert on Friday night or Saturday. It is a real challenge to put together about four tunes in a week. I have noticed that the sight-reading ability of these high school students is weak at best. This is a particular concern when I consider that sight-reading is one of my most critical professional capacities as a professional musician.

I rarely do professional work where sight-reading is not needed. There are those gigs where I just call tunes and improvise and never open a book; but other than that, I have to sight-read at every rehearsal, every concert, and every recording session. If I were unable to sight read successfully, I would severely limit my professional opportunities.

It seems that little emphasis is placed on sight-reading development in most public school programs. I know of schools that work on virtually the same three charts all year as they anticipate region and state jazz festivals. I think there is little educational value in this approach. I mentioned earlier my friend, Jeff Tower from Hemet High School, who would have his band sight-read from the inception of the school year until about Thanksgiving. What a great thing for those students! With my own band, I try to sight-read every rehearsal unless we are right on top of a concert. Sometimes I have the band sight-read on the concert.

A few years ago, I got a call for a quartet for a wedding gig. The bride's mother asked if we could play a certain tune. I told her it was not one we usually played, but we would be glad to play it if she could obtain the sheet music. A couple of weeks later she called me and excitedly told me that she had ordered the sheet music and she now had it in hand. "That's great!" I said. "We'll do it." She asked, "How far ahead of time will you need to receive the music?" I said, "Hmm, oh, about 30 seconds." "What?!" She exclaimed. "You can just read the music like that?" I countered, "Well, when you read something in English, do you have to practice the words and phrasing, or can you just read it?" "Oh, I get it!" she said, "You can just read music like you can read English!" Well, generally, "Yes!"

Learning to sight-read music is very much like learning to sight-read English. How do we learn to sight-read English? Admittedly, at first we are slowly sounding out words; but after a lot of practice, most of us can sight-read words the first time with only few exceptions when something fools us. I have watched my younger kids come home with reading assignments such as: "Read 30 minutes every night and have your parents sign this chart when you have completed it." Or, "Whoever reads the most books this month, wins the reading contest." Or, "Those who read 6,000 pages by the end of the year can come to the ice cream party." **We need to get our music students reading a lot more so they can develop sight-reading skills**. Reading with the ensemble is invaluable; and for my students really focusing on reading skills, I suggest they get a partner they can read with on a regular basis. Both reading with an ensemble or reading with a partner will be more effective than practicing sight-reading alone.

Tips for Swing Sight-Reading Development

I am going to suggest an approach to learning to sight-read swing charts with tempos from medium slow to fast. After getting this approach going with swing, then we can apply it to other styles.

1) The first point we have already made quite adequately: *Sight-read often and regularly!!*

2) *Try to never actually sight-read any more than you have to!* That sounds contradictory! What I mean by that, and I teach this to the students: Use your time before the downbeat goes down to scan the chart and get an advance look at as many key issues as possible. What is the roadmap? Where is the sign and the coda? Where does that repeat go back to? Are there any key changes? Does anything say "Solo" or "Soli"? (Look at that first because you will be more exposed there.) Does anything look particularly black or difficult? (Take a close advance look! Finger through the passage!) It is obvious that the less I am surprised by any of those things, the better for sight-reading.

3) *Learn to read the notes!* So much of note reading mistakes can be traced back to failing to look at the key signature or failing to catch an accidental that carries through the bar. I try to get the students to be able to tell me what key they are in at any given moment without looking. After all, we are jazz players; we should know what key we are in. This may be why key signatures are not usually repeated at the beginning of each line in jazz writing as they usually are in classical notation.

I also try to get the students to call the notes by their correct names, not their enharmonic names. If we are calling a D# an Eb, then we may not catch the accidental carry through on that D at the end of the bar.

The other big help in note reading is learning to read patterns or groupings of notes instead of just note-to-note. If I can see that these sixteenth notes are a G major scale, or a G major scale except for that chromatic C#, or a chromatic scale, or whatever scale, then I can jump right in on it. All I really need to know is where to get on or get off or where to make the turn. The same would be true if I can see that I am dealing with a specific chord—maybe it's a diminished 7th chord or a minor chord with a major 7th. Of course, it would be equally helpful if I can spot any other kind of melodic pattern or sequential movement in the line. I often quiz the students to see if they recognize a particular chord, scale, or pattern. I may even ask them, when it is appropriate, to write in the chord symbols they would place over a particular passage.

I also try to facilitate the students' capacity to use deduction in reading. If I see in a passage of notes that there is an F natural written, then I have to deduce that there must be an F# in the key signature that I have forgotten. This can save me a lot of errors. Unfortunately, it is not fool proof. Because notation is not completely standardized, and because notation errors are made, there are times when that F natural may be superfluous. There may be a cautionary accidental that sends the wrong message when it should be placed there to help. As I have said many times, if the composer uses poor notation strategies, then he gets what he gets, which may be errors on the first reading.

4) *Learn to read jazz rhythms!* It seems to me that rhythmic reading is the biggest issue we have with students when sight-reading. They usually do better with notes than rhythms. At auditions, those who can even maintain a constant pulse while they sight-read are in the top 5-10% of readers for the day. I would like to suggest a method for improving rhythmic reading that I have been using with considerable success. These principles will sound familiar if you have read the previous chapters.

The Keys to Improving Rhythmic Sight-Reading

(a) Help the students learn to think in the longer meter as discussed in Chapter 7. When the students are thinking in long meter, they are far more relaxed and less likely to get into frantic, panic mode in their minds. When thinking in long meter, the students will also be less likely to add a beat or drop a beat, which is so easy to do when thinking in quarter notes. At the half note level, dropping or adding a beat would be dropping or adding an entire half measure. This is easier to detect and prevent when thinking in the long meter. I would have each student beat his foot on 1 & 3 in each bar.

(b) When we are thinking in long meter, then every time the foot drops, we are either at the first of the bar or the middle of the bar. So the second step is to help the students learn to recognize quickly where the middle of the bar is. (See Note.)

Seeing the middle of the bar is really the only challenge, since seeing the first of the bar is a no-brainer. I will have the students take a pencil and in real time mark slash marks down through the staff or vertically just above the staff, on the first of the bar, the middle of the bar, the first of the bar, the middle of the bar, the first......... When they are quick to recognize the first and middle of each bar, then we just have to tie the rhythms to these big beats.

Note: Recognizing the middle of the bar presupposes that the rhythms have been written correctly which is not always the case. The rule for writing rhythms is they need to be written so the eye can immediately discern the middle of the bar. So here is an example of a rhythm that is written incorrectly and then correctly side by side. When someone writes a rhythm so that the middle of the bar is difficult to see, then I say that guy is going to get what he deserves when his chart is sight-read.

should be written

(eye sees the middle of the bar)

(c) Tying the rhythms to the beats, for me, becomes a matter of teaching the students that there are only four places a note will commonly begin—right on the beat, almost on the beat, ricochet off the beat, or right on the upbeat (i.e. when the note is on 2 or 4 which are the upbeats when thinking in 2—the long meter). This is illustrated in great detail in Chapter 8. Please refer back to that chapter on how to get the students using this approach to rhythms.

I have been amazed at what even quite young students have been able to accomplish in rhythmic sight-reading when I have led them through this process over a period of weeks.

(d) Providing correct articulations in sight-reading may be very difficult if we are evaluating and applying principles for articulating each note in each measure rapid fire as we read. If however, we have conditioned the correct articulations for every scale, every chord, and every rhythmic pattern that we have practiced (See Chapter 9); then when we call up that material in sight-reading (or improvising), it will come with the correct articulation already attached. This will keep articulation decisions that have to be made on the spot to a minimum.

(e) At the professional level it is imperative that we can actually turn all these notes and rhythms and articulations into music that is expressive and true to the style. This is a tall order for public school students, and if we can get this part of reading, it will truly be the frosting on the cake. But we do have to strive to get the students to see the dynamics and phrasing and other musical issues while they are reading.

Tips for Applying This Sight-Reading Approach to Other Styles

Once the band has learned to sight-read effectively in swing, then it is not difficult to apply the same approaches to Latin styles or to funk charts. In many Latin styles such as Samba or Mambo, we will be thinking in 2 in the long meter and playing notes that are on the beat, almost on the beat, ricocheting off the beat, or are on the upbeat. It really isn't different from thinking those things in a swing chart.

In the funk chart, we may be thinking sixteenth note figures instead of eighth note figures and thinking in quarter notes instead of half notes. In swing, we think in half notes for the long meter feel, but in funk, we think in quarter notes for the same kind of long meter feel. In funk, the sixteenth-based rhythms are providing a double time feel similar to the eighth-based rhythms in long-meter swing. The same attitudes and approaches listed above for swing are still valid. (See Chapter 8 for an illustration of funk rhythm thinking.)

The ballad is a slow tune that does not lend itself to thinking in the long meter (unless it goes into double time or double-time figures). The rhythmic challenges are usually not extreme, and reading should come fairly naturally for the ballad.

At the slower tempos in whatever style, rhythmically we have to solve for 4 beats in each bar instead of 2. We still need to see the middle of the bar, and we should be subdividing in our minds to make the rhythms accurate. It is still possible to think on the beat or almost on the beat as a general approach. We won't see ricochet notes because the notes that look like ricochet notes will instead be notes that are almost on the next beat because of the slow tempo. (See Example 10 in Chapter 8.) We will often have to play notes right on the upbeat (unless it is a swing ballad), and we have to teach that the upbeat is a definite place, not a nebulous somewhere in the upbeat area.

Be sure to watch the video demonstration of this approach to developing sight-reading skills.

Section 4

The Rhythm Section:
It Don't Mean a Thing if it Ain't in Time . . .

So let's spend some time with the rhythm section . . .

Chapter 14   Helping Your Rhythm Section Players Develop Concept

I am not a drummer or a bass player or a piano player nor a guitarist, and I don't pretend to create a full-on rhythm section reference here. Rather, I would try in the next five chapters to offer something that may be of more value to most of you, anyway: perspectives for working with and buiding your rhythm section from a non-rhythm section player's standpoint. Most band directors are more prepared to deal with the horn sections, but we have to learn to handle the rhythm section to create a first-rate ensemble. The rhythm section is the basis of every jazz group no matter how many or how few horns we add to it. No jazz group can succeed without a well-functioning rhythm section. It cannot be ignored or left to chance. The following five chapters are the things I have done or would do if I were building a school jazz band.

Concept

I would first suggest the director help his student rhythm section players develop a concept of big band playing and rhythm section functions by listening to recordings of great big bands with great rhythm sections. Obviously, the director also needs to do this for himself. For this to be really valuable, and especially as you learn to articulate differences in performance practice between styles, you need to listen carefully to each facet of what is happening on each of the instruments. What is the pianist doing rhythmically? Harmonically? How does the guitar differ from the pianist? And when is it the same? How does the bass player function rhythmically? And how does he create lines? What is the drummer doing on the hi-hat? What about the snare drum? The bass drum? Is there any use of the toms? The higher toms? The lower tom? What is going on with the ride cymbal or other cymbals? Are there any other instruments being used such as cowbell or woodblock? Help your students do this kind of listening, too.

Who should we listen to? All of the rhythm section players will be benefitted from listening to and playing along with any of the major big bands of the modern era (and later, the older big bands as well). These bands include: Buddy Rich, Maynard Ferguson, Count Basie, Woody Herman, Stan Kenton, Rob McConnell, Thad Jones/ Mel Lewis, Bob Mintzer, Gordon Goodwin, Bob Florence, and the like. These model big bands will have great examples of drum set, bass, piano, and guitar playing. Not all of the bands have guitar, but most of them do.

The best plan is when the students play along with recordings of the tunes the school band is currently working on. It is wise to program charts for which you can obtain good recordings. Listening and playing along with these recordings is essential. A picture is worth a thousand words even if it is a sound picture!

A new app that will be hugely helpful with this is called *A-ccompany*. Those behind this new learning tool have selected top musicians (i.e. Wayne Bergeron, Bob Sheppard, Alan Kaplan, Brian Scanlon, John Beasley, Kris Johnson, Jay Lawrence, and many others including myself) to record the most commonly played big band charts in the schools. They painstakingly recorded each instrumentalist in a way that allows your students to isolate their particular part and intimately learn how a real pro would approach it. They can also mute that track at any time and "sit in" with this incredible band.

In addition, they'll be able to practice the music as slowly as needed until they can play it up to speed, practice through solo sections—both with recorded professional solos and with just the rhythm section, and even record their part with A-ccompany's band. There is no better way to learn!

The model band on these tracks sounds phenomenal! This project is similar to what the Jazz at Lincoln Center band has done with Ellington charts with a program called *Tutti* (which is also phenomenal), but *A-ccompany* has expanded to a much wider selection of charts that are most often played by high schools and colleges (and some junior high schools) and has also expanded the practice tools that are available with it. And the library is ever-expanding.

As Suzuki put it, we learn to play the same way we learn to talk. In other words, we learn to play by saturated listening and active emulation. That is what this whole idea is based on, and it takes a major step towards music being an aural art, not just a visual art. And this is especially important for the rhythm section players.

I see this way of learning as the way of the future (and the past, but greatly expanded)—combining the best of technology with personal initiative to be in an apprenticeship situation that has never previously been possible to this degree. The value of having your drummer apprentice with Jay Lawrence, to solo Jay by himself and hear every nuance and then play along with him until emulation is nailed, and then eliminate him and play and record the drum part with the remarkable A-ccompany Band—the value of this process cannot be overestimated! (And this is available for every part in the band—your rhythm section players, the second alto player, the third trombone player, the lead trumpet player!) Oh my gosh, this is a dream come true!! What a tool for us music educators!

And as I mentioned earlier, another significant resource similar to *A-ccompany* comes through Jazz at Lincoln Center (JALC) and is called *Tutti*. The Lincoln Center Jazz Orchestra performs the pieces that are the new Essentially Ellington pieces for the year, and students can play along with the Lincoln Center players while using their own charts from their school band or read them off the screen. Each band director can set this up for the school using a content code which can be obtained by visiting jazz.org/ee or by emailing ee@jazz.org, and then the students can access all of the Essentially Ellington content for free. It works great on iPhone and iPad as well as the computer. The possibilities for playing along with great musicians have never been greater or easier. It definitely beats Louis Armstrong listening to King Oliver through a crack in the door of the club and then trying to imitate what he heard out in the adjacent field—same process but much more primitive means!!

Separate from the JALC connection to *Tutti*, for a small subscription fee, a student or band director can access, with the *Tutti* app, a large number of rhythm section examples played by great rhythm section players including swing, shuffle, jazz waltz, and various types of ballads, funk, second line, Cuban and Afro-Carribean grooves like Mambo and Cha Cha and Reggae, Brazilian grooves like Bossa Nova and Samba and Partido Alto, as well as various rock feels. With each example, it is possible to see the performers as well as hear them. It is possible to isolate, both video and audio, for each instrument as well as to mute each instrument. One can also see the sheet music for each of the instruments or the whole score. This is an invaluable aid to learning how each rhythm instrument functions within a huge variety of styles. This is used at the Berklee School for rhythm section instruction. There is also a separate guitar tutorial in this app. The student can go to www.tuttiplayer.com and join and access all of this. Some of the tutorials for rhythm section styles are free.

Back to the model professional bands of the past, for the drummers there are basically three schools of big band drumming—The Buddy Rich School, the Mel Lewis School, and the Sonny Payne School. So, I would start with listening to the Buddy Rich Band, the Thad Jones/Mel Lewis Jazz Orchestra and Terry Gibbs Dream Band (Mel Lewis), and the Count Basie Band (1954-1965) when Sonny Payne was playing. Of course, it will be helpful to listen to the drummers of any of the other big bands previously mentioned.

With a few of these recordings and a pair of earphones, the rhythm section players can have many hours of playing along with the greats to develop a concept of big band playing. This is such a critical part of learning the art because very little of what a rhythm section player must do is written on the page. The whole rhythm section is improvising their parts the majority of the time unless they have some specific written figures. As previously mentioned, it is true of every instrument in the band, but especially true for the rhythm section, that we learn to play this music by apprenticeship—the models of recorded players of the past, *A-ccompany*, *Tutti*, etc.

I have emphasized big band learning here, but it is equally valuable to listen to and emulate small group recordings. The rhythm section models in small group playing are super valuable for understanding rhythm section functions and interaction and for learning to accompany the soloists in the solo sections of the big band charts.

This principle is documented in a comment made in 1984 by the great jazz drummer, Tony Williams.

"When I was a kid, for about two years I played like Max Roach. Max is my favorite drummer. Art Blakey was my first drum idol, but Max was the biggest. So I would buy every record I could with Max on it, and then I would play exactly what was on the record, solos and everything. I also did that with Art Blakey, Philly Joe Jones, Jimmy Cobb, Roy Haynes, and all of the drummers I admired. I would even tune my drums just like they were on the record.

People try to get into drums today, and after a year, they're working on their own style. You must first spend a long time doing everything that the great drummers do. Then you can understand what it means. Not only do you learn how to play something, but you also learn why it was played. That's the value of playing like someone. You can't just learn a lick; you've got to learn where it came from, what caused the drummer to play that way, and a number of things. Drumming is like an evolutionary pattern."

Resources

There are also a number of great practice resources now for young rhythm section players that are available from Jamey Aebersold (www.jazzbooks.com) and Alfred Publishing (Amazon), etc. For example, Volume 54 *Maiden Voyage* of the Aebersold play-along series has a companion book where all of the drumming from the album has been transcribed, and the young student can study what the drummer did for each of the styles and then play along with the recording imitating the professional drummer. There is also a companion book for piano for that volume where all of the piano voicings and rhythms are transcribed. The pianist can play along with the pianist on the recording; and then using the balance control, he can tune out the piano and play with just the bass and drums trying to imitate how the pianist on the recording handled rhythms and voicings. There is also Volume 30B of the play-along series, *Rhythm Section Workout*, that has a number of tunes where the drummer can see transcriptions of what the drummer did on the recording and can play along with him, but can also tune the drums out using the balance control and play with the bass, piano, and guitar while trying to imitate the drummer from the original recording. The bass player can do the same thing turning the balance control to the opposite side. This seems hugely helpful to me in helping a young student develop.

Volume 30A provides the same possibilities for the pianist and guitarist. With the balance control the pianist can tune out the piano and play with drums, bass, and guitar, or the guitarist can balance the opposite direction to play with piano, bass, and drums. There are companion books for many of the play-alongs that have the transcribed piano voicings and rhythms including Volumes 1, 41, 50, 54, 55, 60, 64 (good for

Latin rhythms), 70, etc. Similarly, there is a companion book to Volume 54 with all the guitar voicings and rhythms transcribed. Of course, it is far more valuable if the students do these transcriptions themselves, but the published transcriptions can provide a point of departure and some inspiration to do one's own transcribing. All of these materials can be found at www.jazzbooks.com.

There are other play-alongs that allow the young drummer to play along with book and CD to Duke Ellington tunes, Latin big band tunes, and other big band classics. Volume 114 *Good Time* provides similar opportunities for the bass to play with just drums or the drums with just bass. Bass lines are transcribed from Volumes 1, 3, 6, 12, 15, 22, 25, 34, 35, 42, 70. The young bass player can study bass line construction—and feel—with some of the greatest bass players like Ron Carter, Rufus Reid, Bob Cranshaw, and the like. After mastering feel and nuances, the student can then tune the bass out with the balance control and play with only the piano and drums. Invaluable!!

Alfred Publishing has a number of the same kind of books with CDs such as the *Gordon Goodwin Big Phat Play-Along: Drums, Volume 1* and *Volume 2*. The young student can play along with Bernie Dressel with the actual Gordon Goodwin band with the sheet music in front of him. Alfred also has *Sittin' In With The Big Band Jazz Ensemble—Drum Edition* for even younger drummers, and there is a Volume 2. For drums, bass, and piano, there is a book in the Alfred *Jazz Play-Along Series, Volume 4*, that provides play-alongs for Gordon's tunes with transcribed piano comping and bass lines. The mp3 CD that comes with the book also provides software for slowing down the tracks for practice tempos. And we're just getting started. [The Gordon Goodwin play-alongs are also available in multiple volumes for trumpet, trombone, alto saxophone, and tenor saxophone.]

By now it should be obvious that the best thing you can do for your rhythm section players is get them recordings of the charts you are working on with the band. Alfred again has been very helpful here because you can get an mp3 of nearly any of the charts you would buy from them by going to www.alfred-music.com. I think most of the other publishers are also trying to make recordings available online of the charts they sell. And we are barely scratching the surface of all the online learning possibilities there are now.

A thoughtful band director has the resources to guide his students to success. There is no reason to show up at the region jazz festival with a dysfunctional rhythm section.

Big Band Recordings

Here are some notable big band recordings valuable for rhythm section players (and the rest of the band as well).

• Count Basie *The Roulette Years, The Complete Atomic Basie, Live at the Sands*

• Buddy Rich *Swingin' New Big Band, Big Swing Face, Wham!, The Best of Buddy Rich*

• Thad Jones/Mel Lewis *Central Park North, Consummation, Live at the Village Vanguard, Body and Soul*

• Maynard Ferguson *The Maynard Ferguson Years, SiSi Maynard Ferguson, The Best of Maynard Ferguson*

• Stan Kenton *7.5 on the Richter Scale, Live at Brigham Young University, Sketches on Standards, Artistry in Rhythm, A Kenton Celebration*

• Rob McConnell and the Boss Brass *Tribute, Louisiana*

- Bob Mintzer *The Art of the Big Band, Live at MCG, Swing Out*

- Gordon Goodwin *XXL*, A*ct Your Age, That's How We Roll, Life in the Bubble*

- Duke Ellington *The Best of Duke Ellington, Digital Duke, Sounds of Music*

- Tom Kubis *Slightly Off the Ground, At Last*

- Tito Puente *Top Percussion/Dance Mania*, Bear Family Records 15687

- Machito *Machito and His Afro Cubans: At the Crescendo*

- Louis Bellson *150 MPH*

- Terry Gibbs *Dream Band Vol. 1-5*

Small Group Recordings

Note that it is also useful to listen to smaller jazz groups for the concepts that relate to different styles and rhythm section interaction. When the soloist steps to the mic, the rhythm section and the soloist are now functioning like a small group, even if the horns are providing backgrounds.)

- Miles Davis *Kind of Blue, Milestones*

- Cannonball Adderly *Quintet Live in Chicago*

- Roy Haynes *Fountain of Youth, We Three*

- John Coltrane *Giant Steps, Live at Birdland*

- Art Blakey *Moanin'*

- Clifford Brown/ Max Roach *The Best of... in Concert, Daahoud*

- Chick Corea *Three Quartets, Light as a Feather*

- Jeff Hamilton *Symbiosis*

- Wynton Marsalis *Live at Blues Alley*

- Peter Erskine *Sweet Soul*

- McCoy Tyner *The Real McCoy*

- Dave Brubeck *Time Further Out*

- Poncho Sanchez *Baila Mi Gente*

- Eddie Palmeri *Llego La India*

- Tower of Power *Great American Soul Book*

- Earth Wind and Fire *Greatest Hits*

- Chicago *Chicago II*

And so many others!

Technical Resources

It would also be good to read books that have been written specific to each instrument by specialists on those instruments.

Drum Books

- *The Drummer's Workbook: A Six-Pronged Approach* by Jay Lawrence

- *Essential Techniques for Drum Set: Book 1 by Ed Soph*

- *The All-American Drummer* by Charlie Wilcoxin

- *Rudimental Swing Solos* by Charlie Wilcoxin

- *Syncopation* by Ted Rees

- *Drum Set Reading* by Ron Fink

- *The Jazz Drummer's Reading Workbook* by Tom Morgan

- *Secret Weapons for the Modern Drummer* by Jojo Mayer (DVD)

- *Stick Control* by George Lawrence Stone

- *Accents and Rebounds* by George Lawrence Stone

- *Master Studies* by Joe Morello

- *The Art of Playing with Brushes* by Steve Smith (DVD)

- *The Art of Bop Drumming* by John Riley

- *Beyond Bop Drumming* by John Riley

- *Advanced Funk Etudes* by Rick Latham

- *Code of Funk* by David Garibaldi

- *Afro Brazilian Rhythms for the Drum Set* by Duduka Da Fonsceca

- *Afro Cuban Rhythms for the Drum Set* by Frank Malabe

Bass Books

• *Big Band Bass by John Clayton*

• *How to Play Bass in a Big Band* by Jeff Campbell

• *The Evolving Bassist* by Rufus Reid

• *The Ray Brown Bass Method* by Ray Brown

• *Michael Moore Bass Method* by Michael Moore

• *Concepts for Bass Soloing* by Chuck Sher and Marc Johnson

• *The Complete Electric Bass Player Vols. 1-4* by Chuck Rainey

• *Modern Electric Bass* by Jaco Pastorious

• *Funk Bass* by John Liebman

• *The Total Funk Bassist* by David Overthrow

• *The True Cuban Bass* by Del Puerto

• *Afro Cuban Bass Grooves* by Manny Patino and Jorge Moreno

Piano Books

• *How to Play Piano in a Big Band* by Bill Dobbins

• *Jazz Keyboard for Pianists and Non-Pianists* by Jerry Coker

• *Voicings for Jazz Keyboard* by Frank Mantooth

• *Jazz Piano Voicing Skills* by Dan Haerle

• *Jazz Piano Masterclass with Mark Levine: The Drop 2 Book* by Mark Levine

• *Jazz/Rock Voicings for the Contemporary Keyboard Player* by Dan Haerle

• *Jazz Keyboard Harmony* by Phil DeGreg

• *Jazz Piano and Harmony A Fundamental Guide* by John M. Ferrara

• *Jazz Piano and Keyboard An Advanced Guide* by John M. Ferrara

• *An Approach to Comping, Vol. 2* by Jeb Patton

• *The Real Latin Piano* by Kiki Sanchez

• *Hal Leonard Jazz Piano Method* by Mark Davis

Guitar Books

• *How to Play Guitar in a Big Band* by Bob Sneider

• *Comping Styles, Chords and Grooves* by Jim Ferguson

• *Mel Bay's Complete Book of Harmony, Theory, and Voicings for Guitar* by Bret Willmott

• *Mel Bay's Complete Jazz Guitar Method* by Mike Christiansen

• *Jazz Rhythm Guitar* by Jack Grassel

• *Three Note Voicings and Beyond* by Randy Vincent

• *A Rhythmic Concept for Funk/Fusion Guitar* by Peter O'Mara

• *Exploring Jazz Guitar* by Phil Capone

• *The Brazilian Guitar Book* by Nelson Faria

• *Brazilian Jazz Guitar* by Mike Christiansen and John Zaradin

• *Salsa, Afro-Cuban Montunos for Guitar* by Carlos Campos

• *Chords Galore* by Jack Petersen

• *Modern Chords* Vic Juris

• *Harmonic Mechanisms for Guitar Vols. 1-3* by George Van Eps

• *The Advancing Guitarist* by Mick Goodrick

• *Jazz Scales for Guitar* by Corey Christiansen

• *Vol. 1 How to Play Jazz – For Guitar* by Jamey Aebersold and Corey Christiansen

• *Guitar Comping* by Barry Galbraith

• *Comping Concepts for Jazz Guitar* by Mark Boling

• *Jazz Guitar Standards Vol. 1 and Vol. 2* (Mel Bay Compilation) Alfred Publishing

• *Getting into Jazz Fusion Guitar* by Scott Miller

• *Chord Chemistry* by Ted Greene

• freddie green.org for help with Freddie Green voicings and approach

• *Quartal Harmony and Voicings for Guitar* by Tom Floyd

• *Chord Tone Soloing for Gt.: Master Arpeggio Based Soloing for Jazz Guitar* by J. Alexander

• *Barry Galbraith #3 - Guitar Comping* a play-a-long available at jazzbooks.com

• *Joe Pass Guitar Chords - Learn the Sound of Modern Chords and Chord Progressions* by Joe Pass

• *Joe Pass Guitar Style: Learn the Sound of Modern Harmony and Melody* by Joe Pass

Professional Help

I think it is also very wise to use some of the funds in the band kitty to bring in a professional drummer from the area to work with your drummer or pianist or bassist or guitarist to work with your other rhythm section players from time to time even within the context of your big band rehearsal. This is, of course, not only individual help for your rhythm section players but also for you. So, pay attention and take notes. What better way is there to learn about things you can do as an educator in the future. The pros can watch and comment, but I would also ask them to sit in and play with the band while your players watch and learn. It may even be possible to bring in a "rhythm section team" of local professionals to work with your rhythm section altogether but also give a lot of individual help.

Private Lessons

This is not just true for the rhythm section players, but for everyone in your band: If you can get them studying privately with area professionals on a weekly, or at least regular, basis; it will make your job so much easier and serve your students in a most valuable way. Having that professional come into your band rehearsal may facilitate the private lesson relationship for the future.

Chapter 15 Helping Your Rhythm Section Players with Good Gear

Rhythm Section Equipment

Drums

Part of the road to sounding good is the best possible gear. Let's start with the drum set. When I have been out in the schools, I have seen some of the most awful drum sets—mismatched sizes, battered heads, broken clutches, poorly tuned, etc. If I were acquiring or upgrading a drum set for my school, I would enlist the help of a professional drummer in the area to help guide size selection and matching, choice of cymbals, etc. Like everything else, cymbals especially are not created equal. I would not just take whatever was shipped or delivered to me. You want to hear the cymbals before purchase. Also, jazz drummers often like to use rivets in the ride cymbal for a more legato sound.

Generally, the jazz drum set is smaller than the rock drum set. The bass drum may only be 18-20 inches, and everything scales down from there. Your big band drummer will not need two large bass drums, for example. The bass drum and the toms should be shallow sizes (not deep drums or power sizes). In jazz, the time is kept on the cymbals; whereas in rock, the time is kept on the drums. Good sounding cymbals help the sound of your band a lot. Get some help!

Get some help to tune the drums as well. Some drum sets in the schools just sound bad because they have not been properly tuned. There are different philosophies on how to tune the drums. For example, Mel Lewis tuned the bass drum, then the low tom, then the high tom to a Bb major triad approximately. But most drummers just suggest tuning each drum until you hear the best resonance from it. No doubt, getting a professional drummer in your area to help you with this is the best solution, but don't just leave it undone or leave it to chance. The sound of jazz drums tends to be coated heads tuned higher than rock tuning. Mounted toms should always be mounted on the bass drum and the floor tom should always be on its own legs.

Sticks are also an issue. The sticks used in the big band are not monster sticks, and jazz drummers use wood-tipped sticks. My friends really like the Jack DeJohnette model of the Vic Firth sticks, but other good choices include any stick that is about size 5A or 5B and has a wood tip. The plastic tipped sticks are useable, but they do make the drums sound thinner and the cymbals sound brighter. It is also essential to have a pair of brushes, and a pair of soft mallets will come in handy at times as well. In a Latin tune, it can be helpful to have a cowbell or a jam block that can be mounted on the set.

Like other instruments, the drum set needs regular maintenance. It is important to replace heads periodically and fix broken clutches and take care of any other issues.

Bass

Let's move on to bass equipment. As far as an instrument, probably nearly all of the bass players are stuck with whatever acoustic bass the school can provide for them. But there is a lot that can be done with the strings, string height, pickup, amplifier, and the like that can really help your bass player.

As far as strings go, most jazz players use the Dr. Thomastik Medium (regular gauge) or Weich (lighter gauge) Spirocore Strings. These strings have a little more stretch, and they have a big sound and will ring longer than the average string, which is very desirable for the walking bass sound we want to create. The D'Addario Helacore Pizzacato Strings are also very good and are less expensive. For bass players who need to use the same bass in the school orchestra and the jazz band, D'Addario also makes Hybrid Strings that would be a good solution.

Adjusters on the bridge are a good investment, especially if your bass player has to use the same bass for orchestra and for jazz band. The string height is usually a little closer for jazz playing than symphonic playing to aid in the long stretches of pizzicato. There is always a trade-off between closeness for ease of technique and facility and farther away for bigness of sound. It is a personal choice that you will have to guide your player through.

The pickup for the acoustic bass is a huge issue. Over the years, the Fishman pickup has been the old standby in the schools; but in recent years, I have become aware of other really terrific pickups made by David Gage—the "Realist", K&K—the Bassmaster Pro, and the Underwood. The important thing is to choose a high quality piezo type pickup designed for upright bass that has a full sound and round quality but also good clarity and definition.

Choosing the right instrument for the job is important, and where possible, the acoustic bass should be used for swing and jazz charts, and the electric bass for rock, funk and some Latin tunes.

The electric bass strings that my friends recommend are the DR or the D'Addario.

Another piece of gear that is critical in the bass sound chain is the amplifier. A smaller speaker size is probably best to avoid boominess and feedback. It is good to use a group of 2-10" speakers or one 12" speaker or 2-12"speakers. The twin 12" speakers are optimal for big band, but the larger they get, the greater the danger of feedback. How the speakers are EQ'd is the bigger factor that we will discuss in Chapter 16.

When choosing an amplifier, we want one that has a clear, warm sound but that doesn't color the sound of the bass, so tube amps are best. Genzbenz makes a small tube preamp that is less colored. Other good brands include Aguilar, Ampeg, Markbass, Hartke, Gallien-Krueger, and Rick Jones Acoustic Image. Amps can be purchased as a separate "head" (amp) with a separate speaker or as a combination amp/speaker in one cabinet. For travel, the lighter combination is nice.

Again, enlisting the help of a local professional player is wise when making these decisions for your school.

Guitar Gear

When it comes to the instrument, the jazz guitar is a hollow body guitar capable of warmer, darker sounds. The jazz guitar should use the neck pickup for a warmer sound. The ideal guitars for a young jazz guitarist would be the Ibanez Artcore, the Eastman Guitars, or The Epiphone SHERATON II. They are in the $800 range but sound comparable to guitars in the $2500 range. Slightly more expensive, around $1100, the Guild Starfire IV also plays like guitars that are two to three times more expensive. The Epiphone and Guild are actually semi-hollow body guitars which are thinner but still have the arch top and arch back and f-holes and tend to be easier to control feedback. If the student will own only one guitar, the semi-hollow body can be a good choice because it is more versatile and can be used in a rock or funk setting if necessary; but if the student can afford more than one guitar, a solid body guitar is yet better for the rock/fusion styles.

A pedal board is a nice addition to the guitar setup, and the student should work toward owning a variety of pedals such as distortion, wah-wah, chorus, reverb, delay pedals, etc. It can also be very valuable in a big band to have a volume pedal to shift quickly between solo volume and comping volume or to create dynamic nuances within the music. My friend, Todd Coolman, uses a volume pedal for those reasons.

When choosing strings, medium or heavier flat wound strings are often the choice. Round wound strings are also used, but they must be medium to heavier gauge strings, not the light ones, and they must be made for jazz by the manufacturer. Check that they are indeed intended for jazz.

When choosing an amplifier, the Fender Twin Amps are good for jazz and are time proven. Roland Cube Amps for good for smaller amps. A little larger, the Roland Jazz Chorus JC120 Amps and also the JC40 are great. Henriksen Jazz Amps "The Bud" Solid State Amps are great. They are a fairly small cube but are loud and have a great sound and only weigh about 12 pounds. The tube amps like the Fender can be a little harder to maintain in a school setting because the tubes get jostled around a lot. The solid-state amps like the Roland hold up better with less maintenance in a school. The most important aspect of choosing a jazz amp is its ability to produce a clean tone. The amps aimed more at rock and blues tend to distort the sound very easily. It is also critical to make sure the amp has the capacity to EQ the low, mid, and high ranges of the tone, not just low and high.

When selecting a pick, use a thicker pick, heavy to extra heavy gauge.

Piano Gear

For the acoustic piano, we are pretty much at the mercy of whatever piano we happen to have, and we pray that it has been tuned in the recent past. In your school, you should make sure that there is a plan for the regular tuning of your classroom and auditorium pianos.

It will be necessary in operating a full jazz program at your school to have an electronic keyboard for use in Latin, rock, funk, and fusion styles. The keyboards with weighted keys are a little more expensive, and a little heavier, but more like a piano and easier to play. Of course, having a keyboard will also necessitate a good keyboard amp. Here are some suggestions based on price levels.

Keyboards $500-1000:

• Casio Privia–good piano sounds, and decent other sounds

• Casio PX300 or 330

• Yamaha P125

Keyboards $1000-2000

• Korg SV-1 73 or 88 key version–tube driver-can overdrive and get a little more crunchy, has a lot of effects on board as well

• Kawai MP7

• Roland SP30 or RD300

• Keyboards $2000+

• Nord Electro

• Yamaha Montage

• Roland RD800

• Kawai MP11

Amplifiers:

• Roland KC series-KC-150 is a great amp but heavy

• Behringer Ultratone Series

• Peavey KB Series

• Motion Sound KB 300 or 500

Chapter 16 Rhythm Section Rehearsal Issues and Approaches

The Rehearsal

Now let's deal with the common things you will need to teach and correct in your rehearsals.

Setup Issues

First, let's ensure that the rhythm section is set up so they can really work together with each other and with the band. Start with the drummer, and place him forward enough that he is in front of the trumpet section so he can hear the lead trumpet and really work with him on all the ensemble figures. This will usually put him in a plane with the trombones (ears equal to the bells) and barely behind the saxes.

The bass can then set up on either side of the drums but should be in close proximity. Some feel the bass should be to the drummer's right between the drums and piano so he is near the ride cymbal for time and near the piano to hear harmonically. The opposite camp feels the bass should be on the other side of the drummer where he can be next to the drummer's hi hat and interface better with the band. Both have been used, and either will work, but I tend to prefer the first scenario.

The piano lid should open into the bass and drums for hearing and eye contact putting the pianist's back toward the audience. If the piano is an upright, the back of the piano should face into the bass and drums for sonic reasons, but this makes eye contact more difficult.

The guitar should sit next to the piano on the pianist's right (high octave of the keyboard) where it is easy to have eye contact with each other and easy to hear each other. Both the guitarist and the bassist should be placed in front of their respective amplifiers so they can hear themselves and judge accurately their personal volume.

I came to do a clinic with a high school jazz band early one morning, and the band room was built with graduated, circular riser-type steps concert band style. The drum set was on about the third riser step and the guitar on about the fifth riser step in the back where he could reach an outlet to plug in his amp. The bass was on the first riser step over against the wall where he could reach an outlet for his amp, and the upright piano was at the front of the room with the sound board pushed against the front wall. It was frankly laughable. There was no proximity and no way these poor students could even begin to function as a rhythm section. The setup was the first thing we changed that morning.

Gear Issues

Please be sure to refer to Chapter 15 for help with guiding your rhythm section players and/or purchasing equipment for the school. Especially note that your guitarist should be using a jazz hollow body guitar, and your bassist should be using appropriate jazz strings on the upright bass. Your drummer should use a jazz type drum set where the drums are not too large (as a rock kit would be).

General Piano and Guitar Issues

Your pianist and guitarist are going to need help with structuring appropriate jazz voicings from chord symbols and using appropriate rhythms for comping. In charts designed for younger bands, the voicings and rhythms are often written out. This may help at first as a guide, but it is more like classical reading than playing jazz. Every young pianist and guitarist should have the opportunity to learn to function in a rhythm section the way real jazz players do, which is to create their own voicings and rhythms from the chord symbols. There is a lot of direction for help on this issue in Chapter 14 where many resources for helping your pianist and guitarist are spelled out. But here are a few basic principles.

The rule of thumb for all modern voicings is that there must be a harmonic rub (dissonance) in every chord. Therefore in general, all chords are voiced to the 9th chord level and dominant seventh chords are voiced with the 6th (or 13th) instead of the 5th. When playing in a minor key, the tonic minor chord will be voiced with the major 7th or 6th instead of the b7th, and all of the dominant 7th chords will be altered (raised or flatted 5ths and 9ths in combination). [Note: The following guitar voicings are difficult fingerings for small hands, and better voicings for the young guitarists are found on the following page. Often young guitarists may begin with the root, third, and seventh—or even just the third and seventh, called shell-voicing technique.]

Piano:

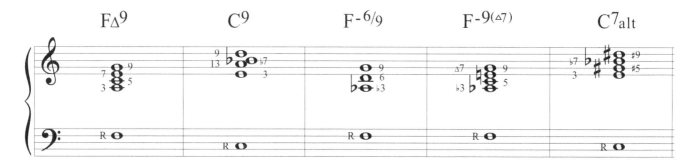

Guitar:

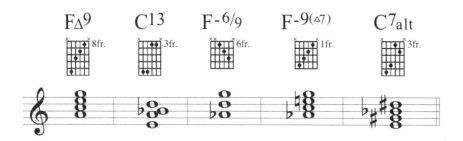

Of course, the pianist and guitarist also need to learn to function with each other as outlined in Chapter 17. The comping instruments normally use rootless voicings in the rhythm section and leave the roots for the bass. However, certain guitar voicings may include the root. (See examples on the next page.)

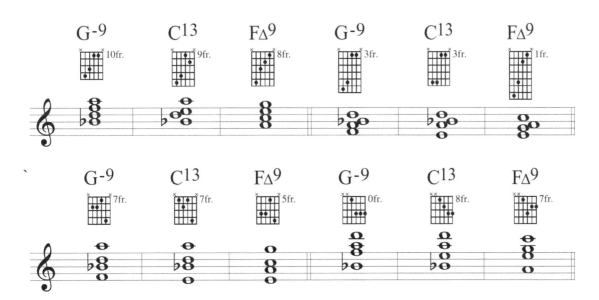

The top line above are examples of one hand voicings that could be played in either the right hand or the left hand. The roots are noted, but would be left unplayed in a rhythm section.

The second example (above) illustrates how the pianist can expand to two hand wider voicings. Again the roots that are notated would not be played in rootless voicings. See Chapter 14 for resources for two hand voicings. Below are similar examples for guitar voicings. These are II- V7 I voicings.

There are some simple guidelines for achieving smooth voice leading between comping chords for guitar and piano and vibes. The following guidelines are exempified in all the examples on this page above. Whether voicings are four notes such as guitar or vibes or one hand of the piano or two-hand spread voicings such as piano, the voice leading for cycle (circle of fourths) movement will move from a chord with the

3rd on the bottom (rootless) to a chord with the 7th on the bottom to the next chord with the 3rd on the bottom. So, some simple block voicings would look like this: Major Chords 3-5-7-9 or 7-9-3-5; Minor Chords b3-5-b7-9 or b7-9-b3-5; or Dominant 7th Chords 3-6-b7-9 or b7-9-3-6. Therefore, in a II- V7 I progression, the numbers to create good voice leading would look like this: b3-5-b7-9 to b7-9-3-6 to 3-5-7-9 OR b7-9-b3-5 to 3-6-b7-9 to 7-9-3-5. That's a lot of numbers! Jazz players always think in numbers so it can be applied quickly to any key, but let's put this in the key of F. The chord progression would be G-7 to C7 to F Major, and the notes would be Bb-D-F-A to Bb-D-E-A (one note moves) to A-C-E-G, or alternately F-A-Bb-D to E-A-Bb-D (again only one note moves) to E-G-A-C. If the smoothness of the voice leading is not yet apparent, sit down at the piano and plunk out these notes (play the examples on the previous page); and you will have an "Aha" moment.

It is a common problem for young pianists to use the pedal too much, thus smearing the chords. The piano must be thought of as a percussion instrument for most comping, except in ballads where the pedal may be more useful. Your pianist will probably have to be coached to put more body weight into the keys and play more percussively. Be sure the lid is open full stick on a grand piano. It is not uncommon for the young pianist to voice too low (muddy) or too high (tinny, tinkly). Voicings should be in the meaty part of the piano—just above and below the middle C area.

Young guitarists usually need help with the amplifier setup and volume. After experimenting with EQ controls for the right tonal concept, turn down the amp and get the player to dig in more acoustically. More human energy and less electrical energy always yields a much cleaner sound and a more percussive, rhythmic performance. Typically, there would also be little or no reverb or chorusing turned on at the amp for a swing tune. There are exceptions to this in rock/pop styles, of course. Many young guitarists come using vibrato and B.B. King style bends. Steer them away from those when functioning as a comping instrument. You will also need to ensure that your guitarist is using only down strokes or strums—no up strokes. For the Freddie Green style of comping which is more felt than heard (see Chapter 17), the amp would be very minimal; but if the guitarist is comping more like the pianist, then the volume would need to be higher for proper tone and projection and so the soloist can hear the comping. In this case, the sound, not just the feel, is important (as it is when the piano is comping). However, the idea of maintaining a clean sound by not overdriving the amp is still very important, and human energy over electrical energy will always help with the clarity. The band director must always give guidance to the guitarist about his or her personal volume in relationship to the rhythm section and to the band.

When the band is expanding to funk or rock or Latin styles, it may be appropriate to use a different guitar body and various effects pedals. It is common in funk, for example, to use a solid body guitar and pedals that may add chorus or reverb or delay and the like. Down strokes and up strokes will be used in the rock and funk styles. It is, again, helpful to look at the reference books in Chapter 14, watch video tutorials (and Tutti Player), play along with recordings, take private lessons, etc. The same is true for the keyboard player if he or she switches to an electric keyboard for different styles.

To summarize and clarify the strumming techniques mentioned above, it is normal in swing and Latin styles to use only down strokes or strums. But in rock and funk styles, both down and up strums or strokes may be used. To expand further, the fingers strum when playing chords, and the fingers "pluck" when playing single notes; the plucking may go either direction, up or down. In certain kinds of comping, the guitarist may pluck instead of strum; and, of course, if the guitarist is playing a solo with single note lines, plucking will be the technique used.

General Bass Issues

The most common instructional need for the bass player starts with the issue of sustain in pizzicato playing. Occasionally, the bassist will play arco; but the vast majority of the time the bassist will be walking a pizzicato bass line. One pizz note must sustain until the next pizz note in a continuum of notes that are connected. To get the right feel in a bass line, the pizz attacks are punchy but sustained continuously in between the notes. The pizz notes are decaying but are still vibrating when the next note is played. To get that sustain with young players can be a challenge because it requires a strong grip in the left hand to hold the string all the way down tight right up until the quick shift to the next note. If the fingers come up a little early to move to the next note, the note will stop vibrating and there will be no sustain or connection and no swing feel. Letting off the left hand early will give the allusion of a duple division in the beat which is anti-swing. (Listen to video example.) Most jazz bassists set their action a little lower to make this easier. It is much more difficult if the bass is set up orchestrally. Jazz bassists also use jazz strings or at least hybrid strings because they vibrate better and sustain longer. (Please consult chapter 15 for more detail.)

Another technical challenge is to get the right hand plucking properly. Bassists use the side of their index finger to pull hard enough on the string that the index finger stops on the adjacent string. Without this technique, there will not be enough percussiveness in the attack. It is easy to find youtube clips where these techniques can be observed, but examples are also easily seen with the tuttiplayer app discussed in Chapter 14.

Constructing bass lines from chord symbols is a vital skill of the bassist. Again, in charts for younger bands, these lines may be written out, but it is essential that the young bassist learn to do this for himself. Chapter 14 cites many resources for helping your bassist with learning this critical ability. A starting place might also be to have your student write out his own bass lines at first. The basic approach would be to write the root of the chord on each beat 1. Then write a chromatic note on each beat 4 that leads to the next note on 1. It can either be from a half step above or a half step below. Now fill in beats 2 and 3 with any notes from either the scale or the chord associated with the chord symbol for the measure. Example:

As with the guitar, the bass player needs to deal with the amplifier. Of course, the first issue for the acoustic bass is obtaining a good pickup so he can plug into an amp. Please refer to Chapter 15 for help with pickups and amps. Most school bass players have the amp cranked way too high, and the resulting sound lacks definition and clarity. I often ask a young bassist to play a walking line, perhaps from a section of the chart being worked on. Then I ask him/her to turn the volume knob on the amp half way down and then play again, matching the volume of the first time. If that isn't enough, I have him/her do it again—cut the amp volume in half but play just as loud. It is amazing how the sound cleans up and how much more attack is heard now. Then I make the point that human energy creates a whole different sound and feel than relying too much on electrical energy. Also, no vibrato should be turned on at the amp if that setting is there.

Especially in the concert hall, we may yet desire more clarity and attack from the bass, so we go after the tone controls on the amplifier. The most common thing I see is to turn the bass EQ knob down and the treble EQ knob up, but I do not think this produces desirable results. The strings are squeaky, and low end is gutted out. I have heard more pleasing results by leaving the bass and treble alone and experimenting with boosting the midrange controls, usually boosting the high mids (maybe lowering the low mids? use your ears!).

Electric Bass

I always want my bass player to play the instrument that is the best choice for the style of the chart. The electric bass is your best choice on a funk or rock chart and often on a Latin style chart. The electric bass is not the ideal instrument for swing charts or ballads unless it is a rock ballad. I strongly believe that swing style is the place to start, so all of my initial comments are about the acoustic bass and swing style. But as the band branches out from swing into Latin or Funk or Rock, the bass player needs to get into the electric bass. A complete bass player needs to double on acoustic bass and electric bass. If your bassist comes more set up for electric bass, then he/she needs to get into the acoustic bass (and get him/her playing in the orchestra and learning the bow, too); if more set up for acoustic, then the electric bass needs to be learned. In the book references in Chapter 14, there are some good resources for both basses and multiple styles.

General Drum Issues

Setting Up the Big Band Rhythmic Figures

The biggest issue to face with your drummer is his capacity to see the rhythmic figure coming in the horns, set it up, and then articulate it with the band. I think of the drummer's job here similar to a conductor when he wants to bring his musicians in on an upbeat. In conducting jargon, it is called a "gesture of syncopation." The conductor gives the downbeat, so the musicians will respond on the upbeat. Similarly, the drummer makes gestures that we call "setups" or "launch pads" so the band will respond together. So, if the band has to play a half note on beat 2, the drummer gives a strong setup note on beat 1. Then the drummer also accentuates beat 2 with the band, but the setup is the most important thing he does. It is important to know that if the setup is played on the bass drum, then the accenting of the figure will be done on the snare drum; and if the setup is done on the snare drum, then the bass drum will accent the figure with the band. Preceding the setup note, the drummer does a fill that leads to the setup. So ultimately, the order of events is play time, fill, setup, punch, then back to playing time. Getting the hang of this really does require a lot of listening and playing along with recordings. The rule for setups is they happen on the downbeat before the figure. I've tried to show a few examples on the videos. The words punch, hit, kick, stab, and figure all refer to what the drummer plays with the horns.

I find that with young drummers I have to actually sing a simple rhythmic idea and show them exactly where to put it in the measure. Then we drill it over and over to get the coordination built up. Being conscientious about this will improve the precision of your ensemble in a remarkable way. Of course, if you as the educator are going to be able to provide ideas for your drummer, then you have also got to pay your own dues listening and "playing drums on the steering wheel" (while you are driving). [Don't tell anyone I said that.]

Here are some written examples of how a drummer would fill, set up the band, and then articulate the figure with them: (The notes that also have X heads on top are the notes being setup and accentuated.)

It seems to be a common problem with drummers that during three months or so of working on the same chart, they tend to lose the chart and just start going by memory on what the figures were and get sloppy. They need to be referencing the chart when they play a concert or a festival, so they can be accurate.

Delineating Form

Another major role of the drummer is to delineate the form of the tune being played. For example, if the tune is based on an AABA form structure, there would probably be a change of color or texture for the B section which is a contrast to the A sections. In addition, the drummer places a fill that accentuates and marks where the section changes. This normally occurs every 8 bars (or 12 in a standard blues). So, in a tune that has 8 bar phrases, the drummer would do a fill in bar 8 that lands on the first beat of the next 8 bar section. This makes it clear to the band where these sections are, but it is especially important to the soloist to receive confirmation that he is still in the right place in the tune as he improvises.

It is also essential that the drummer think in terms of delineating the form for the entire arrangement. For example, he may play one type of color and texture for the original statement of the melody (the head), but then change the color and texture for the sax soli and again for each different soloist. Then there will be a big change for the shout chorus (or whisper chorus). The drummer is not simply a metronomic beat that never changes in sound, but rather a musician who is responding to the changes in the chart and leading out to help the band create music.

It would be great to watch the flow of an entire big band chart and observe how the drummer accomplishes marking the sections and changing colors to make music. It might run something like this:

Drummer starts with many punches and kicks for a big intro; settles into a "2 feel" for the head (meaning that the bass and drums are making it feel like it is an easy 2, playing on 1 and 3 with little embellishments); then goes into a "4 feel" for the first solo (standard time, playing quarters on all four beats) while playing the ride cymbal on the left side; for the next soloist, the drummer changes the ride cymbal sound by going to the right side cymbal—perhaps it is a cymbal with rivets that creates a completely different sound; for the bass solo, the drummer goes to mostly just the hi-hat and/or brushes, and the texture really thins out; then for the sax soli, the drummer switches over to a rim click on the snare drum on 4 or maybe the china/swish cymbal sound (back to sticks); when the chart goes to the whisper chorus, the drummer switches back to brushes and really lightens up the texture; then as the shout chorus comes on, the drummer switches back to sticks and does some heavy fills and setups and punches and might even go to playing heavy accents on beats 2 and 4; then at the end, perhaps there are a series of fermatas for the band with drum solos in between or even a flat-out drum solo that comes to the ending; then for the very ending the drummer does a fill during the last held note and a crash on the cut-off.

This is just an example of how a drummer might think during the flow of a chart. There is an example in the videos that has some similarities to this kind of flow.

In rehearsals, I often use a drum stick on a cowbell to create a pulse for the band (what I call 12 o'clock in my time analogy—see Chapters 12 and 17). It is serious magic that happens when everyone knows exactly where the pulse is. This can help define for the band what locking up the time really is!

Another thing I have found useful for bringing time awareness is this: set a metronome marking for the tune, and set up that tempo on the metronome. Start the tune with the metronome, and then turn it off while the band plays 8-16 bars. Keep the pulse going the band was last playing as you cut them off. Turn on the metronome. How does it compare? Did the band speed up or slow down? We can learn something about ourselves this way. Repeat the process with phrases of increasing length. This can really help to raise awareness of time and of tendencies and personal idiosyncrasies. And it should be done three ways: with just the bass and drums, just the rhythm section, and with the whole band.

I also find that often the drummer will rush in the solo breaks, like two, four, or 8 bar drum fills. The player is so used to having the whole ensemble on his back and having to drive and drag them that when everybody gets off his back for a short time, the burden has been lifted, and the drummer feels much lighter and takes off. This is something that needs a comment in the rehearsal and some drill to make the time solid.

Another common phenomenon is rushing when moving from regular time to double time and then back. Again, this needs to be drilled back and forth to establish the right feel over a constant pulse. This often happens in a ballad that is slow but goes into double time in the middle and then moves back for the ending. I have often heard the time-feel change miserably rushed at a lot of festivals.

Playing the Ride Cymbal

It is important that the drummer learn how to strike the ride cymbal to achieve optimal sound. A little experimentation will quickly show the different sounds that result from hitting the cymbal in different places. Different sounds can be useful, but for the basic ride cymbal sound, the sweet spot is usually 3-3.5" in from the outside edge. This may vary from cymbal to cymbal, so experiment.

The manner of striking the cymbal should be as if the stick was going to go right through the cymbal. This is the attitude of getting the stick *to* the cymbal, not getting *away* from it), not like I'm trying to protect the cymbal and handling it in a polite manner, or like pulling away from a hot stove. The attitude of getting away from the cymbal will not yield the attack and sound that is needed to drive the band. (See the video example.)

Playing the Hi-Hat

I can go all day at a high school jazz festival and never hear a hi-hat. I want my drummer to be dancing with his heel up on the hi-hat with a good, crisp sound. This usually takes some instruction to have the drummer open the distance a little between the hi-hat cymbals and then stomp on that cymbal to make a very crisp sound. (See the video example.)

Playing the Bass Drum

This is an area that can really be problematic in achieving the right sound for your big band. The jazz bass drum, as noted before, is not really large, and it should have heads on both sides. The purpose for taking off the front head and stuffing a pillow in it is to get a much deader sound that can be good for rock. But it is not good for your jazz tunes. There should also not be a hole in the head of the bass drum. The bass drum should compliment the sound of the bass. If the bass player is playing an acoustic bass, then the bass drum should have a rounder, warmer sound. If the bass player is doing slap and pop funk bass, then the tighter, dryer sound for the bass drum makes sense.

In a combo setting, it is common for the bass drum to be played only for accentuating hits (dropping bombs), but it is common in a big band setting for the bass drum to hit all four quarters in the bar (especially in the Buddy Rich/Louis Bellson school of drumming). However, if the bass drum is too loud when playing "four on the floor," then this is too competitive with the bass sound and causes a confusion of textures. The bass drum should be "feathered" or played very lightly except when kicking band figures. Tonight Show drummer, Ed Shaughnessy, called the heavy bass drum playing "gorilla foot." Teach your drummer to avoid this!

Playing The Snare Drum

The rhythmic figures played on the snare drum tend to be complimentary to the piano comping rhythmic figures, and it takes careful listening and coordination between the drummer and the pianist to create a successful texture. More will be said about these comping rhythms in another chapter. (Also, see video examples.)

There is a certain conventional thing that is done on the snare drum during sax solis that would be worth noting. The drummer lays his stick across the snare drum and plays on the rim on beat 4 throughout the sax soli. This technique of clicking the rim is sometimes called "rim clicks or side sticking." Drummers also often play sax solis on the china/swish cymbal.

Another thing about the snare drum is there are times when the drummer will need to play brushes. This is especially true on ballads, but may also happen on more up tempo lighter pieces or sections. Brush playing is an entire art in itself, and you will easily find entire books or videos just about brush playing. Most important is for the drummer to learn the technique commonly called "stirring soup" which refers to the circular way the brushes are played on the snare drum during ballads. Check out the video examples.

Auxiliary Percussion

When extra percussion is added to the texture of the rhythm section, everyone simplifies and plays a bit less including the drum set player. This is based on the principle of keeping the texture clean—less busy and uncluttered.

An additional challenge when working with hand percussion is to make sure it is played correctly. It is very tempting to keep kids occupied by putting a small percussion instrument in their hands. Without adequate instruction, this can really backfire. These instruments are not toys, and there are specific performance techniques and rhythmic patterns that must be practiced to be successful. There are so many of these instruments and patterns that it would be wise to get help from a local professional. Be sure, when seeking help for your percussionist, to seek for the differences between Brazilian and Cuban percussion— they are not the same. Of course, these days you can find tutorials for nearly anything on line. Google it! There are video and audio examples of some of the more common of these instruments on the *Tutti Player* app referred to earlier. Michael deMiranda has over a hundred examples on YouTube that are excellent for learning the different percussion instruments and patterns.

Chapter 17   Helping Your Rhythm Section Players Play Together as a Team

The Bass and Drums: Locking In the Time

The first issue we must deal with is to get the drummer and the bass player to "lock in" the time together. I rarely go into a school and hear the drummer and the bass player even noticing each other, but it is imperative that they learn to play precisely together. Both instruments are playing quarter notes, the drummer on the ride cymbal and the bass pizzicato. When these quarters hit exactly together consistently, we call it locking in the time, or focusing the time, or centering the time. I have compared this to a clock where every time the millisecond hand sweeps around the clock to 12, there is the pulse. The challenge is for the drums and the bass to hit precisely at 12 o'clock together. It is typical that perhaps the drummer is hitting at 5 minutes till 12 and the bass player is hitting at 5 or 10 minutes after 12. This creates a time schism that confuses the band, and the time feels bad. When the time is locked in, the pulse is undeniable and the band has no choice but to recognize the exact position of the beat.

Ideally, I would find time for the bass player and drummer to play together, just the two of them, for an hour periodically, perhaps while the horn sections are in sectionals. Their goal is to focus on each other until they can hit the quarter note exactly together consistently. This is best accomplished if they will simplify. One of the biggest problems the drummer has in keeping time is being too busy and/or too complex. So to simplify, the drummer plays only quarters on the ride cymbal at first, and the bass player also plays only quarters—no triplets or dotted eighth sixteenths, etc. Then the drummer adds in the hi-hat on 2 and 4, and eventually the snare, etc. The bass player can gradually add in some aberrations to the quarter, and the drummer can as well; but these additions do not alter the basic quarter note feel with the quarters hitting exactly together. If the quarter feel changes, then we go back to the simpler approach for a longer time—that could be days or weeks.

While the horns are in sectionals and the bass and drums are working together, it would be an ideal time for the guitar and piano to work together also. This is time where they can work on coordinating comping and how they will play together.

The Piano and Guitar and Other Comping Instruments

In modern swing, each player in the rhythm section has a role to play. The bass player is the anchor of the time and states the quarter note (or basic pulse unit) more or less continuously. He also provides the harmonic foundation. The drummer plays the time and states the quarter note on the ride cymbal a lot, but does not feel any obligation to do so if he needs to do fills or setups or kick the band or create colors in some way. The role of the pianist is to accompany (or comp) by creating conflicts (or syncopations) to the pulse that is being defined by the bass and drums. Louis Armstrong was first to say that jazz does not exist without a conflict of rhythms. This is what the pianist does. In the modern rhythm section, this is what the guitar does, too, and that is what causes all the problems that we will talk about in this chapter.

In the older rhythm section approach, say you were trying to authentically reproduce a style from the 30's, the rhythm approach is what I would call reiterative. That is, everyone reiterates the quarter note. The bass player plays all the quarter notes, the drummer plays all the quarter notes (at least on the bass drum and a lot on the cymbal), the guitar plays all the quarter notes (what we call the "Freddie Green" style from the Basie band), and the piano does quarter note-based things. It results in a very "chunky" feel in the time. In 40's Bebop, the rhythm section started moving away from this with the more modern role assignments. Through the 50's, the rhythm section concept of today matured and smoothed out a lot, with the Miles Davis rhythm sections leading the way.

So, in most of the charts your band plays today, you want this more modern rhythm section approach; unless, of course, you are deliberately working to recreate the style of the older charts. It cannot be emphasized enough the essential necessity of listening to these styles and comparing and contrasting the styles for oneself. There is no way that just reading about it will do the job for you, as the director, or for your students.

So, based on the modern approach, let's deal with the problems of the piano and guitar having carbon copy roles. Having the same roles creates a competitive climate. When both piano and guitar are rhythmically active and harmonically active at the same time, the result is an over-busy, cluttered texture that quickly becomes a mess. This is often compounded in secondary school situations when the director is trying to keep everyone involved. The band may have two guitars and vibes and even two players at the piano plus extra percussion (I've seen this). Now, there are multiple players with the same role, and the texture is thick and cluttered. This should never happen in the jazz band any more than there should be 7 trumpets and 9 saxophones. It is a distortion of the real thing that never yields the best results. Even if a director involves more students in rehearsals, the band should never go on stage (concerts, festivals, etc.) with any of these "extras" at the same time. Work out rotating. Some exceptions to this may be justified at the junior high or middle school level.

But assuming we just have one piano and one guitar, neither will play nearly as much as if the other were not there. [This is also normally true when introducing an auxiliary percussionist into the rhythm section—both the drummer and the percussionist will play about a third as much as usual.]

So, one of the most important concepts is that there should not ever be two instruments comping full bore at the same time. Some years ago, I had Michael Brecker guest soloing with my band. At the rehearsal, Michael suddenly stopped the band and turned around into the rhythm section and said, "Please, only one comping instrument at a time behind me!" And this was on a funk-based tune. A few months later, I saw Mike's quintet at the Salt Lake Arts Festival. He had Joey Calderazzo on piano and Mike Stern on guitar (two of the heavies), and they pretty much never played at the same time as each other. Joey would just sit for long stretches while Mike Stern comped, and then they would trade roles and Mike would just sit while Joey comped. When a player doesn't play for a little while, we call that "strolling". So, this is one option for solving the piano-guitar dilemma—just take turns laying out. This can be a little challenging when dealing with young, less patient players; and sometimes just from a classroom discipline stand point, it makes sense to keep both of them playing.

A second way to coordinate piano vs. guitar, where they are both playing, is to pre-decide who will be the active comper and who will take a secondary role and then when roles will be swapped. The main rule is that there are never two comping instruments that are rhythmically and harmonically active at the same time. So, the primary comping instrument is both rhythmically and harmonically free and active while the other secondary comping instrument is passive both rhythmically and harmonically. So for example, the passive comper will play very simple voicings, often only 3rds and 7ths, what is often called shell voicings, leaving the active comper free to do more complex versions of the chords, often adding altered notes or substitutions. At the same time, the passive comper will use long note, static rhythms leaving the active comper plenty of room to play more complex, syncopated rhythms. The passive comper can listen for a little hole here and there in the active comping where he can interject a little active fill without getting in the way or competing with the primary comping. (The more they have played together and the more they know each other's playing, the better they can anticipate when to interject these small fills.) Then at a certain point the roles can be swapped. These same principles will apply if the other comping instrument is vibraphone.

A third way to have guitar and piano play together really only works well on swing charts. The guitarist in the Count Basie Band was Freddie Green, and Freddie had a style all his own. He played relatively simple voicings in constant quarter notes, and he played unamplified with a hollow body guitar. He wasn't heard in any prominent way, but he was definitely felt. His playing of continual quarter notes would line up with the quarters of the bass and the ride cymbal. It is very important to note that the guitarist should only play down strokes—no up strokes—and there tends to be a gentle accent on 2 and 4 (similar to what would likely be happening on the ride cymbal). With the guitar playing this way, the pianist can comp freely.

The problem I have frequently observed in school bands is the guitarist trying to do Freddie Green style, but the guitar is amplified and way too loud and heavy and often the strokes are both up and down. Strumming is a no no! This is also called 4 to the bar comping and is characterized by simple voicings, usually just roots, 3rds, and 7ths. Freddie often used just two notes, 3 and 7, and sometimes only one. It is probably not reasonable today to play unamplified, but the electrical energy is very minimal and the human energy is maximized. It is still a feel more than a sound. It really is just rhythm guitar.

Another way to use comping instruments without having them clutter the comping is to have them play melody lines with the band. This could be a good solution with either guitar or vibes. It is common, for example, for the guitar to double the lead alto line over a saxophone soli or for the vibes or guitar to double the lead trumpet line over the shout chorus. Often charts are written making use of these ideas; but if not, the band director can do a little orchestrating when desirable.

The same principle of keeping a clean, uncluttered texture also applies within the full ensemble context. When the horn sections get very busy, the guitar and piano should not compete with the horns and clutter the texture. It is often best to just stroll (lay out) and wait and listen for that hole where a little fill can be interjected. Sometimes this may be no more than a well-placed octave "bling" from the piano. In some charts, the arranger will write rests for the comping instruments during the shout chorus or little fills.

There are times, of course, when the piano and guitar parts (and/or vibes) are written out with very specific notes and rhythms that the arranger wants. There is no problem with playing together in this case. It is never a problem to play exactly the same as each other. The problems are created when the comping instruments are playing kind of the same as each other. In other words, when each is playing with their own versions of rhythms and their own versions of chords, then the texture will busy and cluttered and full of clashes. We want to have clean, transparent textures!

Here is an example of how a pianist and guitarist might plan to coordinate with each other in the course of a chart. In the intro, there is a written unison part that they will both play, then on the melody (or head) from letters A to E, they will both be a bit more sparse, but guitar will be the active comping instrument and the piano secondary. Then at E, the piano will comp for the tenor saxophone solo and guitar will lay out. When the trombone solo starts, they'll swap, and the guitar will comp for the solo while the piano lays out. For the trumpet solo, they will switch back, and piano will comp and guitar lays out, or they both play but one is passive. Both will play in the band unison with the horns, then both rest in the shout chorus listening for an opportunity to add a little fill but getting eye contact with each other so they don't both go for it at the same time. In the ending, there are written parts they will both play.

If the chart swings in a more classic swing sense, we may decide to have the guitar play Freddie Green style and the piano would be the primary comping instrument through the chart. It would still be possible to change up textures in the solo section. If the chart is Bossa Nova or Funk style, it may be more appropriate for the guitarist to be the primary comper for a lot of the chart. In Afro-Cuban and Salsa styles, the pianist will be playing montuno patterns and the guitarist would be playing clave patterns depending on the style and clave direction (forward and reverse) of the chart. How will the band director know how to guide this? Again, there is no substitute for listening to the original recording and making sure your students hear it and have access to play along with it and transcribe and study it. Also, a reminder, the *Tutti Player* app has good examples of all these styles, and each instrument can be isolated for careful study.

> Just a reminder at this point that the guitarist and pianist need to be able to see and hear each other. Set up should be in close proximity. The guitar should not be set up back behind the drums out of sight of the pianist, but rather bring the guitar right up adjacent to the piano.

The Value of Combo Work

As noted earlier, the rhythm section functions more like a combo when the soloist gets up to play, so why not form a combo that includes your rhythm section and two or three of your best horn soloists. This is a great way to build your rhythm section and your soloists and can give your brass players a chops break at the concerts. It also helps the rhythm section know what to do during the solos in the big band context.

One of my friends who was teaching at Timpview High School in Orem, David Fullmer, found a way to break his whole big band into about 4 or 5 combos for a period of a few weeks early in the year. Not all of the combos could have the rhythm section during their rehearsals, but the rhythm section(s) could rotate, and meanwhile the other groups used Aebersold play-alongs for their rehearsal. Then Dave would have a combo concert early in the year where each combo played live with the rhythm section, and then Dave would move on to the big band format for the rehearsals the rest of the year. His big band was always terrific, and part of that was the independent musicianship that had been fostered in the combo rehearsals and concert. And part of it was due to having a well-functioning rhythm section and better than average soloists!

Chapter 18   Rhythm Section Solos

Each of the rhythm section players will also be a soloist, but the approach for soloing will be a little different for each from their usual accompanying roles.

Piano and Guitar Solos

The piano and guitar solo approaches are basically the same as the horn solo approaches which will be explored in the next chapters following this one. But there is one basic difference in that the guitar and piano are able to accompany themselves. They don't necessarily need to provide accompaniment with their own solo. It is possible for the guitar to comp for the piano solo and vice-versa. But it is more common with professionals for the pianist to comp for his own solo while the guitar lays out. It may happen more often, however, that the pianist to comps for the guitar solo.

When the pianist comps for his own solo, he will normally improvise solo lines with his right hand and comp with one hand voicings in his left hand. It is, of course, possible for the pianist to play lines in octaves or double octaves during the solo. The guitar can also play in octaves. This was a real trademark sound for the great guitarist, Wes Montgomery. Both instruments can also play block chords in sections of the solo, and this can help to build a climax in the solo. Vibes solos would follow the same ideas.

It also happens occasionally with either guitar or piano that they can play completely unaccompanied. In this case, they need to provide bass notes (at least periodically), comping chords, and solo lines (perhaps harmonized). This is an art in itself and must be learned, again, by apprenticeship. Pianists should listen to people like Erroll Garner, Oscar Peterson, and Art Tatum, etc. Guitarists should listen to Joe Pass, Jim Hall, Johnny Smith, etc.

The Bass Solo

The general approach to the bass solo is also like the approach of the horns—improvising single lines that work with the chord structure. However, the bass is capable of double stops and can also play unaccompanied. In addition, the bass has the ability to play with percussive sounds such as slaps on the body of the bass. The bass can also play an arco (bowed) solo. Some great bass players have even sung along with their solos or hummed. (Listen to Slam Stewart or Michael Moore.) A bass solo can also be a walking solo.

The accompaniment of the bass solo can go more than one way. The most common is for the bass to play with just the drummer. Typically, the drummer will move to the hi hat and keep mostly out of the way. If the piano or guitar accompanies the bass, they will play higher, lighter comping and stay out of the lower frequencies where the bass lives. Always the goal is to be non-competitive and keep the texture transparent and uncluttered. The accompanimental players should always be listening to the soloist and base what they choose to play on what the soloist is choosing to do. This can also be a verbal discussion in rehearsals. "How would you like us to accompany you on your solo?"

The Drum Solo

There are often drum solos in the pieces we play. In fact, I often try to program a piece at the end of the concert that has a drum solo because of the effect it always seems to have on the audience. It is one of the things that can help to ensure a demand for an encore.

Drum solos come in a variety of forms. Some are in time, some are not; many are in the form, but some are not. Some solos are just extended fills between multiple "last" fermata notes—in which case I shape it so each solo is a little longer than the previous. The one thing they all have in common is that they should have a shape that grows in intensity and excitement up to a climax, which is often where the band comes back in. Although, there are times when it may be more appropriate for the drummer to bring it down and re-establish time before the band re-enters.

Soloing is mostly a matter of improvising stickings (often based on rudiments) and orchestrating the rhythms around the various parts of the drum kit with varying dynamics. The soloist must choose which rhythmic level to play at (8th notes, 16th notes, quarter notes, etc.) and then, of course, this can be varied. In jazz, rock, and other related styles, the bass drum will often be performing the function of a third hand in executing rhythmic ideas. Often the drummer will choose a bass drum and hi hat foot ostinato to play over. The drum solo should fit within the particular chart being played so it has relevance to the tune and so it contributes to making the music that is intended in that arrangement.

The fills that we have mentioned earlier in Chapter 16 are really just short solos, and the actual solo is really just a longer fill.

Any attempt to verbalize exactly what to do in one of these solos will fall short if your drummer has not heard recorded drum solos and played along and determined how to approach them. So much of what the drummer has to learn in every facet including these solos is by apprenticeship. Again, try to choose repertory for which you have recordings, especially early on, so the drummer has a model and can play along and learn what he needs to do and how to go about it. That is the whole key!!

In the same way horn players practice scales and chords and patterns, the drummer will benefit from practicing sticking combinations, hand and foot combinations, and rudiments. It is essential for developing drummers to internalize the 40 standard rudiments, and work out of George Lawrence Stone's excellent book, *Stick Control*.

Most drum solos are unaccompanied, but it is possible for the other rhythm section players to play hits or rhythms during a solo. For example, maybe the bass, piano, and guitar hit a quarter note when the harmony changes or maybe every four bars. Some charts are written for the drummer to trade fours or eights with the entire ensemble or for the drummer to solo around rhythmic figures that are being played by the band. Variety is the spice!

Summary

The most important thing the rhythm section players can do to develop as soloists is to learn by listening and emulating (playing along and transcribing). There also needs to be an on-going dialogue in the rhythm section about how each soloist would like to be accompanied (and about how they will accompany the horn soloists). The rhythm section soloists can also profit by going through the same developmental processes as the horn players. That will be the subject of the chapters in the next section.

Section 5

The Soloists:

It Don't Mean a Thing if there Ain't No Jazz....

Let's jazz it up. . . . .

Chapter 19   General Ideas for Helping the Soloists in Your Band

What Can a Band Director Really Do About the Soloists?

We started this book with the premise that to develop a first-rate jazz ensemble, four things are essential: 1-teaching solid principles of instrumental tone production, intonation, section playing, balance, and blend; 2-teaching solid principles of style including articulation and rhythm and time, starting with swing style and then expanding; 3-developing a strong, cohesive rhythm section; and 4-developing strong soloists. If any one of those areas is deficit, the band will fall short of the mark. We have dealt so far with the first three areas. Now we need to deal with how to develop strong soloists. This may seem like the most elusive of the four. If improvisation is a scary thought to you as the band director, if you have never gone through the process yourself, or if you have tried but never felt like you succeeded, then what can you do to help the soloists in you band?

Improvisation is the lifeblood of jazz. A few years ago, I watched Leonard Feather, renowned jazz journalist, and Mark Gridley, jazz history author, debate whether a piece is still jazz if there is no improvisation in it. My own belief is that pieces without improvisation that are still considered jazz are very rare. When we perform at a jazz festival, each chart should include improvisation, even if we have to add a solo up front or create or lengthen a solo section. We have full latitude to modify the form of the chart to accomplish our purposes. Many years back, I adjudicated a jazz band performance that had no improvisation in the whole set of three charts. I felt compelled to comment to the band that even though I heard some jazz-like rhythms and lines, that I had not heard any jazz in their performance. It was like a concert band trying to play jazz charts. We cannot escape our responsibility to deal with improvisation whatever our past experience!

A Right Brain Approach

So, what can you really do to build soloists? It is common for me to have students come to a lesson asking for help with a solo they were given in their school band. It is tempting to jump into theory and chord construction and ideas like I might with a more advanced student, but this approach rarely yields any satisfactory results in any timely way. Instead, we get the recording and start playing along by ear with the whole track, not just the solo section. We get acquainted by ear with the melodic and rhythmic ideas of the chart, and we ear out what the key signature is and where it seems to change key. We improvise through the whole chart and really psyche out the tune. Then we pay closer attention to the soloists and try to copy by ear little ideas we like in the solo or figure out what those notes are that sound cool to us. Sometimes cool ideas can even come from the background figures in the ensemble. In an hour, the student is often already sounding pretty decent and can go home and spend a lot more time living with the recording. If we have no recording, I will pull out something that is in a similar key or style; but this is a strong reason for the band director to choose charts for which there is an available recording.

The process just described is what I call right brain learning. It seems less efficient at first, but it is a far more effective way to learn in the long run. This is something YOU can motivate your students to do! And it is fun! Admittedly, when I do this with the students, I have my horn out psyching out the chart myself; and I am guiding the student in the discovery process and spoon feeding them a little. I do think doing this is more effective, but not essential to the right brain learning process if you are not yet able to do it yourself. Of course, you could take out your instrument in your own privacy (if you are not confident) and do some of this work yourself, and then you can provide more informed guidance in the classroom. The ears are capable of providing a lot of information quickly. It takes a lot of time, training, study and practice for the eyes to yield as much information. (We are certainly striving for that level of proficiency, but I'm afraid it won't come in time for your next performance.)

When playing by ear, we will all play a "wrong" note here and there; but realize the right note is only a half-step away, in most cases in either direction. It is worth practicing the skill of getting out of these wrong notes gracefully. Perhaps a wrong note becomes a grace note to the right note. Or perhaps the wrong note leads to some interesting chromaticism that ends up on a strong target note. It would be impossible to calculate how many grace notes or bends or hip-sounding ideas in the history of jazz started out as a "wrong" note. It is a matter of developing quick reflexes to turn that wrong note into an idea that resolves to a right note. It is important to note that sometimes people talk about repeating the wrong note to make it sound right; but two negatives make a positive only in math. Two negatives in music just compound how bad it sounds. However, if the wrong note has led to an interesting chromaticism in a line, that whole idea could be repeated.

I sometimes assign students to deliberately play wrong notes and practice getting out of them by using them gracefully in a line. This sharpens reflexes and is a skill that often comes to the rescue. The Blues is a particularly good vehicle for this exercise. I used to ask a student why they played that wrong note? But the real question is, "Why did you let that note become wrong?" With a little discretion, pretty much any note in the chromatic scale can be played. It is what is done with it afterwards that makes the difference.

Most Music Education is Left Brained

I think there are good reasons why music education has moved to a much more left brained orientation, but initially it is slow and less effective. Let me explain what I mean. In the field of right brained, left brained thinking, we normally think of the right brain dominant person as the intuitive, spontaneous, artistic, creative type; while the left brain dominant person is more scientific, mathematical, logical, and statistical. So, was our great model, Charlie Parker, right brain dominant or left brain dominant? I think at first, we would be inclined to say right brained because he was an artist. But with further thought, I think we would have to conclude he was double dominant. Both hemispheres were working together to bring forth such brilliance. I actually believe this should be our goal with our students—to aid them in developing double dominance in their playing. That means we need to help them develop both right brain skills and left brain skills. (We will expand this idea in Chapter 20.)

Unfortunately, there is little attention to right brain development in most education today. Right brain skills, like playing by ear and transcribing and playing our emotions, are difficult to teach, to measure and evaluate, to base a grade on. Right brain teaching is not cut and dried and quantifiable; it's very imprecise. Left brain skills, like theory and scales and notation reading, are easy to put on the blackboard and to base tests and grades on. They are specific and exact and dependable. Small wonder that academic education is more left brained. But I think most private lessons are left brain centric, as well, because it is partly a matter of job security. If you come to the lesson, and I give you a right brain assignment like go home and play by ear with the radio two hours a day, what happens at the next lesson? "Did you play by ear with the radio for two hours a day?" "Yes." "Great! Do that again this week—$80 please." How long does it take you to realize that you really don't need me in that loop? And it would be the same if I assigned some transcribing or asked you to turn off the lights in your bedroom at night and just try to play your emotions. It is hard for us as educators to trust the process and step out of the way and let the students have their own experience directly with the music. Plus, it just may look like we are not doing our job, but we really are. We are helping students know what they should do, motivating them to do it, and following up with an opportunity to be accountable by reporting and demonstrating their progress. You will be so much more helpful to your students that way than by trying to teach theory and coming at it with numbers.

Should we not teach theory and hold students accountable for scales and chords then? Of course we should! But not at the expense or in lieu of helping them have right brain experiences directly with the music. In the next chapter, we will look at ideas for developing double dominance. We will also get into jazz theory and jazz nomenclature. But in priority, it is better for the right brain development to start first. And all band directors can do that for their students even if their own experience with improvisation is minimal or non-existent.

Since you passed your music dictation and sight singing classes, we know you can hear; although those classes were difficult for you because college was the first time you were asked to really use your ears. (Secondary music education has largely turned music into a visual art.) If you are conscientious and want to grow as an educator, push yourself to do the right brain developmental exercises. The more you are growing personally, and the more you are able to model what you are teaching, the more you will inspire your students. In bands that have strong soloists at the festivals, there is always right brain work going on somewhere behind the scenes.

That is where it starts for you—and your students. But we also need to push on into jazz theory and harmony, chord construction, functional analysis, jazz melodic construction, jazz rhythm, and jazz style. The earlier chapters of this book give a lot of ideas for working with jazz rhythm, jazz articulation, and jazz style. These issues are the same whether reading or improvising. So, in the next chapter we will focus on the left brain territory; but remember if this gets too scary, you and your students can go a long way with just the right brain approach suggested in the present chapter.

Chapter 20 Developing Double-Dominant Improvisers

In Chapter 19, we discussed the meaning of double dominance where the right brain creativity is combined with the left brain math to create a musical product which neither orientation would be capable of producing independently. (No, double dominant is not the name of a chord.) I have a metaphor for the interaction between the right brain and the left brain. In the computer, there are two types of memory, the hard disk or permanent memory and the RAM or temporary memory. All the permanent storage of numbers is held in the hard disk which is analogous to the left brain, and the creative work is done in RAM which is analogous to the right brain. When we click on a word processing icon, the necessary information is appropriated from the hard disk so we can create our document in RAM. As we are working along, we realize we want to insert a picture. RAM must re-access the hard disk to bring up the information necessary to work with graphics, and then we can proceed. In a similar manner, the right brain says, I want to play "this" (a melodic idea), and the left brain immediately responds with the necessary material (why that is a minor 7th chord from the 9th: 9-b3-5-b7-9, and since you are in F# that is G#-A-C#-E-G#, and here are the fingerings......)! And all this happens faster than nanoseconds.

This right brain-left brain/computer metaphor suggests a two-fold process for developing as an improviser. First, we have to accumulate materials for storage in the left brain; and second, we have to learn how to access and organize those materials in the right brain to create a solo. (I am aware that any good metaphor taken too far can go bad, but I think the general notion of what we are talking about here is healthy.) So, let's look at the activities included in each side of the equation.

Right Brain Developmental Activities

• listening continually

• play by ear with the radio

• play by ear with CDs

• play by ear with play-alongs

• transcribe solos to the instrument

• transcribe licks (short melodic ideas)

• play simple melodies in all 12 keys

• just play your emotions

Left Brain Development Activities

• learn theory

• practice scales

• practice chords

• analyze chord progressions and form

• notate transcriptions on paper

• read notes, read chords

• play 3rd of every chord in a tune, etc.

• learn patterns in all 12 keys

Motivating students to do all of these things and teaching them the techniques and/or theory necessary for each activity is the role of the jazz music educator.

Helpful Thoughts on the Right Brain Development Activities

Listening

Everything starts with listening! Remember Suzuki's "mother tongue" principle—we learn to play the same way we learn to talk. It is really impossible to learn to speak a language authentically if you have never heard it spoken. You can't get it by reading the language or by using a conversion dictionary (i.e. French-English Conversion Dictionary or "Classical-Jazz Conversion Dictionary"). This is the first step, then, get them listening! You may have a requirement each grade term for a certain amount of listening and live concert attendance. The students can begin by listening to the charts you are working on in the band, but they need to listen to the source models for their specific instrument (they can expand to other instruments later).

I believe we should go back to our common practice period, the Bebop Era of the 40's, and then work forward from there (and later, even back from there). However, some students may be really enthralled with current fusion type music. Build on that enthusiasm, and then lead them back to the real source people. That means Charlie Parker (saxophone), Dizzy Gillespie (trumpet), J.J. Johnson (trombone), Bud Powell (piano), Ray Brown (bass), Max Roach (drums), Charlie Christian (guitar), etc. Then move into the next era with John Coltrane and Sonny Rollins and Cannonball Adderley (saxophone), Miles Davis and Lee Morgan and Clifford Brown and Freddie Hubbard (trumpet), Frank Rosolino and Carl Fontana and Curtis Fuller (trombone), and McCoy Tyner and Bill Evans and Wynton Kelly (piano), Charles Mingus and Paul Chambers and Jimmy Garrison (bass), Jimmy Cobb and Elvin Jones and Tony Williams (drums), Jim Hall and Wes Montgomery and Johnny Smith (guitar). This list is, of course, way over-simplified and reflects some of my own bias, but you can't go wrong with starting with these players. More comprehensive lists are all over the internet when you want more.

Playing by Ear

Start by motivating the students to play along by ear with the things they are listening to. When I was in high school, I spent a lot of time playing along with Charlie Parker and Cannonball Adderley and John Coltrane. I couldn't keep up with them, but I was absorbing how they approached things and checking out cool notes and figuring out keys. Then when the piano solo came up, that was like a play along for me; and I would keep playing, trying to sound as much like Bird or Cannon or Trane as I could (no offense to the pianists, but I could get over the volume of the piano solos).

Also play along with different radio stations by ear. I used to do this sometimes a couple of hours each night in high school. I would be on a rock station, then KLUB 57 Easy Listening, then to the classical station, then back to a different rock station. I would psyche out what key the tune was in, then what the rhythmic basis was, and then see if I could fit in with the style. I had no one giving me guidance or feedback. I had no one to tell me if I was right or not—just my ears. I really had no way of knowing, at the time, how much good I was doing for myself. At one time, I could play all the sitcom themes and commercials and top 40 tunes on the radio—oh so good for my ears!! Apple iTunes has made access to radio so easy now. You can access hundreds of radio stations from all over the world. I always have the students start with classic rock and reggae stations where the tunes tend to stay in one or two keys for the whole tune. Then they can gradually graduate to more difficult tunes (jazz). This is fun for them and usually highly motivating.

Also, have the students play by ear with any play-along CDs or materials they own. Jamey even suggests that when you buy a new Aebersold play-along CD, play by ear with it for a while, even a month. Then open the book and see what else you can learn.

Transcribing

Transcribing is the single most important thing an aspiring musician can do. It is a difficult, slow process and requires patience and persistence. It seems very inefficient to transcribe a solo. Why don't we just buy a transcription book and practice the solo? This would be more efficient all right, but not nearly as effective as doing the transcription ourselves. If we read someone else's transcription, it becomes a reading exercise not an ear exercise—now it's left brain work. When we read a transcription, we see the notes and an approximation of rhythms; but there is no information about tone, intonation, vibrato, articulation, rhythmic feel, scoops and other dramatic devices or inflections. When we do our own transcribing, all of that information is there. Nothing is missing! Yes, it takes more time, but we are getting so much more for our effort.

Another major benefit of doing our own transcription is the development of ear to finger coordination. (When we read, we develop eye to finger coordination.) With transcribing, we develop the ability to hear a pitch (either internally or externally) and our mind/body automatically produces the correct fingering. This is obviously invaluable when we are improvising and trying to translate melodies we are hearing in our heads into fingerings and notes.

The other question that always arises about transcription is, "Should I transcribe just to my instrument or to paper or both?" Many years ago, *Downbeat Magazine* published an interview with Wynton and Branford Marsalis. The interviewer asked Wynton the inevitable question about transcription. Wynton said, "I never transcribe. I don't believe in it." I puzzled over this answer, and re-read it a couple of times; and concluded that it must be a typo. Finally, I read on, and Branford said, "Yeah, I don't either. I just learn to play it on my horn." Then I realized Wynton was referring to the literal meaning of transcription which is to write it down. They were both using the term more loosely and saying that they transcribe to the instrument, not to paper. One of the great New York alto saxophone players, Jim Snidero, told me that he first learns to play the entire transcription on his horn, and then he put the horn down and makes himself write down the solo without the aid of the instrument. The first effort is a right brain exercise, and the second effort is more of a left brain exercise although there are still elements of right brain involved. The line is not always clear. Many activities go across both lines, and we are trying to build the marriage of the right and the left.

I think part of the issue with writing down the solo (which does have some value) is that the information is now stored on an external storage medium. It is like having your storage on a flash drive or a CD. What if I don't have it with me or cannot find it quickly enough (which will always be the case)? But if I have learned to play the solo on my horn, I have stored it to the hard disk (brain), and it is immediately accessible even sub-consciously and will have a much more far-reaching effect on my playing over time.

There is a technique for transcribing that saves a ton of time and makes it more fun. Depending on the difficulty and speed of the passage being transcribed, decide how many notes to listen to. If it is easy, more notes; if it is difficult, maybe only 2-4 notes or even just one. Press the pause, and sing it first before trying it on the instrument. Sing it enough times to get it clear in your head, then find it on the instrument. This will save re-referencing the track over and over and ultimately save a lot of time.

Playing in All 12 Keys

It is essential for a jazz musician to be equally fluent in all 12 keys. We will often play in half of the keys or more in the course of a single tune. Transcribing and playing by ear help a lot with developing this capacity, but another exercise is to play simple melodies in all 12 keys. Start with nursery rhyme tunes—*Mary Had a Little Lamb, Row Row Row Your Boat, Three Blind Mice, Twinkle, Twinkle Little Star*, etc.—and just play them up by half steps through all 12 keys. Graduate to ballad heads that are a little harder but slow—*Over the Rainbow, The Christmas Song, Greensleeves*, etc. Later, move on to more difficult tunes and bebop licks. Again, the line is not cut and dried between right brain and left brain work here. It is probably valuable for both sides. There is something very positive that happens to players when they work in all 12 keys—a certain cognitive clarity and technical facility.

Playing Your Emotions

Many nights when I was in high school, I would go into my bedroom, where I usually practiced, and turn out the lights and just try to play my emotions. It would be different from night to night, but it really helped me get in touch with my heart and my horn and bring the two together. This is not a very precise kind of assignment, but can yield valuable growth for a soloist. I saw Bobby Shew one time talk about taking an F major scale and trying to play it with different emotions—happy, then sad, then angry, then sentimental, etc. On a different day, pick a different key and go through the same process. Most right brain activities are not especially precise and measurable. As I said earlier, I think this is why traditional education has veered away from right brain approaches. But this does not negate their value and importance. As I think I have already illustrated, if I had to choose between the two, right brain would be the clear winner. But fortunately, we do not have to make that choice; so on to left brain activities.

Helpful Thoughts on Left Brain Development Activities

Learn Theory

It is important for all musicians to learn theory. This is the math part of music or the grammar part of music; and for the jazz musician, theory must really live on the horn and become part of performance. The basics of theory are no different for a jazz musician or a classical musician. Your college theory will be helpful. We need to teach basic things like clefs and key signatures and time signatures and intervals and scales and basic rhythmic concepts. In jazz, we take the scales further and build more complex chords and deal sometimes with more complex rhythms. Like your college theory classes, there should also be an ear training component of theoretical learning. I always have the students sing any scales or chords they are working on, but I also test their ability to respond by ear with their instruments to chords on the piano.

Learn Scales

In my experience, students don't really know their scales until they take on all 12 keys at the same time. Knowing all 12 major keys and scales is the beginning of all jazz theory. In jazz, we often do things in the circle order, but never in the Circle of Fifths. The Circle of Fifths was fine for Pythagoras and his mathematical mind, but it has no practical value in music, either classical or jazz. The Circle of Fifths is chord *regression*, and it just isn't the way music works. Now, the Circle of Fourths is chord *progression*, so that is the way we use it. But in jazz, we called it the Cycle of Dominants because C is the dominant of F is the dominant of Bb is the dominant of Eb. The cycle is the strongest of all chord progressions because it is V-I, V-I, V-I. So, this is a good place to start: learn all 12 major scales in the cycle order. Then it becomes easy to expand to other scales.

In theory, we can think of things in either a relative way or a parallel way, and we always think in the easiest way we can. For example, if the goal is to play a Dorian scale (mode), there are two ways to think about it—relative or parallel. A relative approach would be to recognize that Dorian is the second mode of the major scale, so it is related to the major scale down a whole step and uses the same key signature. Therefore, C Dorian would be a scale with two flats. The parallel approach is where we compare the C Dorian scale to the C major scale and discover that it has a b3 and a b7. So to play Dorian, we just play the C major scale with a b3 and a b7. We get the same answer either way; but if there are only one or two changes, it is easier and quicker to think in the parallel approach. Mixolydian scales are just major scales with a b7. It is much slower to think of the relative scale down a 5th. On the other hand, if we are trying to think parallel on a Locrian scale, it would be a major scale with a b2, b3, b5, b6, b7—five changes. That is too much to think about, so in this case, relative thinking is easier. Just go up a half step to the relative major scale (and key signature). So, playing an F# Locrian scale is a matter of thinking up a half step to G, and just play a G major scale starting on F#. So, relative thinking works better for Phrygian (related down a major 3rd), Locrian (up a minor 2nd), and Aeolian (natural minor—related down a minor 3rd). Parallel thinking works better for Dorian (b3, b7), Lydian (#4), and Mixolydian (b7). Therefore, first help the students learn all 12 major scales and then learn all the other modes derived from the major scale. (We often loosely just call them scales instead of modes.)

Learning Chords—The Chord Study

Most music education focuses on the scales and hardly touches the chords. We read arpeggio exercises and perhaps learn the basic triads, but it is fairly superficial compared to what jazz players need. Of course, we need to learn our scales; but if I had to choose between the two, chords are vastly more important. My students really start to blossom when they work on the Chord Study that we willl get on the next page. With the younger students, I start with just the three basic chords.

As we go along, notice that all jazz chord construction is based on parallel construction with alterations based on what the notes would have been in the major key of the bottom note. I should also point out that I am not going to use the correct, specific chord symbols for 9th chords. Typically, the only time you will see chord symbols with 9ths on all of them is in some published charts where the publisher feels a need to be very specific. Players in the jazz world don't worry about writing that way for each other. We all know that all chords that have a possible 9th always go to the 9th. So if I see D-, it means to me D-9. If I see D-7, it means to me D-9.

Jazz chords always go to the 9th chord level, so we arpeggiate this way:

    CΔ   C-   C7

1-3-5-7-9-7-5-3- | 1-b3-5-b7-9-b7-5-b3- | 1-3-5-b7-9-b7-5-3| then up a half step to the next key around the cycle—the 3rd of the dominant is the leading tone into the new key, now:

    FΔ   F-   F7

1-3-5-7-9-7-5-3- | 1-b3-5-b7-9-b7-5-b3- | 1-3-5-b7-9-b7-5-3- | up a half step from the 3rd to the new root.

    BbΔ   Bb-   Bb7   etc.

Repeat the pattern until mastered in all 12 keys. (See the video example.)

[The Δ means major, the – means minor, and the 7 by itself means dominant.]

For most instruments, about every 3 or 4 keys, the range becomes an issue; so we can adjust by descending on the dominant chord this way: 1-3-5-b7-9-b7-5-3-1-b7-5-3 | then up a ½ step to the new key.

This is challenging at first, but with persistence becomes easy; and I have junior high school private students who can rip through this in all 12 keys in about 5 minutes. Gradually, we begin to expand to other chord colors. It is easy to add a new second chord, the minor with a major 7 chord = C-Δ. Then we add the half-diminished chord = CØ7, or may be written C-7b5. Then we add C diminished = C°7 and finally the augmented triad = C+. This is only the triad; everything else goes to the 9th, except the diminished 7 chord which doesn't have a 9th. So to keep the rhythm working the same way for the exercise, I have the students go up to the 3rd—1-3-#5-8-3-8-#5-3 |.

So, the more complete exercise becomes: (I give the whole thing right off to college students and some more advanced high school students)

    CΔ7   C-Δ7   C-7   CØ7

1-3-5-7-9-7-5-3- | 1-b3-5-7-9-7-5-b3- | 1-b3-5-b7-9-b7-5-b3- | 1-b3-b5-b7-b9-b7-b5-b3- |

    C°7   C+   C7

1-b3-b5-bb7-8-bb7-b5-b3- | 1-3-#5-8-3-8-#5-3- | 1-3-5-b7-9-b7-5-3- | up a ½ step to F.

Most of the chords are really easy to learn with the parallel approach. However, three of the chords are more difficult and need specialized teaching and learning approaches. The hardest chord is the half-diminished (Ø). But when the minor 7 chords have already been learned, the half-diminished is a matter of playing a minor 7 chord from the b3rd of the half diminished root. So, play the root and go up to the b3 and play the -7 chord based on that note. Example: F#Ø7 would be F# then A-C-E-G (A-7). More difficult would be AbØ7 which spelled correctly is Ab-Cb-Ebb-Gb-Bbb—kind of ugly. We don't mind thinking enharmonically in the jazz world, so now it is Ab up a minor 3rd to B-D-F#-A (B-7). I tell my students that if they are in a theory class, then they must spell correctly. It's like being in an English class, where you have to spell correctly. But when you are practicing (and improvising), no one cares how you spell. No one knows how you are spelling it. Spell it in a way that works for you!

The diminished chord is actually very easy to learn, but it looks very difficult at first. When we spell a C diminished 7 chord, it looks a little daunting: C-Eb-Gb-Bbb-C. But realize this is a symmetrical chord—

every interval is a minor 3rd. Therefore, it is same no matter which note of the chord we start on. It is a C°7, an Eb or D#°7, a Gb or F#°7, and an A°7. We get four chords for the price of one! Therefore, I only have three different diminished chords to learn. Since I have four different spellings for each chord, why don't I choose the simplest spelling for each chord? My options on C are: C-Eb-Gb-Bbb-C, Eb-Gb-Bbb-Dbb-Eb, F#-A-C-Eb-F#, or A-C-Eb-Gb-A. They are all the same notes spelled different ways. I don't know about you, but I am going to use the spelling on F#. It has an interesting architecture for a chord—a # on the bottom, a b on the top, and white keys in the middle. So if I am spelling it on C, it is C-Eb-F#-A-C. If I spell it on Eb, it is Eb-F#-A-C-Eb. If I spell it on A, it is A-C-Eb-F#-A. It is always the one on F# no matter where it starts.

Using the same thinking, my other two diminished spellings are C#-E-G-Bb-C# (same architecture) and G#-B-D-F-G# (this is a bit arbitrary, could also spell it B-D-F-Ab-B if you like it better). The point is that we only need three total spellings for diminished 7 chords. I can then practice them as families and then around the Cycle of Dominants. When I put it back into the extended chord study (above), it is a piece of cake.

The augmented chords work exactly the same way because they are also symmetrical chords, but they are constructed of all major 3rds. So we only get three for the price of one, and we are going to need to have four distinct spellings. I have arbitrarily decided those spellings are: C-E-G#-C, F-A-C#-F, Bb-D-F#-Bb, Eb-G-B-Eb (G-B-D#-G if you like it better). Therefore, for example, a C#+ chord would be spelled C#-F-A-C# instead of its correct spelling C#-E#-G##-C#—the F spelling is much simpler. Again, I would practice the augmented chords as families and then around the Cycle and then put them back into the extended Chord Study. Example of the full Chord Study:

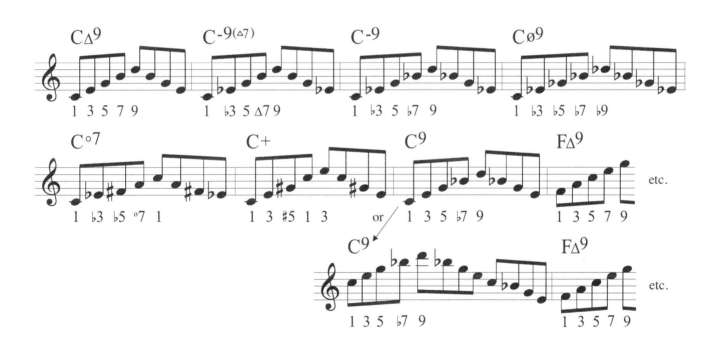

Now we have all the chords up and running in the full Chord Study described and shown above; and we practice it every day. I would think the C diminished 7 chord as C Eb F# A, and notice how the 3rd of the C7 chord is the leading tone to the new key of F. After warming up on the Chord Study, we take the next step of applying it to real tunes. So we sight-read chords in the fake book every day.

If you are not familiar with the meaning of fake book, these are books of often 500-600 tunes that show the melody and chord symbols for each tune. From these pages that we call lead sheets, we fake arrangements on the spot at various gigs—hence, fake book. One of the most common fake books in use is *The Real Book* (play on words—there is also *The New Real Book* and many others). A serious student should own a fake book. They make good birthday and Christmas presents. I have the students read 4-6 tunes a day in the fake book. They can read the melody, too, but I want them focusing on reading the chord symbols. They arpeggiate the chords in the correct harmonic rhythm for the tune. So, if the chord lasts a whole measure, they can play 1-3-5-7-9-7-5-3; but if the chord only lasts for two beats, they can only play 1-3-5-7 before running out of time. With repetition, the students can get quite fluent with reading the chords, with a steady pulse, in most tunes. This may be the most important and helpful left brain activity of all. (Note: we have not yet dealt with altered dominant chords, so I just have the students play the plain dominant they know for now. In other words, if they see a C7#9 chord, I just have them play a regular dominant arpeggio 1-3-5-b7-9 until we expand to the altered dominant chords.

Adding the Altered Dominants to the Chord Study

Once the student is becoming fluent with all the chords of the Chord Study, then I do extend the study to include the altered dominants. These could be tacked onto the Chord Study, but I often make it a separate Chord Study Set. For example:

C7   C7sus   C7#11   C7#5

1-3-5-b7-9-b7-5-3- | 1-4-5-b7-9-b7-5-4- | 1-3-#4-b7-9-b7-#4-3- | 1-3-#5-b7-9-b7-#5-3- |

C7b9   C7#9 (always implies a #5 in jazz, written or not)

1-3-5-b7-b9-b7-5-3- | 1-3-#5-b7-#9-b7-#5-3 | and up a ½ step from the 3 to the new root (F).

Sometimes with a younger student, I just add the most common altered dominant—C7#9—on the end of the original chord study instead of adding all the altered dominant types at once.

Practicing Chords and Scales in Chord Progressions

The most common chord progression in modern music is the II- V7 I. While the student is practicing many II- V7 I chord progressions when he/she is reading in the fake book, it is also good to create an exercise that requires the student to do them systematically in all 12 keys. The simplest way to do this is to use the Cycle of Dominants (4ths). The roots are already automatically in II-V-I order. We just need to put in the correct qualities of the chords. That means: C- F7 BbΔ, Eb- Ab7 DbΔ,   F#- B7 EΔ, A- D7 GΔ, –one time around the cycle, and we have done II V7 I progressions in four major keys. In order to do the other keys, we have to go around the Cycle two more times but shift our starting point twice. Example is: shift start to F- Bb7 EbΔ, Ab- Db7 GbΔ (or G#- C#7 F#Δ), B- E7 AΔ, D- G7 CΔ—shift again, Bb- Eb7 AbΔ, C#- F#7 BΔ, E- A7 DΔ, G- C7 FΔ equals all 12 keys in II V7 I format. This same format can also be used with scales—around the Cycle with Dorian, Mixolydian, Major and shift the starting point twice for all 12 keys. The scales and chords could also be done as companions at the same time using the same format for practice. In other words, C-7 chord with C Dorian Scale, F7 chord with F Mixolydian Scale, BbΔ7 chord with Bb major scale, then repeat with Eb-7 Ab7 DbΔ7, etc.

When this is mastered, we should use the same approach with II V7 I progressions in minor keys. Of course, the roots are the same for minor, but the chord/scale qualities must change. The II chord is half-diminished, the V chord is still dominant but must be altered (most typical is dominant 7#9 (includes #5); and the I chord is, of course, minor, but it will typically have a major 7th (even though the 3rd is minor) or a major 6. So for the II V7 I practice in minor, I would have the students go around the cycle doing CØ7 F7#9 Bb-9Δ7, EbØ7 Ab7#9 Db-9Δ7, F#Ø7 B7#9 E-9Δ7, AØ7 D7#9 G-9Δ7—then shift the starting points to FØ7 and then to BbØ7 for two more trips around the cycle to master all 12 keys.

Turn right around and repeat the process with the scales that fit the chords (if you haven't dealt with jazz theory thinking before, this may be a new concept; but we have a scale to fit the sound and intent of every chord): Locrian scales for the half-diminished chords, Super Locrian (or Diminished/Whole Tone) for the Dominant #9 chords, and Melodic Minor (ascending version only) for the minor tonics with major 7 chords. The easiest ways to approach learning these scales are: Locrian—up a half step to the relative major scale and just use that key signature (relative thinking), Melodic Minor—just play a major scale with a b3 (parallel thinking, no need for all the old rigmarole since we don't use the descending form in modern music), and for the Super Locrian—a combination of the first two approaches, go up a half step to the relative melodic minor scale (major with a b3, a combination of relative thinking and parallel thinking).

Example: II V7 I in B minor

  C#Ø7   F#7#9   B-9Δ7 (B-Δ)

C# D E F# G A B C# (2#s) | F# G A Bb C D E F# (1#, 1b) | B C# D E F# G# A# B (b3) |

 (related to D major scale)   (I'm not afraid of non-Bach   (B major scale, but flat the 3rd)
                 key signatures if I can make one)

> Please note that I am never afraid to conceptualize an unconventional key signature if it makes things easier. Unfortunately, not all of the keys lend themselves easily to this; but why not when it does work? So any scales derived from C Melodic Minor have one flat=Eb (C melodic minor, Eb Lydian Augmented, F Lydian Dominant A Locrian #2, and B Super Locrian all have this same key signature). Any scales deriving from G Melodic Minor have one sharp=F# and one flat=Bb. Any scales deriving from A Melodic Minor have two sharps=F# and G#. All scales deriving from D Melodic Minor have one sharp=C#. All scales deriving from F Melodic Minor have two flats=Ab and Bb, and so forth.

Most of the tunes your students will need to improvise on for your big band are made of a combination of major II V7 I's and minor II V7 I's; so, if they are practicing both major and minor II V7 I's in all 12 keys, they are basically practicing all tunes at once. For application to a specific tune, they just have to apply the II V7 I's in different orders and juxtapositions. There are other possible formats for practicing these materials, but I am trying to keep this as clear-cut, straight-forward as possible.

Chord Functional Analysis

As my students practice sight reading chords in the fake book, I begin having them do functional analysis of the chords as they go. "Okay, you can play the chord, but how is it functioning in the bigger picture?" This starts with just recognizing at sight the II V7 I progressions. Sometimes, a II V7 does not go to I, but it is still a II V7 and should be recognized as such. As we begin to refine our analysis, I give this guide:

• If it is major, it is a I (unless by context, we can see that it is really a IV such as when two major chords are in a row—the second is a IV in the key of the first).

• If the chord is minor, it is a II (unless we see by context that it is functioning as a III or VI or a I or IV in a minor key).

• If the chord is dominant, then it is a V (unless we are in a Blues where it can be anything—I, IV, V, VI, II, III).

• If the chord is half diminished, then it is a II in minor (but could be VI in minor).

• If the chord is diminished, then it is substituting for, and therefore functioning as, a dominant chord (possible, but rare, to function as a chromatic passing chord).

An important difference between classical and jazz analysis is that in classical analysis, it is important to try to keep our chord functions all in one key until we can show clearly that there is a modulation. This idea would drive you crazy when trying to analyze most jazz tunes. In jazz tunes, when we see a II- V7 in a different key, we just figure that we have momentarily tonicized those chords in a key other than the primary key—and that is the way we treat it when we are improvising. I will illustrate this in a moment.

One other important difference in classical analysis is the use of capital letters for major chords and lowercase letters for minor and the like. In jazz analysis, we use capital letters for all chord symbols and look to the attached symbol to determine quality.

Let's look at a few analysis examples the way a jazz musician would view it.

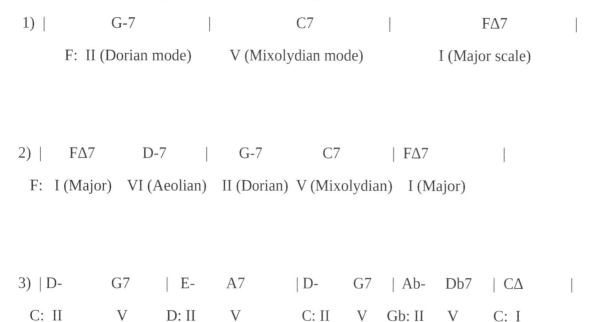

1) | G-7 | C7 | FΔ7 |

    F: II (Dorian mode)   V (Mixolydian mode)   I (Major scale)

2) | FΔ7   D-7 | G-7   C7 | FΔ7 |

  F: I (Major)   VI (Aeolian)   II (Dorian) V (Mixolydian)   I (Major)

3) | D-   G7 | E-   A7 | D-   G7 | Ab-   Db7 | CΔ |

  C: II   V   D: II   V   C: II   V   Gb: II   V   C: I

4) | EbΔ | A-   D7 | EbΔ | G-   C7 | F7 | |
    Eb: I   G: II   V   Eb: I   F: II   V   F: I (as if in blues)

5) | F#Ø7 | B7#9 | E-9Δ7 |
   E-: II (Locrian mode)   V (Super Locrian Mode)   I (Melodic Minor)

6) | D-7   BØ7 | EØ7   A7#9 | D- |
   D-: I (Mel Min) VI (Loc. #2) II (Locrian) V (Sup. Loc.)   I (Melodic Minor)

7) | F-7 | Bb-7 | Eb7 | AbΔ | DbΔ | D-   G7 |
   Ab: VI (Aeolian)   II (Dorian)   V (Mixolyd.) I (Major)   IV (Lydian)   C: II   V

8) | C-7 | F7 | BbΔ | EbΔ |
   Bb: II (Dorian)   V (Mixolydian)   I (Major)   IV (Lydian)

9) | F#-7   B7 | G#Ø7 C#7#9 | F#-7   B7 | EΔ |
   E: II   V   F#-: II   V   E: II   V   I

10) | C-7 | F- | | D-7b5 | G7 | C- | |
   C-: I (add the Δ7)   IV (Opt. add Δ7)   II (Locrian   V (add #9,#5)   I (add Δ 7)

11) | BbΔ7 | | Bb7 | | EbΔ7 | | Ab7 | || BbΔ7

     Bb: I   Eb: V (opt. #9#5)   I   V? add #11   Bb: I
                                                                  (substitution)

12) | CΔ7 | | D7#11 | | D-7 | G7 | CΔ | G-   C7 ||

    C: I   V? (Lydian/Dom   II   V (may add #9,#5)   I   F: II   V

There are a few things to notice in the analyses above:

In #2, the D-7 is not functioning as a II which would be our first thought. Since it is functioning as a VI, then we use Aeolian (mode 6) instead of Dorian (mode 2).

In #3, we are free to view each II V7 in the key in which it lives, not the prevailing key of the piece.

In #4, the last chord is dominant, and therefore our first thought is that it is functioning as a V; but the context and ears will help us decide to treat it as a tonic as if we were playing a blues (see next chapter).

In #6, the first and last chords are functioning as tonic in minor; therefore, I will add the major 7 and use a melodic minor scale, even though the chord symbol does not indicate the major 7.

This is an example of our musicianship informing us what needs to be done. Also in #6, two half diminished chords in a row means they can't both be a II, and context shows that one of them is a VI. When it is a VI, we would want to use the Locrian #2 scale—the #2 reflects the Major 9 we would add to the chord, even though it is not in the chord symbol. (This is also an option on the II chord in minor.)

In #7, it becomes apparent that when in a major key you play a VI chord function, you match it with the 6th scale mode (Aeolian). When you play a II chord function, you match it with the 2nd scale mode (Dorian). When you play a V chord function, you match it with the 5th scale mode (Mixolydian). When you play a I chord function, you match it with the 1st scale mode (Major or Ionian). When you play a IV chord function, you match it with the 4th scale mode (Lydian). So simple!

In #7 and #8, we see the situation of two major chords in a row which nearly always means the second chord is functioning in the key of the first. Therefore, the progression is I to IV; and since the IV is functioning in the same key as the I, it must have a #11 whether written or not.

In #9, we can loosely call this progression II V7 | III VI7 | II V7 | I |, but the way we would approach it in improvisation is to play the first measure as a II V in E, the second measure as a II V in F# minor, back to a II V I in E.

In #10, when a jazz player recognizes the C- is functioning as a tonic in minor, he feels license to add the major 7th on the minor chord. He may also take license to add the major 7th on the IV chord, F-. The D-7b5 is the same as half diminished (Ø), and it is functioning as a II chord in the key of C minor. That means the G7 is functioning as the V, and so we must add the #9 (and the #5). The dominant chord *may* be altered in a major key at will, but it *must* be altered in a minor key. These things are often left out on the lead sheet (especially in the old *Real Book*), and we always just add what should be there as soon as we recognize an omission.

In #11, the Ab7 chord is functioning in a strange looking position. It is not the V chord of Bb. It is the V chord of Db, but then resolves to Bb. It is actually functioning as a substitution for the F7. You can take it as a principle that when a dominant chord is functioning in an odd position like this, you should add the #11 even if it is not written. If the dominant is functioning as a true V in its primary position, then the best altered notes to add are #9, b9, and #5. If it is in this odd, secondary kind of position, those alterations will not sound good; add the #11 instead. (I am not using the words "secondary position" here with the same meaning as secondary dominant.)

In #12, we see the same thing with the D7 functioning in an odd, secondary kind of position, but the #11 is already written on it in this case. The G7 is functioning in a primary position, and so I would usually add #9 and #5. It is optional, but most jazz players would take the option to alter more often than not.

More Scales (Ascending Melodic Minor Scale Derivatives)

After we have learned the Major scale and all of its modes (Ionian, Dorian, Phrygian, Lydian, Mixolydian, Aeolian, and Locrian), we should do the same with the Melodic Minor scale. As noted earlier, the Melodic Minor scale is simply a Major scale with a flat 3 (parallel thinking); but if we revisit the modes, we get some nice new colors. If we compare each mode of the Melodic Minor with its parallel major, we can see easily what each scale/mode can do for us.

Mode 1: The Melodic Minor scale best colors the tonic minor chord because it reflects the b3 and the major 7 (ex: C-9Δ7).

Mode 2: This is a Dorian scale with a b9 which is totally un-useable because b9 on a minor chord sounds horrid and is never used.

Mode 3: The Lydian/Augmented scale is a major scale that has a #4 and a #5, so it is very useful for the less common situation (but increasingly more common in modern music) of a major 7 chord with a #5 (ex: CΔ7#5).

Mode 4: The Lydian/Dominant scale is a Mixolydian scale with a #11, so it works great with a dominant chord that has a #11 (ex: C7#11)

Mode 5: This is basically a Mixolydian scale with a #5, but it is not used much because we have another choice that is more often used for the dominant chord with a #5. (The Wholetone)

Mode 6: The Locrian #2 scale (not a very inventive name) is used with a half- diminished chord that has a major 9 (ex: CØ7Δ9). As students become more advanced, they will increasingly use this scale for half-diminished chords.

Mode 7: The Super Locrian or Diminished/Wholetone scale (can also be called just The Altered scale) is perhaps the most useful scale in this family, coloring the altered dominants with #9 or b9 and #5 in combination. These always happen in minor II V7 I progressions and are optional in major II V7 I progressions.

More Scales (The Symmetrical Scales)

Another "family" of scales is what I call the Symmetrical Scales. These scales are so symmetrical that they do not have 12 distinct entities. For example, the Chromatic Scale is so symmetrical that there is only one of them. No matter what note you start on, it is still the same scale—the same fingerings. (We already saw this with the diminished 7 chords and the augmented chords.)

A second symmetrical scale in the Wholetone. It is all whole steps, so no matter which note you start on in the scale, the scale is the same. Therefore, we get six for the price of one. We only need two Wholetone scales to know all 12 of them—the one on C and the one on C#. The Wholetone scale is the best fit for the C7#5 mentioned earlier. If we spell the notes of the scale—C D E F# G# Bb C; the E is the major third, and the Bb is the b7 which equals a dominant function. The G# is the #5, and the D means the 9th is not altered.

I should clarify right here that when I am numbering the notes in a scale so that I can see what chord tones it will color, I number 1 9 3 11 5 13 (or 6) and 7. This is what we did in the predeeding Wholetone scale paragraph to detemine what the scale would color (C7#5). If we did the same with a Lydian/Dominant scale— C D E F# G A Bb C, we can see that is it a dominant function scale with a major 3rd and a b7, but that it also colors the #11 and 9 is major. If we numbered the Locrian #2 scale—C D E F Gb Ab Bb C, we see that it has the b3, b5, and b7 that makes it fit a half-diminished chord but the 9th is major.

The other important symmetrical scale is the Diminished Scale. In classical analysis, this is sometimes called the Octatonic Scale. It alternates half and whole steps, so ½, W, ½, W, ½, etc., or it may alternate W, ½, W, ½, W, etc. Every time we move a half step and a whole step, we are starting over again with the pattern. So every time we move a minor 3rd, the scale repeats itself, thus giving us four for the price of one. Therefore, we will only need 3 distinct Diminished Scales to make all 12 keys. The C, Eb, F#, and A diminished scales are all the same notes as each other. We just need the diminished scales on C, C#, and D, and we have them all. If we number a diminished scale—1 b9 #9 3 #4 (or b5) 5 13 b7 8, we see that it has a dominant application since it has a major 3rd and a b7; but it colors a dominant chord that has altered 9ths. It would take care of a C7b9, a C7b9#11 (or C7b5b9). It could cover a C7#9, but as we noted earlier, a dominant chord with a #9 always implies a #5, written or not; and we see in our number analysis that the diminished scale does not contain a #5. The Super Locrian (Diminished/Wholetone scale) would be a better choice in that instance. If we number that scale—1 b9 #9 3 #11(b5) #5 b7 8, we see why it is better fitted to handle the sound of a C7#9#5.

Here is a tip for learning the Diminished Scales. They should be learned with the half step first (classically, the Octatonic Scale is usually thought of as having the whole step first). Instead of learning this scale by thinking intervals—half step, whole step, half step, whole step, etc.—learn it by descending in the following way: For a C Diminished scale, C Bb A G which is the top of the C7 Mixolydian scale; then F#7 down F# E D# C# which is the top of the F#7 Mixolydian scale. After learning it descending, it becomes much easier to ascend.

Finished Product: The C Diminished Scale

Using this idea, the Diminished Scales can be learned quite quickly; whereas, trying to learn the scale thinking intervals is very slow. Once the scale is learned with the half step first, it is easy to adapt it to starting with the whole step first when needed.

More Miscellaneous Scales

There is a fourth category of scales that I call Miscellaneous for lack of a better description. In this category, we have the Blues scale 1, b3, 4, b5, 5, b7, 8 and the Pentatonic scales—major 1, 2, 3, 5, 6, 8 and minor 1, b3, 4, 5, b7, 8. We will look at the uses for these scales in the next chapter.

In summary, if a student learns the four families of scales—Major derivatives, Melodic Minor derivatives, Symmetrical, and Miscellaneous, he/she now has all the materials that would be needed to function in any jazz context. There are other scales that we could throw in, but virtually every tune can be covered with these materials.

> If you survived all of that, but are not sure you understand it all; I would recommend two things:
> •Go back through it sitting at a piano where you can plunk out and visualize and hear, and things will begin to clarify themselves in your mind.
> •View the videos that are related to this chapter for demonstrations that will also help to clarify these things in your mind.

Form Analysis

Another part of left brain functioning is to understand the form of the tune or piece being worked on. Some of the most common jazz forms are The Blues, AABA (of which Rhythm Changes is an example), ABAB1, AABC, and AAB. Form designations are a way of describing repeat structure. When analyzing the form of a tune, I want the student to be more detailed. Is it really AABA, or is it A, A1, B, A2? If we more accurately realize the form of our tune, we can keep our place and not get lost so easily. One jazz tune has the form ABCDAB, so tunes can get a little more complex. In classic jazz styles, the melody of the tune (head) and the chord structure for improvising tend to be the same form pattern repeated over and over; but in more modern forms, the changes for the head and the changes for the blowing (solos) may be distinctly different from each other. I like to have students first examine the form of a tune from a right brain standpoint—listening and counting bars and hearing the repeat structure of the tune. Then we can study it visually and see if there is any detail we didn't hear—left brain work second.

Learning Patterns

Patterns are melodic formulae that fit over certain jazz progressions. For example, we learn major II V7 patterns that last for one bar (2 beats each) but also for 2 bars (one measure each). We also learn patterns for II V7's in minor, both one bar and two bar patterns. We also learn patterns that work on the tonic Major or tonic Minor chords, both one bar and two bar pattern ideas. We may also learn blues patterns or hip pentatonic patterns. In the jazz world, patterns are often called "licks". I view this whole matter as learning vocabulary words and phrases. We learn words and phrases, not so we can sound programmed, but rather so we can know the basic language and then use it to express ourselves, perhaps in terms we haven't used before until right now. In the metaphor we have used since the beginning of this section that learning jazz language is like learning any other language, we learn to speak jazz very much like we learn to form words from the alphabet and then phrases and then sentences and paragraphs. I believe this is the most effective way to get students to go from being able to play their chords and scales to being able to use them to create new melodies. As a young teacher, this was a mystery to me. I can teach the students theory and scales and chords and chord progressions, but how do I get them to apply all of that to make a melodic improvised solo? I believe, on the left brain side, that patterns are the answer. (This will, of course, still fall short if we don't have a lot of right brain development paralleling this process.)

As I was coming up, I believe I stunted my growth for some time by refusing to practice patterns. I didn't realize that the "canned" effect was a temporary phase, and I was encouraged in my dereliction by friends who told me I sounded fresh, not like those other guys. But over a period of time, I changed my mind as I saw friends who had practiced patterns start to blossom as improvisers. I suddenly felt behind and realized I needed to get started on the pattern work. Learning a pattern is like learning a vocabulary word. After a while we may use a different suffix or a different prefix or only part of the word. When many patterns are internalized, they start to cross breed and become combined in all kinds of unusual ways. This is a very important aspect of developing a rich jazz vocabulary! When we have a vocabulary, we can speak at will and express ourselves in an appropriate way for each new circumstance.

Years ago, I had a college student who I was assigning and encouraging to practice his scales and chords and patterns. One day he walked into my office and told me he didn't want to practice that stuff anymore. He felt it was stifling his creativity, and he affirmed that he just wanted to play like John Coltrane. I asked him what he meant, and he said he just wanted to be creative and compositional like Trane. I said, "Okay, let me see if I understand you correctly. You want to play like John Coltrane, but you want to skip all the steps that Trane went through to get there." He thought for a moment and smiled as he said, "Okay, I get it." We call it paying dues. It takes a lot of effort to establish a rich vocabulary that can then be used to express ourselves in creative and meaningful ways. When that begins to happen, it is one of the most rewarding things in a musician's life.

A great source for beginning pattern work is Jamey Aebersold's Vol. 3 of his play-along series, *The II–V7–I Progression*. This book comes with a play-along CD and gives opportunity to practice with the rhythm section on II V7 I progressions in all 12 keys in both major and minor. In the back of the book, Jamey gives 72 patterns for major II V7 I's and 17 patterns for II V7 I's in minor. It is not 72 or 17 hip patterns, but there are plenty of good ones to keep students practicing for a long time. I ask students to play through every pattern and put a mark by the ones they really want to know and then start working through them.

The patterns are given in one key, and the student has to put them in the other 11 keys. There may be a temptation to write them down transposed. While this may be helpful to get some clarity started in the brain, this should not be a regular practice, and we should not get stuck continually looking at anything we have written down. Again, we don't want to store our materials on an external storage source where they lose usefulness. We need to store these materials on the hard disk where they are always immediately available and where they can incubate and cross breed. For a developing improviser, we also don't want to reinforce having to see things on paper. We have to be able to function from our minds and our ears.

There are other published sources for patterns; search at jazzbooks.com. But these patterns can also come from our listening and transcribing, from fellow musicians and teachers, and from transcriptions done by other musicians. Jamey's play-alongs have patterns interspersed throughout the series, but one of my favorites is Vol. 15, *Payin' Dues*. Jamey writes new melodies on a handful of standard jazz tunes that are loaded with great ideas and patterns for improvisation.

Hopefully, these sections have given you some good ideas for helping young musicians experience right brain and left brain development. Remember that our primary goal is to facilitate double dominance in our students. Let's move on to another critical learning activity for young musicians that brings this all together.

A Double Dominant Approach to Learning Tunes

I said before that the single most important thing a person can do to develop as an improviser, and as a musician for that matter, is to TRANSCRIBE!! That is number one! But the second most important thing a person can do and an important companion to transcribing is to LEARN TUNES—tune after tune after tune after tune.

JB Dyas tells of when he was in high school as a budding guitarist and finally got up the nerve to call the guitar teacher at the local university and ask for lessons. The college teacher was not really into teaching high school students, but relented. JB was able to ask all the questions he had had for a long time. In the fourth lesson, the teacher said, "I am going to give you an assignment; and when you get it done, call me and we'll have the next lesson." JB responded, "Okay, what is the assignment?" "Learn 100 tunes." "Why would I learn 100 tunes before coming to the next lesson?" The teacher responded, "Because by the time you learn 100 tunes, you won't have all those stupid questions!" Perhaps not the best teaching strategy, but an excellent point. There is amazing learning that comes by learning tunes. And to be able to function professionally and make any money playing jazz, we must know tunes—lots of them.

So here is my "double dominant" approach to learning tunes. First, we have right brain experiences with the tune and then left brain experiences, and then, hopefully, they come together.

1) Learn the head (melody) of the tune first. This should be a right brain approach and learned by ear. Transcribe the melody, or learn it from your mind if you can already sing it. If you have no source for it, record yourself playing it from the book, and then close the book and transcribe yourself. You will know the tune a lot better and retain it a lot longer if you learn it this way.

2) Play by ear with the recording, either the real recording or a play-along, and learn everything about the tune you can with your ears—the key, the modulations, the rhythmic basis, the style, the form, etc. If you can take the time, you could even transcribe a solo or solos from a recording of the tune. Learn everything you can with the right brain first!

3) Now involve the left brain. Start by arpeggiating all of the chords in harmonic rhythm through the tune (like the sight-reading in the fake book). I would follow this up with running the corresponding scales through the tune in harmonic rhythm. Then choose a pattern for major II V7's and a pattern for minor II V7's and a pattern for the tonic chords—one bar and two bar as needed for each chord scenario, and then run patterns through the entire progression, patterning every chord.

4) Analyze chord functions and put Roman numerals on all the chords. At the same time examine the form in a detailed way. Figure out how you are going to remember the tune and the way the chord progression is structured.

5) Do more ear training. Play the 3rd of every chord, then the 5th of every chord, then the 7th of every chord, then the 9th of every chord. Then figure out the guide tones and play them. (The concept of guide tones will be explained soon.)

6) Sing everything that has been worked on so far—sing the arpeggiation of the chords, sing the scales, sing the patterns, sing the 3rds, 5ths, etc., sing the guide tones.

7) Play the tune and improvise using the materials and your ears with the real CD and with the play along CD if you have one.

8) Work on the tune now with no backing track. It is essential that we become self-reliant—independently keeping the time and the harmony and the form. Ultimately, our improvising should be recognizable as the tune even with no backing track.

> I always have the students sing everything they are working on, starting with the chord study and scales and then patterns. Then later, we sing the arpeggiation of chord progressions of the tunes we are working on along with the guide tones, roots, thirds, fifths, sevenths, and ninths.

In a simplified form, we first have right brain experiences with the tune, then left brain experiences with the tune. Then we work on ear training based on the left brain materials. Then we work on application and bringing the two hemispheres together. This obviously takes time and patience, and the first tunes will take longer; but it gets much faster with succeeding tunes. Gradually, a student begins to function in a double dominant way—the ears and intuition are contributing and the mind and knowledge are contributing to the finished product.

There is an important ground rule for this process. We want to come out of the process really knowing the tune—that is, I don't want to have to look at anything to know the melody or the chord progression. This is less a matter of memorization (where I am looking at something and trying to commit it to memory), but more a matter of learning the tune without dependence on the page in the first place. In the right brain phase, I am not looking at anything. In the left brain phase, I have to begin by looking at something; but my goal is to look at the page as little as possible. So once, I have figured out the form and structure of the progression and how I am going to remember it, the rule is to never play again with the book open. I may open the book and double check, using the book for either confirmation that I've got it right or for correction; but then I close the book and go back to work. If I learn it this way, I will retain it much better and longer than simple memorization.

Guide Tones

So let's deal with the concept of guide tones and playing changes, and then we will look at the application of the double dominant approach to a specific tune. The guide tones form what I call the framework of the tune. These are the notes that must move by half steps as we move from one chord to another. They are the notes that define the chord progression; and when incorporated, the progression is clear even without a backing track or rhythm section. We often hear the terms "playing the changes" or "Do you know the changes?" These tend to be used in the generic sense of "Do you play the chords?" or "Do you know the chords?" But the more specific meaning of playing the changes is "Do you play the notes that need to change as one chord moves to another?" The guide tones are the notes that have to change by half step as one chord moves to the next and which define the sound of the chord progression. The acid test for an improviser is whether the listener can hear the tune and identify it with no reference to the melody or to an accompaniment.

In a simple illustration of guide tones, let's say that the chords move from C major to C minor. What notes have to change by half step from the first chord to the second? E must move to Eb, and/or B must move to Bb. The line we generate should include at least one of those note changes, i.e. E on the left side of the bar line to Eb on the right side of the bar line, or B to Bb. Incorporating this half step change will give a clear signal to the listener that we have changed from major to minor, even when the chords are not being sounded by an accompaniment. So, we are always looking for these half step movements. It is half steps that make the world go around. Whole steps do not have the same definitional power. These pitches are like dots in a connect the dots puzzle. How many different sound pictures can I make connecting the dots (guide tones) in various ways?

C major to C minor is very straight forward, but it is more challenging to figure out how to make a II chord sound like it moves to a V chord and a V chord to a I chord. The problem is that all three chords are functioning in the same key signature, so we don't have any obvious half step changes to define the progression, or do we? If we examine the II to the V chord and compare each note of the II chord to the V chord and then the same for the V chord to the I chord, it looks like this.

Chords:	| D-	|G7	| CΔ
Scale Tones	D	D (5th)	D (9th)
(D Dorian)	E	E (6 or 13th)	E (3rd)
	F	F (b7)	F (4th) cannot be used, so go to E (1/2 step)
	G	G (root)	G (5th)
	A	A (9th)	A (6 or 13th)
	B	B (3rd)	B (7th)
	C	C (4th) can't use so move to B (1/2 step)	C (root)

As you can see, all the notes are in the same key, and most of them work; but from the II chord to the V chord, the b7th has to resolve by half step down to the 3rd. The same is true for the V chord moving to the I chord—the b7th has to resolve down a half step to the 3rd. These are the definitional notes that, when incorporated into the line, will signal to our ears that we move from the II to the V to the I with no reference to any accompanimental chords. The reason this works this way is that the 4th note of the scale cannot be played on a chord that has a major 3rd. Therefore, when moving to dominant or major chords, the 4th note must resolve down to the 3rd. The 4th is a horrid sounding note on those two chord types. From this, we can formulate a principle that in a major II V I, the guide tones will always be the b7th going down to the 3rd (half step) II-V, and the b7th goes down to the 3rd (half step) V-I. [same note numbers for both chord changes]

In a minor II V I, for the same reasons just stated, the guide tones are the b7th to the 3rd when moving from the II to the V; but when moving from the V to the I, there is a difference. The b7th to the b3 (since the tonic chord is minor) is a whole step. Guide tones must be half steps. The whole step will not sound bad, but it is not definitional and will not provide enough information to hear the chord change clearly when there is no accompaniment. So where are the half steps in minor? Since the V chord in minor must be altered (#9, b9, #5) we have several options shown in the next example.

In minor: IIØ | V7#9 | I-9Δ7 |

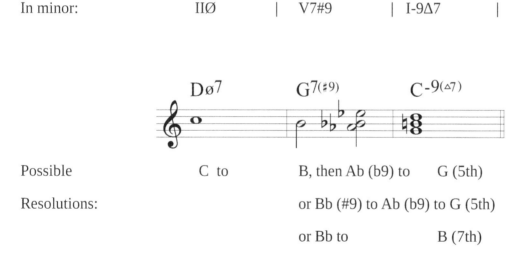

Possible   C to   B, then Ab (b9) to   G (5th)

Resolutions: or Bb (#9) to Ab (b9) to G (5th)

                                 or Bb to   B (7th)

                                 or Eb (#5) to   D (9th)

These all sound great. When defining guide tones in minor for a young student, I just arbitrarily use the b9 to the 5 for V to I; therefore b7 to 3 for II to V and b9 to 5 for V to I. But the other possibilities are there.

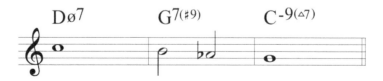

Most patterns for either major or minor II V7 I's incorporate these guide tones. The first many patterns I always give to a young student will be based around the guide tones, which trains the fingers and the ears to gravitate toward them.

If we elect to alter a dominant chord in a major II V7 I, we have the same additional resolutions as minor and a couple more because of the M3rd on the tonic.

In major: II- | V7#9 | IΔ7 |

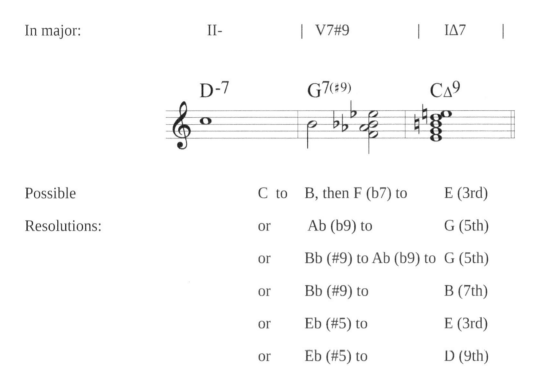

Possible   C to   B, then F (b7) to   E (3rd)

Resolutions: or   Ab (b9) to   G (5th)

                             or   Bb (#9) to Ab (b9) to G (5th)

                             or   Bb (#9) to   B (7th)

                             or   Eb (#5) to   E (3rd)

                             or   Eb (#5) to   D (9th)

Because of all the additional resolution possibilities, jazz players tend to alter a lot; and we have the license to alter anytime it fits our purposes even when the chord symbol does not show any alteration, and even when the rhythm section is not altering.

Admittedly, this is a lot of theory, but this is what the left brain domain is about; and the double dominant jazz player will have mastery of all this theory, both in his mind and on the instrument. For a jazz player, theory is not a separate and unrelated topic in music. THEORY LIVES ON THE INSTRUMENT AND IS A WAY OF LIFE!

Example of the Double Dominant Approach to All the Things You Are

If you were setting out to learn the tune, *All the Things You Are*, I would first have you listen to recordings of the tune—several different artists and versions if possible. I would have you live with it until you could sing the melody and scat-sing solos along with it (this may happen in the car or walking, while getting dressed, while getting ready for bed, etc.). Then I would have you pick up your instrument and learn the melody—from your mind if possible or with reference to a recording if needed. If you have listened to more than one recording, you may hear little variances in the way the melody is played. It is often best to listen to the melody at the beginning from a singer; it may be more accurate. It is also possible to refer to a book for, perhaps, more clarity, but remember the rule: we don't play when the book is open.

Then I would have you play by ear and try to improvise with recordings, the real recording and the play-along version if one is available. Then you should try to decipher what the key centers are and how they change. Figure out by ear what the repeat structure is, the form. Consider what the rhythmic basis is—does it swing? Or is it straight-eighth based? Learn everything you possibly can about the tune with your ears. Play along with the jazz players on your recordings and check out cool-sounding notes and melodic ideas.

Then I would have you open a lead sheet if you have one, and see what you can learn with your eyes and your mind. Let's look at the chords and analyze function and form. The chord layout is printed begining below.

First, we should go through and arpeggiate all of the chords in the proper harmonic rhythm. Remember, if the chord lasts a full measure, we can only play 8 eighth notes, 1-3-5-7-9-7-5-3-. If the chord lasts two measures, we play that twice. If the chord lasts only 2 counts, we can only play 4 eighth notes, 1-3-5-7. We can also go through and play all of the scales that fit the chords. We need two measures to play up and down a scale. If we have one measure, we can only go up (or down). When we are looking at a II V7, we can play the same scale up or down through the both chords—it's all the same key. So, for a II V7 that lasts one bar, just play the Dorian Scale ascending.

We could also go through and pattern the whole tune. We will need a pattern for each type of chord event. Perhaps when there is a single bar minor chord (VI) not attached to a II V7 I, we will choose this pattern: 1 2 b3 4 5 b3 2 1. When we have a II V7 that lasts two measures, we will play 1 2 b3 4 5 b3 2 1 | 8 7 b7 9 6 5. When we have a II V7 that lasts one bar, we will play 1 b3 5 b7 3 2 1 b7. When we have a one bar II V7 that is in minor, we will play 1 b3 b5 b7 3 b2 1 b7. When we have a major chord that lasts one measure, we will play 7 1 3 5 7 5 3 1. When we have a major chord that lasts two measures, we will play 7 1 3 5 7 9 8 7 5 3 1 7 6. This exercise helps us become much more proficient at the juggling of all these materials which prepares us for real-life improvising. See the application of this on the chord sheet below. We could then choose different patterns for another practice run.

All the Things You Are

|Form: This is the A Section

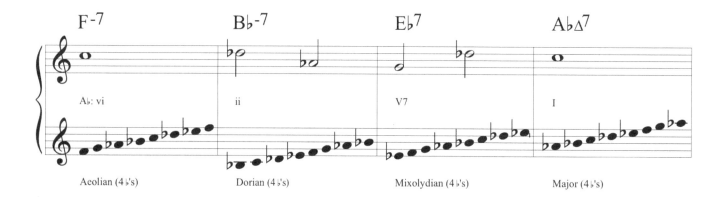

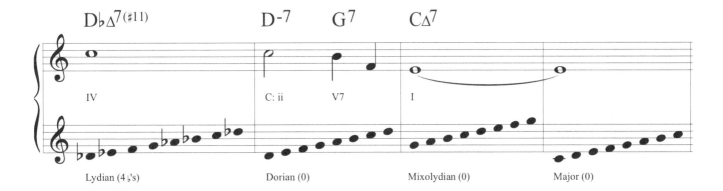

FORM: This is the Second A section, same format but different key, so this is A1

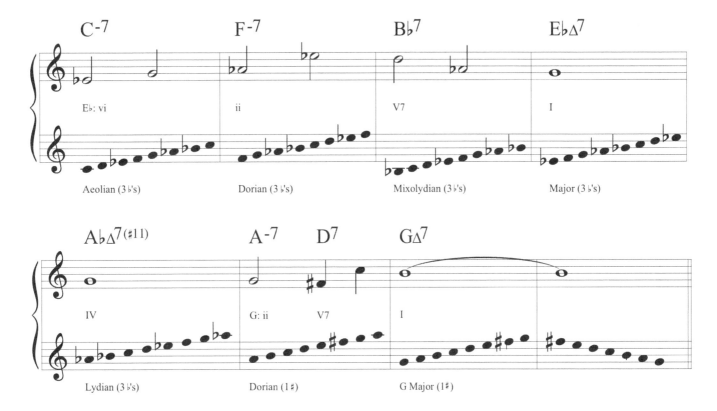

FORM: This is the Bridge or B

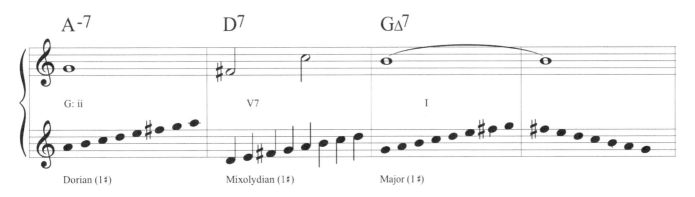

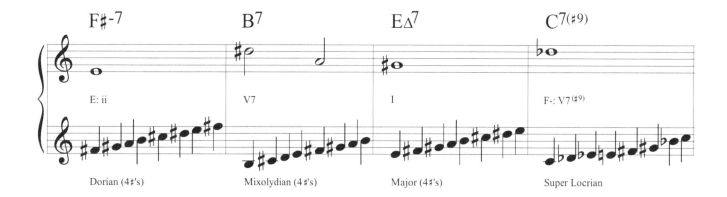

Form: This is the Last A, but it is extended to 12 bars, so this is A2

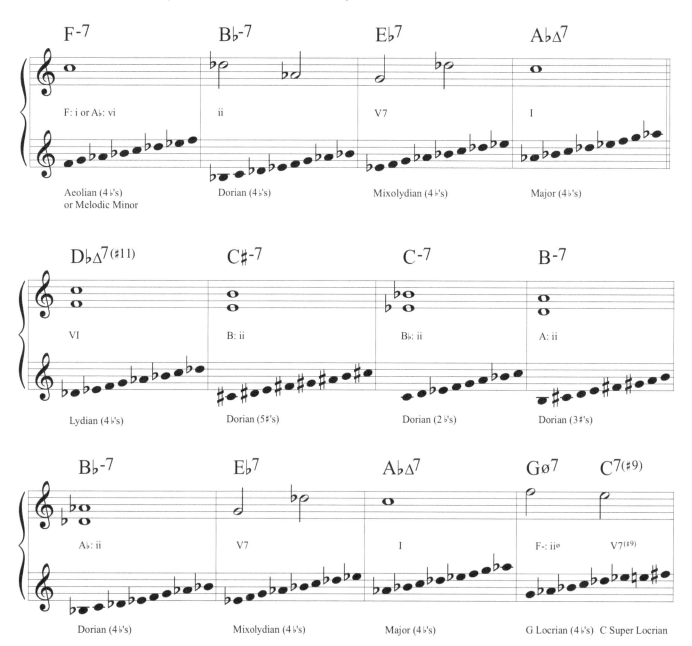

You can see above all the ways I would be analyzing this chord progression to play on it: 1) The chord functions, 2) the chord construction, 3) the accompanying scales and key signatures, 4) the form—A A1 B A2, 5) the guide tones which yield a framework of pitches that make the tune sound like the tune. In this step, I want to learn everything I possibly can with my eyes about this tune through left brain analysis.

Ear Training

Now let's work on ear training for this tune. I want to learn to hear everything I have learned with left brain analysis. I would sing everything (in harmonic rhythm) I have identified in the chord progression above:

   •Sing the melody

   •Sing the chords as arpeggios

   •Sing the scales

   •Sing patterns

   •Sing the guide tones

And add:

   •Sing the 3rd of each chord

   •Sing the 5th of each chord

   •Sing the 7th of each chord

   •Sing the 9th of each chord

Bringing It All Together

Let's improvise on the tune now. If you are playing with a play-along, turn it off and work on the places that are weaker. Drill keys that are more difficult. Practice connecting the guide tones for phrases in as many ways as possible, in time! Do your solo lines sound like the changes and the tune with no backup? If not, go back and play the guide tones some more and rework ideas for connecting them. Again, the guide tones are like dots in a dot-to-dot puzzle, and we try to make different pictures by connecting the dots in different ways (but we are not discarding the dots). In a way, we are also in a crossword puzzle where we are trying to solve in each measure for both horizontal (melodic) and vertical (harmonic) considerations at the same time. Add to this the emotional expression that can accompany these two simultaneous puzzles, and we have the greatest game going! Let's turn the play-along back on and have a party. Hopefully, the right brain skills and the left brain skills are coming together to produce an exciting solo. This is the payoff time! (This is a lifelong pursuit by the way.)

Chapter 21   Teaching Improvisation with Different Tune Vehicles

With the foundational approaches for improvisation from Chapter 20, let's look at ideas for teaching basic jazz tune types or vehicles. The tune types we will approach will be Blues, Modal, Rhythm, Bebop, and we will save Ballads for the next chapter. When Charlie Parker was asked how he learned to play (improvise), he answered that he first learned how to play the Blues in all 12 keys, then Rhythm Changes in all 12 keys, and then *Cherokee* (Bebop) in all 12 keys. He said that took him about two years; but after that, he could play anything. There is an early story about Bird (Charlie Parker) that in his infancy as an improviser he went to a jam session. When they called the tune, *Honeysuckle Rose*, he ventured up because he had been practicing that one. But the rhythm section was playing it in F, and Bird had learned it in Bb. They laughed him off the stand. As he came down, he said, "That's the first time I know'd there was different keys." We all start somewhere, even Charlie Parker.

Blues Tunes

The Blues is the most fundamental jazz form, and all jazz musicians must master and play blues in all keys. There are probably hundreds of tunes written on blues progressions. Some people feel that it is a mistake to start with Blues because it may result in a young person always playing Blues Scales on every tune. This does sometimes happen; but it is only because instruction stops at that point, and the student is left to do the only thing he knows. I have never had a student get stuck playing Blues Scales all the time when we have continued on to other alternatives. I have no problem whatsoever with using the Blues as a starting point. All the great jazz innovators were blues players at heart.

> There is also a stigma in some regions about playing a Blues Scale even in a blues tune. This is ridiculous!!! Blues Scales are in full use by professional players, and there are plenty of Charlie Parker solo transcriptions to prove it. The problem arises when that is the only thing a student knows how to do. We should always use any jazz materials as a conscious choice for expressive reasons, never because that's all we can do. But again, we have to start somewhere.

When I start a student on a blues, I do it with a little Sonny Rollins tune called *Sonny Moon for Two* (*Live at the Village Vanguard*, Vol. 2). (They should listen to the original recording and, ideally, play along with it.) The tune itself is a descending minor pentatonic scale (1, b3, 4, 5, b7, 8) repeated three times with some rhythmic interest to make it into a melody. It is a real jazz tune, but it is easy to teach by ear to students; and they can all succeed right away. Once everyone knows the tune, I point out that the melody is a scale; and we play it as a scale. Then I do some call and response with them to give them ideas about how to make melodic ideas from the scale. I play two bars, they repeat those two bars. I start simple and gradually give them more. If they don't get one, I will repeat it and then move on. (Refer to videos for a demonstration.)

The beauty of this approach for beginning students is that the Pentatonic Scale fits over all the chords, and they don't have to think about chords or progressions yet. It is impossible to play a wrong note or get lost.

Everyone can succeed and live through it and thereby gain some confidence and motivation. They do it by ear, so it is right brain and does not reinforce dependence on the written page.

I call this approach "horizontal playing" when the materials used are blanketing the whole progression. The material is based on a horizontal consideration such as the key of the piece instead of on the vertical chords as they go by. Pentatonic Scales make great blanketing scales, and so do Blues Scales. There is really no such thing as "The Blues Scale". There are many possible configurations of blues scales, but the one that is usually referred to as "The" Blues Scale is very close to the Minor Pentatonic Scale—only one additional note. Minor Pentatonic is 1, b3, 4, 5, b7, 8, and Blues Scale is 1, b3, 4, b5, 5, b7, 8. So after having students play for a while with the Minor Pentatonic, I will add that b5 note and have them experiment with that. I will repeat the call and response and give them ideas for how to incorporate the new note (blues licks). We are still playing horizontally, and no one will play any wrong notes or get lost.

When everyone is succeeding pretty well with Minor Pentatonic and Blues Scale horizontal playing on the Blues, then I will move on to "vertical" playing on the Blues. Now it becomes necessary to know what the chord progression is and how to deal with changing our note choices when the chords change. Fortunately, the Blues is still very approachable vertically for most students. Here is the basic entry-level progression I normally use. It is followed by a version with a few substitutions that are most frequently added. The numbers in parentheses are the guide tones (the half-step movements that define the progression).

12 Bar Blues

	I7 (3)		I7 (3)		I7 (3)		I7 (b7)	
	IV7 (3)		IV7 (b7)		I7 (3)		I7 (3)	
	V7 (3)		IV7 (b7)		I7 (3)		I7 (3)	||

This progression would be good at a junior high school or beginning level. I normally use a little more advanced progression for high school beginners as follows.

12 Bar Blues With Standard Substitutions

	I7 (3)		IV7 (b7)		I7 (3)		I7 (b7)	
	IV7 (3)		IV7 (b7)		I7 (3)		VI7 (3)	
	II- (b7)		V7 (3 then b7)		I7 (3)		I7 (3) or V7 (b7)	||

If we use the V7 chord in the last bar in the above example, it becomes what we call a simple turnaround (turns us around back to the top of the progression). Very soon and certainly at the college level, we expand the turnaround to look like this (last line of the progression):

| II- (b7) | V7   (3 – b7) | I7 (3)   VI (3) | II- (b7)   V7 (3) ||

These guide tones (the framework of the tune) can be sustained as whole notes and half notes at first, but I try to make it more interesting by adding a simple rhythm and fleshing out a few notes around the guide tones:

The students should run the chords and scales through the progression just as we do when we approach any other tune. But then I have the students play the framework (seen on the staff above) and repeat this over and over and over until they are sick of it; but by doing so, they are creating an intuitive sense of what those critical note changes are and when they need to happen to outline the sound of the Blues. I will have the whole class play the framework while each person has an opportunity to solo over it. I will demonstrate how to expand around the framework notes (guide tones) while still touching into them. When this is done well, the blues progression is clearly heard even with no accompaniment. (Please refer to the video demonstrations of this approach.)

Another Sonny Rollins tune, *Tenor Madness,* makes a great teaching vehicle for vertical playing on the Blues. The melody itself outlines the guide tones that we want to teach.

Partially dependent on the age of the student, I usually introduce the first approach to the Bebop Scale during this time. The Bebop Scale is based on the dominant 7th chord, and nearly every chord in the basic Blues is dominant in quality; so this is a perfect time to introduce this scale. It is simply a mixolydian scale with one additional note, the major 7th. No, the major 7th cannot be played against the dominant chord (b7) except in passing; but that is the way we will use it. This simple addition gives a couple of advantages: first, the scale now has 8 notes to better fit the timing of a measure; and the best target (chord) tones fall in strong positions on the beat. Without the additional note, all the wrong notes fall in strong positions including the dreaded 4th note of the scale. Virtually all of the great players since the Bebop era have used this additional note.

Here is how the Bebop Scale would look on the Blues progression. I like to have the students start getting this note configuration in their fingers and in their ears early on. As usual, we always apply materials to the progression in harmonic rhythm.

By the time the students have experimented with horizontal playing using the Pentatonic and Blues Scales and with vertical playing using the guide tones and Bebop Scales, they can begin to mix it altogether to create a solo. While most rock/fusion improvising is horizontal in approach; in a bebop approach to the blues, it is normal to play vertically while still choosing to intersperse blues or pentatonic scales at times for expressive purposes. See the following Charlie Parker example from *Au Privave*.

Notice in the above example that Bird is using the Blues Scale in bars 1-3. Then he is playing the changes closely in the rest of the chorus. Notice in bar 10 that he is using altered notes (b9 and #9) on the A7, and then he uses the bebop scale the rest of the measure (A G# G—adding the major 7 as a passing tone).

When students begin to master these materials and approaches in one key, they should start expanding into other keys until they have mastered all 12 keys. Remember that it is essential during this process to listen to the Blues and transcribe blues solos.

Modal Tunes

Another way that many teachers start young improvisers is on a modal tune such as *So What* or *Impressions* (same chord progression). *Impressions* is on Volume 54 of the Aebersold play-along series titled *Maiden Voyage*, which is another common modal tune also on that album. There are three features of a modal tune that make it attractive as a starting point. First, we only need one kind of scale to get started, usually Dorian. Second, the chords last for a long time, so we don't have to deal with fast moving chords. Third, there are no wrong notes to play as long as we stay disciplined to the scale. Here is how *Impressions* looks:

|| D- (8 bars) | D- (8 bars) | Eb- (8 bars) | D- (8 bars) ||

Notice that it is a 32 bar form, AABA. All the chords are minor and require the Dorian scale; so the student only needs to learn the D Dorian scale and the Eb Dorian scale (concert pitch).

I would approach this tune by first having the students listen to the form and to solos played on the tune, *So What*, on the Miles Davis *Kind of Blue* album and on *Impressions* on the John Coltrane album, *The Very Best of John Coltrane*. Have the students learn the two Dorian scales needed and then take them through standard variations for scales such as are seen in most scale etude books, but don't use a book because these scale variations need to be done without using the eyes. Variations could include:

1234, 2345, 3456 etc. || 1231, 2342, 3453, etc. || 123, 234, 345, 456, etc. || 135, 246, etc. ||

1353, 2464, 3575, etc. || 1 3, 2 4, 3 5, 4 6, etc. (3rds) || 1 4, 2 5, 3 6, etc. (4ths) || etc.

The point of these pattern exercises is to gain familiarity with the materials, which is essential because we will be using the same materials for extended amounts of time. I would also have them learn the chord arpeggios and broken chord arpeggios. As mastery is gained, an expanded approach would be to also have them learn the Bebop Scale on the progression. This is not as simple as on the Blues because the Bebop Scale is a dominant phenomenon, and we are dealing with minor chords in this modal tune. If you have already taught the Bebop scale on the Blues, then it is just a matter of adaptation. To play a Bebop Scale on a D- chord, figure out what the dominant chord would be if the D- were the II chord in a II V7 progression: answer would be G7. Therefore, I would apply the G Bebop scale to the D- chord. (Note that anything we can play on the V7 chord we can play on the II chord and vice-versa.) It is also possible to codify from this process that the Bebop Scale for minor chords adds the major 3rd as a passing tone, whereas, the dominant version adds the major 7th as the passing tone. I have decided to just apply the dominant version on D-, and I think it will be apparent why this may be better choice as the chapter goes along and we apply a lot of variations to the Bebop Scale.

Once the students are familiar with the materials, then it is a matter of how to apply and organize the materials to improvise on the tune. This is largely a matter of combining the different scale patterns (previously page) in various, less predictable ways and adding rhythmic variation. A large challenge of playing on a modal tune is keeping one's place when the chords last so long. With considerable experience, it is possible to feel when 4 bars or 8 bars has gone by; but students will need a little help with this at first. Help them hear the key change so they can at least respond to it, and make sure the drummer is delineating 8 bar sections. These delineating fills by the drummer make it far easiser to hear the form and when the key is about to change. I think it is more difficult for young students to deal with these long-lasting chords than to deal with chords moving at a more natural rate, and it is more difficult to give them exact materials to play.

However, the modal tune is a great vehicle for working on more general organizational principles such as motivic development, both melodically and rhythmically, and question and answer structure. I may give the student a rhythmic motif such as a dotted quarter and an eighth note, and ask them to see what they can do with it. Developmental techniques such as augmentation or diminution or inversion are fair game. Or I may ask the student to create an idea that has an upward inflection at the end, as in a question, and then create a similar idea or shape that has a downward inflection on the end, as in an answer. It is also possible to give the student the challenge to sequence the same or similar idea originating from each scale degree. This really is a wonderful way to teach some traditional developmental techniques.

Another very important aspect of playing on the modal tune is reflecting the key change in the note choices at the double bar lines. D- has no sharps or flats, but Eb- has five flats. I would give the student the challenge of playing an idea on the D- side of the bar line that has a D in it that has to move to a Db on the Eb- side of the bar line. Or have them play an idea in D- that has an A in it that has to move to either Ab or Bb when they hit the bar line, etc. I might even have them create an idea that has common tones for both sides of the bar line but other tones that have to move by half step or an idea where all three tones have to move by half step. Some examples are below—left of double bar line is D- and right of double bar line is Eb-:

Give the student a set of three or four pitches at a time to work with, and see what they can come up with. This is something each student can have success with, and success begets success. (Refer to videos.)

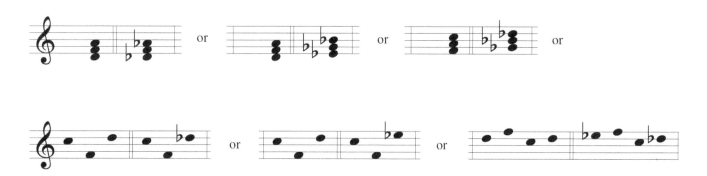

Rhythm Changes

Rhythm changes are the chords from the George Gershwin tune, *I Got Rhythm.* The bebop players loved playing on this chord progression; and since a chord progression cannot be copyrighted, they wrote many other tunes on these same chord changes. It is vital in jazz to learn to deal with this chord progression.

I Got Rhythm Chord Changes (one version)

A Section: | BbΔ7   B°7 | C-7   C#°7 | D-7   G7 | C-7   F7 |

Function: I   V (G7b9)   II   V (A7b9) II (III) V7 (VI)   II   V

Guide tones: Bb   B   C   C#   C   B   Bb   A or Eb

Framework:

In Numbers:

    1 2 3 5   Chord (up)   5 b3 1 5   Chord (up)   5 b3 1 b7 3 8   5 b3 1 b7   3 8 b7

                                           1st Ending

    | BbΔ   Bb7 | EbΔ   E° | D-   G7 | C-   F7 ||

Function: I   V   I   V (A7b9) II (III) V (VI)   II   V

Guide tones: D or A   Ab   G   C#   C   B   Bb   A

Framework:

|In Numbers:

    3 2 1 7   b7   ½ step   3 5 6 5   Chord from C# 5 b3 1 b7 3 8   5 b3 1 b7   3 8

2nd A Sect.: | BbΔ7 B°7 | C-7   C#°7 | D-7   G7 | C-7   F7 |

Function: I   V (G7b9)   II   V (A7b9) II (III) V7 (VI)   II   V

Guide tones: Bb   B   C   C#   C   B   Bb   A or Eb

Framework:

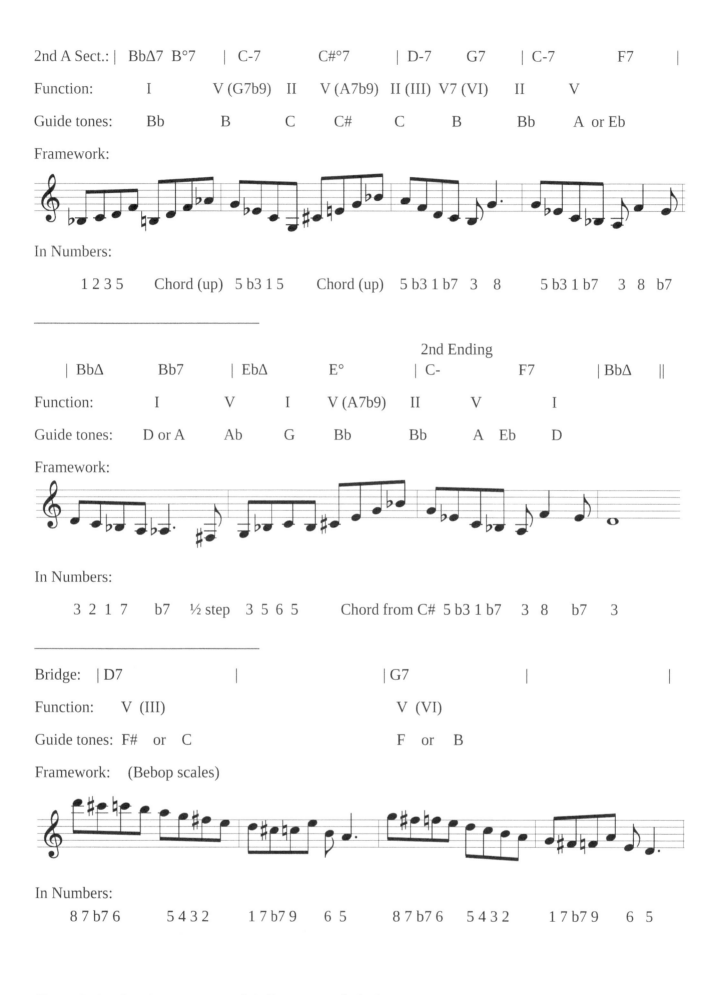

In Numbers:

        1 2 3 5   Chord (up) 5 b3 1 5   Chord (up)   5 b3 1 b7 3 8   5 b3 1 b7   3 8 b7

_____

                                                              2nd Ending

    | BbΔ   Bb7 | EbΔ   E° | C-   F7 | BbΔ ||

Function: I   V   I   V (A7b9)   II   V   I

Guide tones: D or A   Ab   G   Bb   Bb   A   Eb   D

Framework:

In Numbers:

    3 2 1 7   b7 ½ step 3 5 6 5   Chord from C# 5 b3 1 b7   3 8   b7   3

_____

Bridge: | D7 | | G7 | |

Function: V (III)   V (VI)

Guide tones: F#   or   C   F   or   B

Framework: (Bebop scales)

In Numbers:

    8 7 b7 6   5 4 3 2   1 7 b7 9   6 5   8 7 b7 6   5 4 3 2   1 7 b7 9   6 5

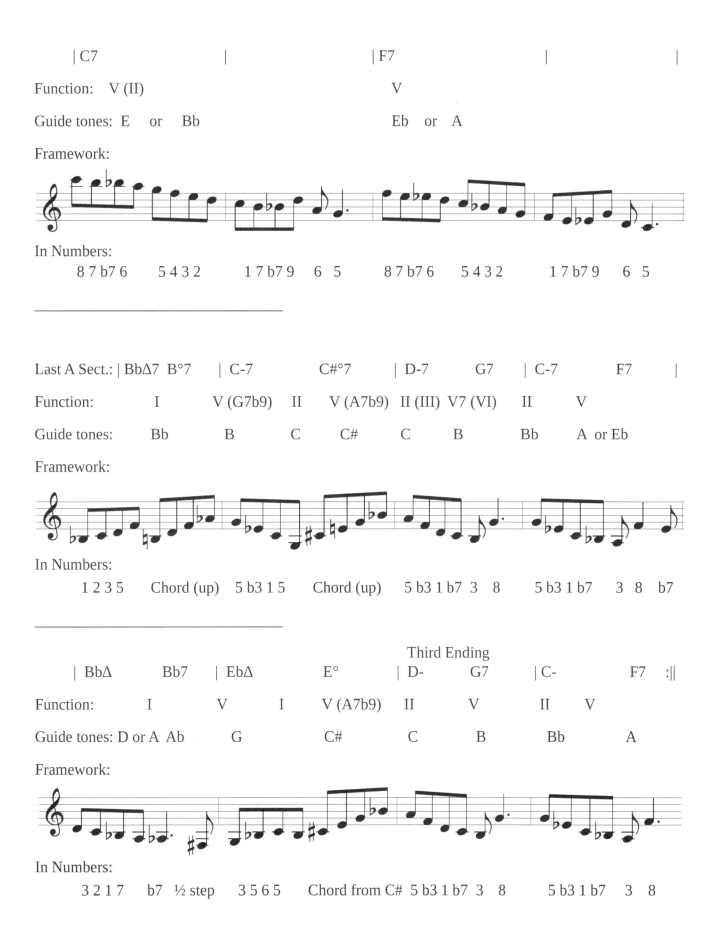

| C7 | | | F7 | | | |

Function: V (II)   V

Guide tones: E   or   Bb   Eb   or   A

Framework:

In Numbers:

8 7 b7 6   5 4 3 2   1 7 b7 9   6 5   8 7 b7 6   5 4 3 2   1 7 b7 9   6 5

Last A Sect.: | BbΔ7 B°7 | C-7   C#°7 | D-7   G7 | C-7   F7 |

Function: I   V (G7b9)   II   V (A7b9) II (III) V7 (VI)   II   V

Guide tones: Bb   B   C   C#   C   B   Bb   A or Eb

Framework:

In Numbers:

1 2 3 5   Chord (up)   5 b3 1 5   Chord (up)   5 b3 1 b7   3   8   5 b3 1 b7   3   8   b7

Third Ending

| BbΔ   Bb7 | EbΔ   E° | D-   G7 | C-   F7   :||

Function: I   V   I   V (A7b9)   II   V   II   V

Guide tones: D or A Ab   G   C#   C   B   Bb   A

Framework:

In Numbers:

3 2 1 7   b7   ½ step   3 5 6 5   Chord from C# 5 b3 1 b7   3   8   5 b3 1 b7   3   8

Rhythm Changes Framework in Full Form:

It is as important for a jazz player to be able to play Rhythm Changes in all 12 keys as it is to play the Blues in all 12 keys. Rhythm Changes go through many different versions because of substitutions, but the version I am going to use is pictured on the previous page in the standard concert key of Bb.

To approach this tune, as with other tunes, I would have the students listen to some examples of Rhythm Changes on recordings of such tunes as: *I Got Rhythm*, *The Flintstones* (TV Show Theme), *Oleo* (Sonny Rollins), *Rhythm-A-Ning* (Thelonious Monk), *The Theme* (Miles Davis), *Cottontail* (Duke Ellington), *The Eternal Triangle* (Sonny Stitt and Sonny Rollins with Dizzy Gillespie), etc. Decide on one of the heads and learn it by ear. (Note that some Rhythm tunes do not have a written bridge (B section), but rather it is improvised.) Then do the usual arpeggiation of the chords in harmonic rhythm.

When the basics are in control, start into the guide tones and play them in half notes and whole notes. Then flesh out the guide tones with the framework pitches written on the chord sheet (previous page). Play the framework over and over across the course of many days to really internalize it. The rhythm and sound of the pitches will gradually become intuitive as they are programmed into the brain. I have found this framework idea (given for both Blues and Rhythm Changes) to be invaluable as a starting place and can be done with a whole band in the warmup period of the rehearsal.

Before we go further, let's make a few notes about the Rhythm Changes progression. The form is AABA 32 bar song form. The A sections of rhythm changes are based on I VI II V7 I's with a short excursion to the IV chord for variety, really very simple; but with all the substitutions, it can look a bit more difficult. The B section (or bridge) is just the Cycle of Dominants bringing us back to the A section. The framework I am suggesting, will provide a good point of departure that will work on nearly any normal version of Rhythm Changes. Often though, either the A section or the B section will be fairly substituted. For example, on the tune mentioned above, *Eternal Triangle*, the A sections are quite standard, but the bridge has been altered quite a lot by substitution.

In the chord sheet on the previous page; in bar 1, the second chord started out as a G-7. But then we substituted G7 for it, so it became a secondary dominant of the next chord C-, the II chord. Then we decided to alter with b9, so it became G7b9. The top four notes of G7b9 are B°7, so that is what we ended up with in our progression.

Example: Bb G- | C- F7 | D-

Bb G7 | C- F7 | D-

Bb G7b9 | C- A7b9 | D-

Bb B°7 | C- C#°7 | D-

Add a similar process for the second chord of bar two, and we end up with a nice chromatic progression | BbΔ B°| C- C#° | D- G7 |. In the sixth measure with the IV, Eb E°7, it is hard to put a roman numeral on the E° because it is probably really like what often happens on the second bar of the IV chord in the blues, where the substitution is to raise the root so that it becomes diminished. Even aside from that, the E°7 is another version of A7b9 which would lead to the next chord opf D- in the first ending. Note that the last two bars of the whole tune (3rd ending) are set up for repeating from the top and are acting as a turnaround. If the tune is ending, then the cadence ending at the end of the second A (2nd ending) would be used instead.

Getting Variation

Now the stage is set to really have some fun, and it is this next step that brings such incredible growth in young improvisers. This is often the real turning point. By now we should have the framework really internalized and can almost play it in our sleep, and certainly we are ready for some kind of variety . What are the ways to get variety and still play the guide tones? There are really four ways to get the variety:

- Directional changes

- Register or octave changes

- Rhythmic changes

- Alterations (mostly on the dominant chords)

I have the students take just the first two bars and explore as many ideas as possible for creating variety. The first three methods for variety (above) work well for bars 1 and 2, but the idea of alteration does not help a lot in those bars because we have already altered about as much as we want to. Remember the B° and the C#° are substitutions for G7b9 and A7b9 respectively which are already altered, and the Bb∆ doesn't want to be altered nor does the C-7. The first task is to see how many ways we can vary directions on those first two bars. (Note: always play one more note over the bar line for the resolution.) In the framework, we used the directions up, up, down, up. What else can we do?

Direction: Bar 1   Bar 2

Up, Up   Up, Up

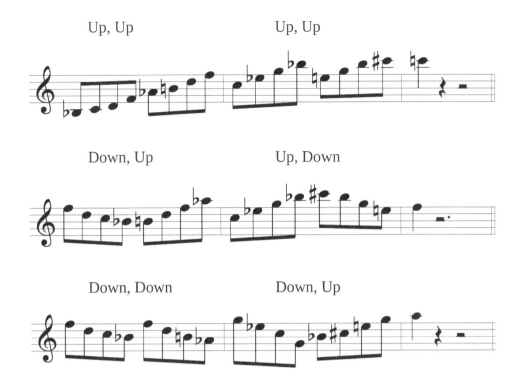

Down, Up   Up, Down

Down, Down   Down, Up

Etc. (16 different combinations are possible.)

Some of these directional changes can be changed up even more by using more of the range of the instrument.

Register: Bar 1   Bar 2

        Up, Up (but in higher octave)   Down, Down (to the low octave)

A number of additional variations are possible when using more extreme registers.

Even more variation can come with rhythmic change. So far, we have played all eighth notes. How many more rhythmic ways can we still play the same 4 notes?

Rhythm:

What variations are available if we only play 3 of the notes?

What variations are available if we only use 2 of the notes?

etc.

Bars 3 & 4 Alteration:

When we have explored as many variations as possible for bars 1 and 2, we move onto bars 3 and 4 (which are the same as bars 7 and 8). We can change directions and register and rhythm on these bars, too, but I usually emphasize, first, the variation available through altering on the dominant chords.

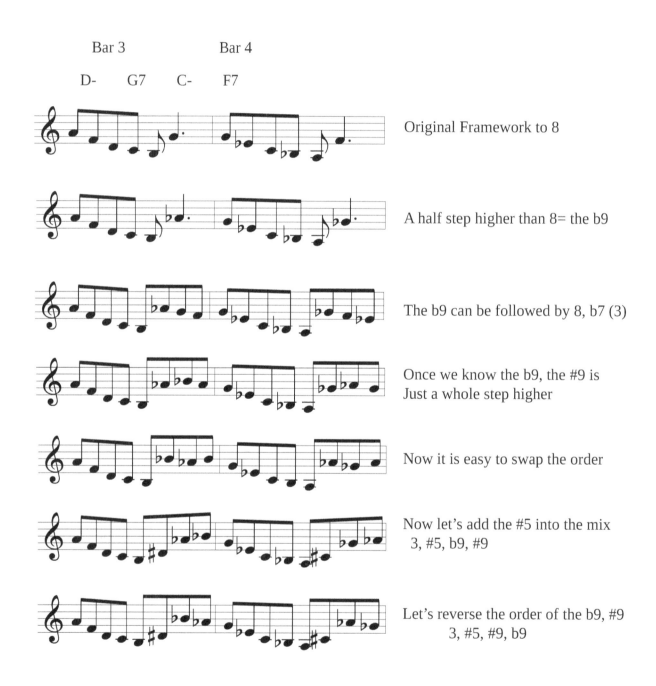

Bar 3   Bar 4

D-   G7   C-   F7

Original Framework to 8

A half step higher than 8= the b9

The b9 can be followed by 8, b7 (3)

Once we know the b9, the #9 is
Just a whole step higher

Now it is easy to swap the order

Now let's add the #5 into the mix
    3, #5, b9, #9

Let's reverse the order of the b9, #9
        3, #5, #9, b9

Now let's revisit these alterations with different direction (ascending instead of descending):

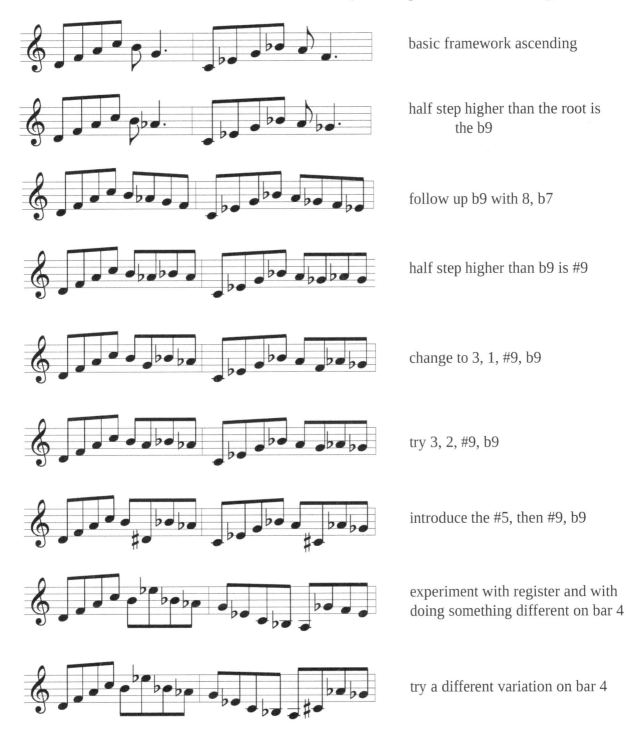

basic framework ascending

half step higher than the root is the b9

follow up b9 with 8, b7

half step higher than b9 is #9

change to 3, 1, #9, b9

try 3, 2, #9, b9

introduce the #5, then #9, b9

experiment with register and with doing something different on bar 4

try a different variation on bar 4

The possibilities with varying direction, register, rhythm, and alteration are seeminly endless (and also seem to be a lifelong pursuit).

We can experiment with similar ideas for bars 5 and 6, and now we are ready to see how many ways we can blow over the first A section. How many ways can I connect the dots? This is basically three fourths of the tune. Now I need to work on variations for the bridge (the other fourth). Since our bridge framework is the Bebop scale, how many ways can I vary the Bebop scale?

Bebop Scale Variations

Basic scale with standard ending (All examples on D7):

Simple variations by going up 1, 2, or 3 notes before descending, plus alternate endings:

Ascending the scale never happens. The ascending material is based on the major chord built on the b7. This illustration is still based on a D7 and shows ascending one octave and then two octaves.

Another way of getting varation is to use enclosures. The following illustration shows an enclosure for the root. We start a half step above and then go a half step below and then hit the target note. Can happen in either or both octaves.

Here is an illustration for enclosing the 5th.

Enclosing the root and the 5th.

Enclosing the 3rd comes from two half steps below since a half step above is the 4th note of the scale.

Here would be an example of enclosing all three targets, the root, 5th, and 3rd.

Since the enclosure for the 3rd is by far the most useful, here are some other enclosures for the 3rd.

The first example uses the ascending variation to then create a diatonic double enclosure to the 3rd. The second example is the same except for putting the first three notes up an octave. The third example is a chromatic double enclosure to the third.

In the next example, we see an illustration of combining two versions of enclosures for the 3rd and using more range.

Charlie Parker would also sometimes arrive at the 3rd in the line and then descend chromatically all the way to the b7 (still D7).

Work through the bridge over and over with these Bebop Scale variations, and then play through the whole tune over and over experimenting with every way to make variations you can imagine. Hey look, Mom, I'm improvising! (I am always blown away by what happens to students when they are willing to pay this kind of price.)

Another Bebop Tune Application

Let's look at the use of patterns in approaching one more tune, *Afternoon in Paris*. This is a great tune by John Lewis, pianist in the Modern Jazz Quartet or MJQ. Again, it would be important to find recordings and listen and play along by ear and even transcribe. But let's see how patterns can create a framework out of the guide tones for this tune. Working on this tune in this way is another real turning point for students. The chord chart for the tune shows 10 pattern choices for realizing the A section of the tune. Notice all of the patterns incorporate the guide tones.

Afternoon in Paris (A section only) —First Four Bars

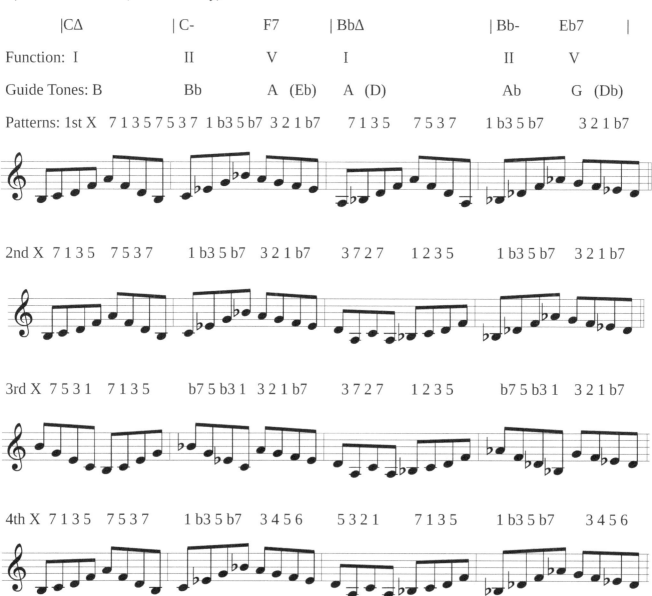

	|CΔ		C-	F7		BbΔ			Bb-	Eb7		
Function:	I			II	V		I			II	V	
Guide Tones:	B			Bb	A (Eb)		A (D)			Ab	G (Db)	

Patterns: 1st X   7 1 3 5 7 5 3 7 1 b3 5 b7 3 2 1 b7   7 1 3 5   7 5 3 7   1 b3 5 b7   3 2 1 b7

2nd X 7 1 3 5   7 5 3 7   1 b3 5 b7   3 2 1 b7   3 7 2 7   1 2 3 5   1 b3 5 b7   3 2 1 b7

3rd X 7 5 3 1   7 1 3 5   b7 5 b3 1   3 2 1 b7   3 7 2 7   1 2 3 5   b7 5 b3 1   3 2 1 b7

4th X 7 1 3 5   7 5 3 7   1 b3 5 b7   3 4 5 6   5 3 2 1   7 1 3 5   1 b3 5 b7   3 4 5 6

5th X 7 5 3 1 7 1 3 5   b7 5 b3 1   3 4 5 6   5 3 2 1   7 1 3 5   b7 5 b3 1   3 4 5 6

6th X 7 5 3 1 7 1 3 5   b7 5 b3 1   3 2 1 b7   3 7 2 7   1 2 3 5   1 b3 5 b7   3 4 5 6

7th X 7 1 3 5   7 5 3 7   1 b3 5 b7 3 4 5 6   5 3 2 1   7 1 3 5   b7 5 b3 1   3 2 1 b7

8th X   7 1 3 5   7 5 3 7   5 b3 1 b7   3 8 b7   3 7 2 7   1 2 3 5   1 b3 5 b7   3 1 #9 b9

9th X 7 5 3 1   7 1 3 5   b7 5 b3 1   3 b9 #9 b9   5 3 2 1   7 1 3 5   b7 5 b3 1   3 #5 b9 #9

10th X 7 1 3 5   7 5 3 7   5 b3 1 b7   3 #5 #9 b9   5 3 2 1   7 1 3 5   1 b3 5 b7   3 2 #9 b9

Afternoon in Paris (A section only) —Second Four Bars (all patterns continue from the first 4 bars)

|AbΔ | DØ   G7b9 | CΔ | D-   G7 || C

Function: I   II   V   I   II   V   I

Guide Tones: G   (C)   C   B (F, Ab   B (E, G)   C   B F   E

Patterns: 1st X 7 1 3 5 7 5 3 7   1 b3 b5 b7   3 b2 1 b7   7 1 3 5   7 5 3 7   1 b3 5 b7   3 2 1 b7   3

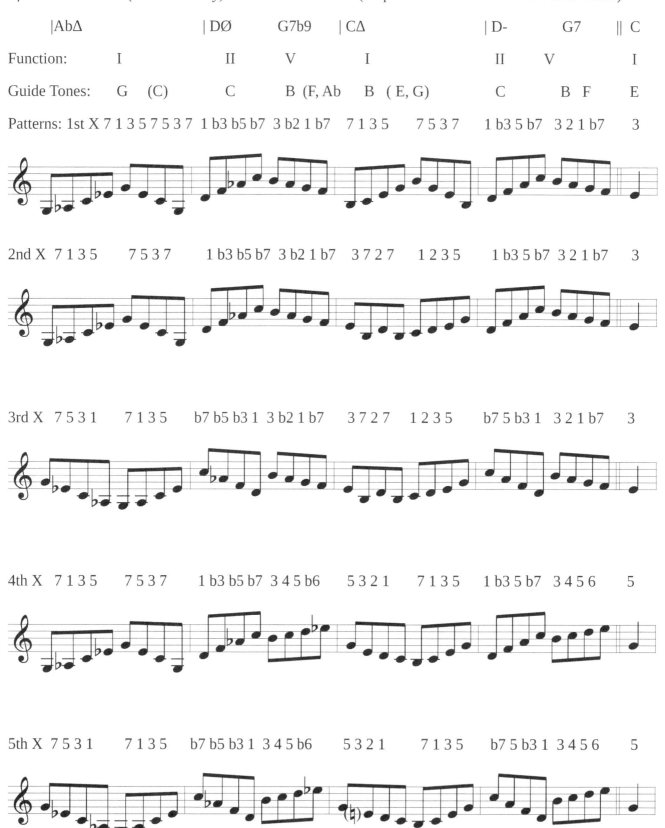

2nd X 7 1 3 5   7 5 3 7   1 b3 b5 b7   3 b2 1 b7   3 7 2 7   1 2 3 5   1 b3 5 b7   3 2 1 b7   3

3rd X   7 5 3 1   7 1 3 5   b7 b5 b3 1   3 b2 1 b7   3 7 2 7   1 2 3 5   b7 5 b3 1   3 2 1 b7   3

4th X   7 1 3 5   7 5 3 7   1 b3 b5 b7   3 4 5 b6   5 3 2 1   7 1 3 5   1 b3 5 b7   3 4 5 6   5

5th X   7 5 3 1   7 1 3 5   b7 b5 b3 1   3 4 5 b6   5 3 2 1   7 1 3 5   b7 5 b3 1   3 4 5 6   5

6th X   5 3 2 1   7 1 3 5   b7 b5 b3 1   3 b2 1 b7   3 7 2 7   1 2 3 5   b7 5 b3 1   3 4 5 6   5

7th X   3 7 2 7   1 2 3 5   1 b3 b5 b7   3 4 5 b6   5 3 2 1   7 1 3 5   b7 5 b3 1   3 2 1 b7   3

8th X   5 3 2 1   7 1 3 5   b3 1 b5 b7   3 #5 #9 b9   5 3 2 1   7 1 3 5   5 b3 1 b7   3 5 8 b7   3

9th X   7 5 3 1   7 1 3 5   1 b3 b5 b7   3 1 #9 b9   5 3 2 1   7 1 3 5   5 b3 b7 5   3 #5 8 3   9

10th X 5 3 7 5   9 7 5 3   1 b3 b5 b7   3 5 b7 b9   5 3 2 1   7 1 3 5   b7 5 b3 1   3 4 5 6   5

The A section is three quarters of the tune, so let's just deal with that much for now. I have found that internalizing these patterns goes a long way toward developing a jazz vocabulary. In preparation for going through the different kinds of repetition, I often have the students practice each type of pattern in the keys needed for the tune. For example, practice the patterns needed for major chords in the three keys of the tune. Then practice the variations of the II V7 patterns in the four keys needed. (Example on next page.)

Major 7 Patterns (3 keys—C, Bb, Ab)	II V7 Patterns (4 keys—C, Bb, Ab, C minor)		
7 1 3 5 7 5 3 7 (1)	1 b3 5 b7 3 2 1 b7	| 3	(Always practice
7 5 3 1 7 1 3 5	b7 5 b3 1 3 2 1 b7	| 3	the resolution)
3 7 2 7 1 2 3 5	1 b3 5 b7 3 4 5 6	| 5	
5 3 2 1 7 1 3 5	b7 5 b3 1 3 4 5 6	| 5	
	5 b3 1 b7 3 8 (as in the rhythm framework)		
which again leads to:	5 b3 1 b7 3 b9 8 b7	| 3	
	5 b3 1 b7 3 b9 #9 b9	| 5	
	5 b3 1 b7 3 #9 b9 #9	| 5 or 7	
	5 b3 1 b7 3 #5 #9 b9	| 5	
	5 b3 1 b7 3 #5 b9 #9	| 5 or 7	
and change directions for these:	1 b3 5 b7 3 b9 #9 b9	| 5	
	1 b3 5 b7 3 #5 b9 #9	| 5 or 7	
	etc. etc.		

Then we should put these patterns into the format of the tune, one at a time, in the proper sequence of the progression. But as shown in the 6th time and the 7th time above, the fun comes when mixing them all up. This now becomes improvisation and becomes even more interesting when we start using rhythmic variety and range variety with the directional variety. Later, we could add the variety of adding alterations in the II V7's as we did in the rhythm changes—8th, 9th, and 10th examples above.

As with all other exercises, it is also a great idea to sing all of these patterns for ear training. A lot of ear training occurs just from playing the patterns over and over, but growth is enhanced that much more by singing. Add to that, singing the actual chord progression in harmonic rhythm. İt may be helpful at first to sit at the piano and check in here and there, but the goal is to become independent of any instrument in our singing exercises.

By the time a student has paid his dues on the Blues, the modal tunes, Rhythm Changes, and other bebop tunes, the student (or the band director) is well on his or her way as an improviser. Keep in mind through this process that our primary goal is to help the student develop double dominance; and while it is easy to get caught up in all the theory and these cool patterns, we must not forget that first in importance is the development of the right brain. Also, a reminder that if all this theory is a bit daunting; you, as the band director, can still accomplish a great deal with your soloists by just getting them playing by ear with the piece you want them to solo on. (Chapter 19)

All of these approaches will be much more understandable if you consult the video demonstrations!

Pepper Adams was one of the truly great baritone saxophone soloists in jazz. A fellow saxophonist and roommate observed this about Pepper's practice routine and the ultimate end of this kind of practice.

> When he practiced changes, he attacked them [with] what scales he could use against the changes, what arpeggios he could use, and then he would try to attack every note in that change from every angle. After a while he said, 'I don't even think of changes anymore. When a piano player plays a chord, I know what it is. I can hear all phases of it and I can fit it into what I want to do. I don't let technique hang me up because I practice all the scales going in all different kinds of directions, going up one scale, coming down another scale, and then doing them in fourths.' He said, 'I've done this to such an extent that I can attack any change from any direction and go to any direction I want to go.' He was just progressing until it got to a point where he would have so much under his fingers, he could do anything he wanted with it." —Pepperadams.com (Facebook blog)

It is the disciplined practice that brings the mastery required for freedom of expression!

Chapter 22   Helping the Featured Soloist on the Ballad in Your Festival Set

In most states, you are required to program a ballad in your festival set. This is because the ballad is the true test of musicianship. The ballad separates the men from the boys. The ballad is a slow tune and typically features one soloist from your ensemble. When choosing the ballad, consider who your strongest soloists are; and choose to put your best foot forward. This soloist will need to play a personal version of the melody, improvise, and probably play a cadenza. This is a tall order!

Initial Preparations

As with all the other tunes we have looked at, our first priority is to help our soloist develop double dominance for the ballad. This must start with listening to great players playing the ballad, so be sure to choose a tune for which you can access at least one recording. The soloist must play along with the recording(s) by ear and learn the melody and ideas for melodic variation. The soloist should figure out the key and key changes for sections of the tune and learn the form of the chart as much as possible by ear. Ideally, all of this has happened before you ever pass out the chart to the band; but, of course, it can also happen along the way.

Playing the Melody

Playing the melody is a big deal for a couple of reasons. First, this is the thrust of the ballad—a beautiful melody. But also, the melody must be personalized by the soloist. The melody is not played as it is written, nor is it played exactly like anyone else ever played it. The soloist must find his own ways of expressing himself while still being true to the basic melody and intent of the composer. This is why the great Lester Young (Prez) said he could not play a ballad unless he knew the words. When we know the words, we have a feel for what we are trying to express and where the natural places are for pauses and the like. Knowing the words would probably, as Jerry Coker put it, "curb some of the unnecessary re-attacks of pitches (commonplace among instrumentalists) where they are not called for by the syllables within the lyric." This re-attacking almost seems like an epidemic sickness among students, and I see it as an indicator of immaturity when I am adjudicating soloists at a festival.

However, before we get into personalizing the melody, first things first, realize that the soloist is particularly exposed; and it is essential that we also do coaching that can help with sound production and intonation. Otherwise great aspects of a performance can be totally undermined by sound and pitch problems. We must also help the soloist play legato articulation and to play dynamically. Vibrato is an essential expressive element in a ballad. Some notes are played without vibrato while others are started straight and vibrato is introduced toward the end of the note. Occasionally, some notes might have vibrato throughout. Teach the technique of vibrato, but also help the student listen to vibrato on ballads by great vocalists and instrumentalists.

I often find myself coaching students to put a lot more soul into their performance. We think of the ballad as "pretty", and that typically connotes (in white society) soft, gentle, dainty, lace around the edges, etc. But the jazz ballad is based more in a black aesthetic where "pretty" is pure, raw emotional expression. We need the soloists to bare their souls.

Personalizing the Melody

To help the soloist accomplish his or her own personalization, I have students take one phrase of the melody at a time and see how many permutations they can come up with on the original melodic phrase using rhythmic and melodic variations. They should also experiment with devices like scoops and bends and glisses. Often these phrases will be played multiple times (as many as 6); and there is a stigma around playing the same phrase the same way multiple times, so we need to come up with several ways of varying each phrase. This is part of the creative expectation of a ballad. The soloist should continue and do this with each phrase of the tune. Then when it comes time to play the full melody, the soloist is equipped with many ideas. These ideas should always be used with this time-proven principle in mind: We always move from simple to more complex, not the other way around. The first statements of the melody phrases are closest to the original, then gradually expand. When the form of the tune is AABA, the first A would be the most plain with a little improvisation on the turnaround (bars 7 and 8). Then the second A would be more personalized with more improvisation around the melody. The B would probably be more plain again for at least the first half since it is being heard for the first time. The last A would be more like the second A and may even get a little more complex in the variations.

Another incredibly important principle that comes to the fore in the ballad could be summed up in what I call "back-phrasing". The ballad tempo is slow and doesn't naturally lend to a lot of motion. But without motion, there is no emotion! So, our challenge is to use other means to create motion. The main motion in a bar should be in the second half of the bar. We often hang back in the first half of the bar, so we can justify creating more motion in the second half to carry the phrase across the bar line into the next bar. This also applies to larger units like every two bars, every four bars, and every eight bars. We want to create the allusion of stronger motion, but we can't rush the tempo to do it; so we hold back and pay for the time first, and then we can push the movement forward without actually rushing the tempo. There is no such thing as a credit card in nature. If we try to move first and then pay later, it is backwards; and it sounds awkward and unmusical. We back-phrase so we can pay for the time first and then move.

This motion (emotion) is accomplished by using tension and release patterns in the music. They are built into the harmonic structure and form of the tune, and we have to ensure the rhythm section is doing its part to create this tension and release at the appropriate places in the form. The soloist has various musical parameters available to him or her to help create tension. It is good to for each player to have his own catalog of these devices. The following is a start that can be expanded by the indiviual.

Tension-Building Devices:

- rephrasing surface rhythms for increased motion

- playing louder or using crescendo

- playing higher on the instrument

- playing faster notes

- repetition

- playing more complex or more syncopated rhythms

- choosing notes with higher dissonance or more color

- using dramatic devices such as bends, growls, etc.

- silence, if set up properly

  etc., etc.

There are those who believe that this is the very reason music has its ability to touch our hearts and change our emotions. The music captures in a symbolic way the rhythms of our own emotional life. Usually not consciously, but subconsciously, we identify the tension and release in the music with the tension and release patterns we have felt in our own past lives, and we feel something in response. This can help give meaning to the experiences and emotions of our lives and becomes an enriching experience. The soloist must become conscious of these things that create deeper expression of emotions.

When approaching a ballad, we must determine if the rhythmic basis is straight eighths or swung eighths. If it swings, then the rhythm is basically tripletized and the information back in Chapter 8 can be very helpful. Probably the most common ballad basis, though, is straight eighths, but we still have to be careful about playing too many straight eighths in a row without rhythmic variation. When consecutive straight eighth notes are played on occasion, they must be inflected and accented with variety so they do not sound equally the same (singers are good at this). Remember that when all notes are created equal, there is no phrasing—because phrasing depends on some notes being more important than others. All known musical phrasing principles are especially critical in ballad playing.

The Improvised Chorus

The soloist usually gets at least part of a chorus where he or she needs to improvise without the responsibility of staying around the melody. The soloist should prepare for playing the changes by paying the same kinds of dues as we talked about in last two chapters (Chapters 19 and 20). Arpeggiate the chord progression in harmonic rhythm. Run the scales that fit the chords. Look for places to try out alterations. Get familiar in every way with the basic materials available, but then apply them in a ballad-specific way to express emotion appropriate to the context. This would be a great time to turn off the lights at night and play emotions alone and along with the ballad recording. There is no way to escape living with the tune to internalize it.

Some years ago, Jan Kanipasek (Woody Herman, Thad Jones-Mel Lewis) and I were featured soloists on a fund-raising concert. Among other tunes, we each played a ballad. Jan played *Skylark* in a very seasoned way. I decided to try a ballad that was brand new to me at the time, *Easy Livin'*. After the concert as we were packing up, I commented to Jan that I didn't feel like my ballad went all that well. Maybe I was a little premature airing it? Jan said, "Yeah, man. It takes 20 years to really internalize a ballad." I have found he is right. With ballads I have lived with for years, I don't even think about what the changes are; I just bare my soul, and yet it's all intact. But with limited time, we have to do the best we can for our festival set, and I have at times been blown away by what a young person has accomplished with a little coaching and a lot of live-with time and effort.

During the solo section, it can be appropriate to use a variety of rhythmic levels. The ballad is proceeding at the quarter note level. The soloist is probably working a lot at the eighth note level, but may go back and forth between eighth note and quarter note levels. The soloist may also elect to go back and forth into the sixteenth note level which is called double time. And some advanced soloists even use the double of the double time on occasion (quadruple time). If different rhythmic levels are to be used, they must be practiced; and I often coach a young player to play a half time idea and then repeat the same idea in double time making sure the articulation and time feel remain the same. Then do another half time idea and repeat it in double time. This can also be done with phrases of etudes or transcriptions if ideas aren't immediately plentiful. It is normal, but not desirable, for the soloist to rush when going into double time and when returning to half time. It is imperative to use a metronome while practicing going back and forth.

The Ending

Toward the end, the melody will typically simplify, similar to the beginning, as we put on the brakes to come to a close. In many charts, there will be a written space for a cadenza just before the last chord or last phrase. In charts designed for younger bands, the cadenza may be left out. When there is not a written space for a cadenza, I frequently insert one if it is appropriate to the soloist.

The cadenza, similar to classical cadenzas, is intended to be a virtuosic burst from the soloist to create a climax just before the end. This can be a challenge for young players who may not have built up much in the way of virtuosity. I have found, however, that by giving them good structural ideas and good materials to work with, it can be surprising and gratifying what they come up with. Let's look at a few scenarios.

A short, simple cadenza may just be an elaboration on the V7 chord, the penultimate chord. The band would play the chord to send off the soloist, the soloist would play unaccompanied and bring the band back in for the last chord. This V7 chord in a ballad will always be altered. It is often written b9 (most common) or #9. If it is b9, elaboration on a diminished scale or diminished chord can be very effective. The diminished scale (refer to Chapter 20) will be the one with the half step first. Just running the scale itself with some rhythm and some articulation will work very well; but there are some common patterns for diminished that can also be very useful. Every time we move a half step up the scale, we have a new whole step pair. It is common to move these whole step pairs around in different ways. See the following examples based on a G7b9 chord. (next page).

It is also possible for a student to succeed using diminished 7 chord arpeggios, and they can also be mixed with the diminished scales patterns or just the diminished scale itself. Remember that the correct sounding diminished 7th chord is NOT built on the root of the chord symbol, but rather occurs starting on the 3rd of the chord. For example: G7b9 will sound bad if the student plays a G°7 arpeggio. The top four notes of G7b9 –B D F Ab --spell the correct sounding diminished 7th chord for this occasion. Similarly, if the chord is D7b9, the correct diminished chord is F#°7. I have had students sound great on a cadenza after practicing these materials and planning a shape to bring the cadenza to a climax, and then deciding how to bring the band back in. Here is an example of playing a broken diminished 7 arpeggios on a G7b9 (B°7).

Note:
It is important to realize that the diminished 7th chord is an incomplete chord—it has no root. Any note in the chord could be a root. The real root of a diminished chord is found a major 3rd below what looks like the root. Therefore, if looking at a B°7, it is really a G7b9. The two are synonymous. Therefore, the scale that fits them is also the same scale. Since a diminished scale on G is spelled G Ab Bb B C# D E F G; if I start the scale on G, it begins with a half step; and if I start the same the scale on B to fit the B°7, it is at a point in the scale that begins with a whole step (B to C#). From this observation, we can codify a principle that when applying a diminished scale to a dominant chord, it should be the one with a half step first; and if we are applying a diminished scale to a diminished 7th chord, it should be the one with a whole step first.

It would also be very effective to play a cadenza based on the Super Locrian scale that fits the penultimate V7 chord. Let's say your lead alto saxophonist is featured on a ballad that ends in concert Eb. This would put the alto player in C, and the V7 chord in his key would be G7#9. The Super Locrian scale that fits G7#9 is the seventh mode of Ab Melodic Minor (major scale with b3), so the scale is G Ab Bb B C# Eb F G. (Refer to Chapter 20.) This scale sounds great when it is simply played, but it also contains the #9 b9, #5 which are really pretty notes. I give the students what I call the #9 pattern that looks like this for G7#9: Bb Ab Eb B Bb Ab, with the Ab ultimately resolving to G on the C major chord. (See the example at the end of the paragraph.) Those are the cool notes. They don't have to be played in that order. I have the student experiment with putting the notes in different orders, ascending, descending, different rhythms, etc. Again, with a little structure, this could become a good cadenza. It would also work to mix the materials for Diminished scales and chords and Super Locrian. Start with the diminished stuff and end with the Super Locrian stuff. Here is the #9 pattern:

Sometimes the cadenza may start on the II chord (Dorian or Melodic Minor or Bebop Scales) and then move into the same kinds of elaborations on the V7 chord that we have already just discussed. For extending the cadenza more, the student could even go through the whole progression for the A section (not necessarily in time), end up on the V7 and do similar elaborations to bring it to the final resolution. If the A section progression is used, it does not need to be in the same harmonic rhythm. It could go through much faster, or it could have a rubato elaboration on each chord.

Another extended cadenza idea could be to play a fragment or phrase of the melody (maybe slower) and then elaborate (faster—maybe softer?); then play the next phrase of the melody and then again elaborate. This continues until all the phrases of the melody have been played (maybe melody phrases from only one A section) and the progression has arrived at the penultimate V7 chord.

There are many more ideas for extending the cadenza. Listening to recorded examples is the best source for ideas. My teacher, David Baker, once said, "Originality is quoting from obscure sources."

It is also a great idea to borrow ideas from classical cadenzas.

> For example:
> • sequence an idea, moving it through different scale or chord tones or chromatically
>
> • repeat motivic ideas in augmentation or diminution or both
>
> • repeat an idea with different dynamics (loud, soft, loud again)
>
> • use unusual articulations (play an idea legato, then repeat it staccato, perhaps with a contrasting dynamic level)
>
> • use thematic fragments from the melody and elaborate on them or sequence them
>
> • use rubato and speed up and slow down

The Last Note

When the band comes back in after the cadenza and sustains the last note of the chart (or just sustains the last note if there is no cadenza), the featured soloist should add an improvised fill over the band, using the Major 7 as the starting point or hinge point in the line, and come to rest on one of the "pretty notes" to end the tune. The dumbest sounding note is the root. It should never be played as the last note even if it is the last written note. The 3rd and the 5th sound okay and may be appropriate at times, but the really pretty notes are the Major 7, the 9th, the 13th (6th) and the #11. One of these notes will be the most satisfying.

Conclusion

The ballad is usually one third of your program at a festival. The soloist deserves your close attention. The band will only sound as good on that tune as the soloist. In a figurative way, the soloist is standing out there naked. The slow tempo totally exposes his or her strengths and weaknesses. As Jerry Coker puts it, "In the other vehicle-types, you can remain clothed in patterns, licks, change running, humorous quotes, bits and pieces of transcribed solos, linear substance, blues scales, and repetition. But in the ballad, all of that must be stripped away, revealing your true musical nature, which could result in anything from a humiliating void to inspired greatness! Hipness and musical fads won't help you, either. Ballads force you into as state of sincere honesty, allowing the listener to look deeply into your musical soul. What will they find?"

Chapter 23   Helping the Vocalist in Your Band

A good singer adds a wonderful touch to the ensemble performance. It is not common in a junior high school or high school big band to have a regular singer, but now and then you will have an opportunity to work with a singer. So, let me pass on a few thoughts for helping the vocalist with your big band.

Charts

The first issue will be to find charts that work for your band with a vocalist. There are a lot of charts that are published specifically for vocal features. Most all the major publishers have an area of their catalog dedicated to vocal charts, and I will give that information in Chapter 24. I often adapt an instrumental feature to become a vocal feature. For example, the Basie chart on *All of Me* is a piano feature, but it can also be a great vocal feature. Eric Richards' arrangement of *The Nearness of You* is a great trombone feature, but I adapted it to be a vocal feature with an improvised trombone solo. Some of the Stevie Wonder charts arranged by Mike Tomaro (*I Wish*, *Higher Ground*, etc.) are written instrumentally, but it works great to add a singer. It is a matter in that case of deciding which horn parts will not be played when it would be competitive to the singer who has the melody. (It is usually best not to double the melody that the singer is covering.) Whether using charts published for vocal or adapting charts to feature a vocal, you have to be sensitive to key and range considerations. Don't just assume a chart will work for your singer; evaluate the chart versus your singer's range.

Auditions

Not everyone that wants to sing with your band should be given the opportunity. I always audition singers before making any commitments. A poor singer will not add to your concert or your band's experience. I would evaluate based on the following:

- What is the quality and power of the voice?

- What is the range? Where is the meat of the range?

- How is intonation and pitch security?

- Can I work with the present state of style? Is it too far away from what I need?

- Is there any personality or stage presence with this person?

- Will this be a good experience for my other musicians?

Once you have determined that you will use a particular vocalist, you will have to work with them to get them ready for the performance.

Right Brain Preparations

The first thing I would do is make sure the singer is listening to a good recording(s) of the tune or tunes you will be doing. Choose charts (at least at first) for which a recording is available. If you are adapting a chart for vocal, you may not have a recording with vocal of that specific arrangement; but be sure your singer can listen to the original recording. The singer must go through the same right brain learning on a tune that your instrumentalists go through. Make sure the singer is listening, singing along and imitating, getting a feel for key (range) and style and inflection and vibrato. I would even have the singer scat (improvise with non-word syllables) with the recording and do some transcribing. For most singers, the vocal chart (if there is one) will not be that helpful anyway; they should learn everything they can about the chart and the style with their ears.

Vocal Technique

In the rehearsal, you will need to give coaching on sound production and intonation—basic vocal skills. You may not feel very qualified to do this; but if you can play your horn, the principles are the same. Many years ago, Lynn Skinner invited me up to adjudicate at the Lionel Hampton Jazz Festival in Moscow, Idaho. He told me I would be doing a day of high school vocal jazz ensembles and a second day of college vocal jazz ensembles. I said, "Lynn, you realize that vocal is not my specialty?" He paused and said, "Hey man, pitch is pitch!" I found that he was right; I had plenty to offer to those vocal groups. So often, we are coaching singers to imitate how an instrument would to it (and instrumentalists to imitate how a singer would do it). If the singer needs drastic help in the vocal production area that you can't solve; you may need to involve the vocal teacher at your school or enlist a private teacher for that help. (You may have made a mistake in the audition process.)

Suffice it to say that you do need to worry about things like abdominal support, opening the mouth and throat, and projection. Usually some little reminders will make these things come together. Intonation is huge in a finished product, and I would give lots of comments as needed to bring it to an acceptable level. It is common for singers to sing on the flat side, so some encouragement to sing on the upper side of the pitch usually helps. Do not leave intonation to chance.

Coaching Style

Capturing the style, especially swing style, is a challenge for young singers. Again, this starts with listening and imitation, but there are some common reasons swing style is elusive to singers. The first is what I would call "Broadway Swing". If singers have had any vocal training, it is likely they have done Broadway style songs from musicals in the past. The problem with Broadway swing is that it doesn't swing. Help the singer get into the real rhythmic aspects of swing which are exactly the same as they are for your horn players. (See Chapter 7 and 8.) Another aspect of Broadway swing is the use of a more classical type of vibrato. This does not work for swing at all; and I find myself always coaching singers to get rid of the constant vibrato and add it like a jazz singer—what we call terminal vibrato, or vibrato on the ending of the note. In other styles, the vibrato is part of the color of the tone on the note. In jazz, it is more like an ornament at the end of a note, almost in the category of a trill or turn or mordent. Occasionally, the long notes can be colored a little more with vibrato, but it is not the default norm. Listen to jazz instrumentalists and singers, and you will find that only a few notes will tend to have vibrato across the value of a longer note;

most of the time there will only be vibrato at the ends of notes. There are, of course, always exceptions, and listening to the style involved is clearly the key! There will be differences when crossing stylistic lines.

The vocalist's approach to interpreting the melody of the tune is very similar to what we outlined in the previous chapter about your featured soloist on the ballad. It is important that the melody be recognizable, but it is also important for your singer to personalize the melody. Similar to your ballad soloist, I would have the singer practice each phrase of the melody experimenting with small melodic and rhythmic variations. Add to this using bends, scoops, glisses, and other inflections, and even occasionally a growl. The singer should experiment with ways to express more emotion and soul. Your singer should always be asking himself/herself, "How can I play with the melody lyrically, dramatically, dynamically, rhythmically? And even, "Are there any places where I might be more flexible and take some time liberties, maybe even changing the tempo for a section of the chart, or can I get the rhythm section to change textures with me?" Realize that some vocal parts for big band charts are written in what we call "lead sheet" style. The rhythms are all half notes and quarter notes and whole notes. A jazz singer would never use these stagnant rhythms. We have to jazz up the rhythms—anticipations with ties across the bar lines and syncopations and rhythmic variety.

When playing with the rhythms, the singer should not lay back so much that nothing ever lands on the beat, and the audience is wondering if there is any consciousness of where 1 is. However, singers do need to use back-phrasing as discussed in the previous chapter on ballad playing. At the risk of redundancy, I will repeat the concept in this context. Without motion, there is no emotion! So, our challenge is to enhance the feeling of motion without changing the tempo. The main motion in a bar should be in the second half of the bar. So we often hang back in the first half of the bar, so we can justify creating more motion in the second half of the bar across the bar line into the next bar. This also applies to larger units like every two bars, every four bars, and every eight bars. We want to create the allusion of stronger motion, but we can't rush the tempo to do it; so we hold back and pay for the time first, and then we can push the movement forward without actually rushing the tempo. There is no such thing as a credit card in nature. If we try to move first and then pay later, it is backwards; and it sounds awkward and unmusical. We back-phrase so we can pay for the time first and then move.

We do have to breathe periodically, but we should never break up grammatical phrases or prepositional phrases or breathe in other weird places where the meaning of the words is undermined. The question of where to breath is big! The singer must plan breathing places carefully, never just suddenly breathing because of running out of breath. They must think about the meaning of what they are singing.

Also, vocalists in a jazz setting are very exaggerated in how they end words with little inflections. They often caress the consonants in a non-classical way and add texture into their pronunciation. For example, lingering on an M or N can add a nice texture.

Another of the concepts discussed in the previous chapter that applies also to the singer is that when personal variations are introduced by the singer, they should follow the plan of simple to gradually more complex. The original statement of the melody should be simpler and more true to the melody than the second time through the melody where more variation can be introduced. In a typical vocal feature chart, there will be a time where the band is featured and the singer lays out. When the singer re-enters, he/she may use considerably greater variation and more complex personalization but then may simplify again towards the end of the chart to bring it to a close. Again, there is no substitute for hearing how this works on a recording; you can verbalize these things to the singer, but a sound picture is worth a thousand words.

As a summary, the plan of a chart might run something like this, assuming a hypothetical layout for this chart: Intro—the band, A1—singer stays simple and close to melody, A2—singer sings with more variation and personalization, B—singer is a little simpler since this is the first time this part of the melody is being heard, A3—the singer embellishes and personalizes more than ever since this is the third go around for this part of the melody, A4—tenor sax solo, but the singer stays engaged and helps to bring focus to the soloist, A5—band feature and the singer may dance or add a little improvised fill a time or two, B2—singer re-enters at a high level of embellishment, A6—singer starts to simplify and brings the chart to the close, Coda—band plays a little additional phrase bringing the chart to the last note, Last Note—the singer does a solo sfill.

It is important for the singer to listen to the chart as it plays through and consider how to respond to the band. Is there a sax line that the singer could play off of and add a little solo fill or melodic response? In a way, there is a call and response that goes on between the singer and the band. The singer must learn to respond to what is happening all around him or her.

Vocal Improvisation

Sometimes a chart may leave room for some improvisation by the vocalist; and if not, I may open some space for a solo if I have the right singer. When a vocalist improvises we call it "scatting" or "scat singing". True scatting would reflect guide tones and changes, and would be all the same considerations and approaches as the instrumental solos. This ideal is not often realized in vocal solos. (Even the great Bobby McFerrin was a disappointment to me when he recorded a scat solo on the Charlie Parker tune, *Donna Lee*.) It is common in school vocal ensembles for the instrumentalist, who also wanted to sing with the vocal group, to be the best soloist. With private jazz vocal lessons that I have done, I have had the singer working on the Chord Study and singing scales and patterns just like the horn players. I also have them work on guide tones and ear training in the same way. (See Chapter 20) Admittedly, it will only be the most serious vocal student who would go to these lengths. But short of this, a lot can still be done with the ears only (as discussed in Chapter 19).

We can help a singer learn the tune from a right brain standpoint just like an instrumentalist. The fact is, the vocalist has some advantages over the instrumentalist in the right brain domain. There is no need to translate sounds heard in the mind (or externally) into fingerings and embouchure and tonguing coordination. Everything is much quicker to the voice than to the horn. But a little help to hear the changes, the guide tones, may be necessary.

One of the other big concerns with scatting is the syllables used. Since the vocalist is not improvising with preset words, the usual thing is to use "scat syllables" although actual words or phrases can be made up or borrowed from the tune as well. Scat syllables are just non-word syllables made up on the spot to fit the line. Some people use the term nonsense syllables; but, unfortunately, that is what I often hear—totally silly syllables that detract from making music. I avoid that term because I want my vocalists to use musically informed syllables. These are the syllables that horn players use when they are singing imitations of what they play. I use these syllables all the time when I am directing the big band horns to illustrate phrasing.

A good way for the jazz vocalist to work on good syllables for scatting would be to listen and imitate verbally what they are hearing in the big band and what they are hearing when instrumental soloists improvise. Another good approach is to listen to the great scat singers of the past including Ella Fitzgerald, Clark Terry, Denis DiBlasio, Chet Baker, and Louis Armstrong (who invented scat singing), and any of the other great singers like Sarah Vaughn, Billie Holliday, Dinah Washington, Frank Sinatra, Tony Bennett, etc. There are also more recent singers who have interesting scat styles like Dee Daniels, Kitty Margolis, Kurt Elling, Diane Reeves, Diana Krall, Catherine Russell, etc. In the book section at the end of this chapter, there is a book of Chet Baker's top scat solos with all notations of the syllables he used. This would make a great study. The Bob Stoloff book, listed at the end of the chapter, also has syllable help in it. In addition, see Justin Binek's doctoral dissertation on Ella Fitgerald's scat syllables: Binek, Justin Garrett. *The Evolution of Ella Fitzgerald's Syllabic Choices in Scat Singing: A Critical Analysis of Her Decca Recordings, 1943-1952*, dissertation, May 2017; Denton, Texas. (https://digital.library.unt.edu/ark:/67531/metadc984212/). A PDF version is downloadable at that site. This dissertation is a very useful study of syllables for the aspiring young scatter (and the more seasoned ones, too).

Microphone Technique

It is also necessary to give a little coaching to your singer about microphone technique. The mic's we use on the stage are tight pattern microphones; they are not wide pattern like the average public address microphone. Therefore, it is necessary to sing directly into the mic. It will not pick up the same way when the sound source is off axis. Holding the mic too high or too low or too far away does not work. Instruct your singer to be on mic, straight down the center bore of it. The mic should be held horizontal to the ground, not pointed up where the mic covers the face or pointed down. The more the mic is pulled away from the face, the more the sound thins out. The closer the mic, the more resonant and rich the sound. Most of the time we want this resonance, but sometimes it can be appropriate to thin it out a little. Many singers kiss the mic. It is a good idea for a singer to buy a personal mic and get used to how to use it. This is the singer's instrument. It is also common for jazz singers to pull the mic a little farther away when singing a really loud high note to temper the volume a little.

It is imperative that the band director help the band play dynamics and stay under the soloist until it is time to unleash. Sometimes, say in a shout section, the singer may need to come up and use a brighter timbre to cut through; but other times it will be appropriate to be warmer in timbre. The singer and the band should not be in competition.

Fronting the Band

Last but not least, the vocalist is in a real way fronting the band. Help them be conscious of this and to dress accordingly and perform with energy and personality. For those short minutes, she or he is the show. However, caution them not to be over the top or fake—physical movements and gestures must genuinely fit the musical intent. The singer may also help to introduce the tune (before starting) or soloists (in the middle of the chart) or to transition back to the big band (toward the end of the chart).

In a performance, the singer needs to guage what his or her space on the stage looks like and assess what movement is possible in the space allotted. When making a move, the singer should shift weight back to move forward; and if walking to the right, hold the mic in right hand and the cord in the left (or vice-versa if moving to the left). If the singer feels the cord getting stuck, they should stop and take a step back so the cord is not hanging at a weird angle (this could be very distracting to the audience if it looks precarious).

Perhaps one of the hardest things about stage presence for the singer is dealing with the time they are not singing. They need to still be present when they are not singing but not distracting. Good advice would be for the singer to take a couple of steps back from the front position but still face toward audience. The singer can show her/his appreciation or love of what the soloist or band is doing in an interaction that brings the focus to the soloist or the band. This is something that has to be thought about and practiced.

At the end of the last note of the chart, the singer should hold the pose and not break character too soon. "The glitter settles before you move." Follow through!

It is a great plan for the singer to join the rhythm section during their sectionals and get things worked out and more solid. This can save a lot of rehearsal time and make the singer more comfortable and confident. The band director could also attend the sectional with the singer to offer some coaching.

Resources: Books and Sing-Along Volumes

Sing-Alongs

Jamey Aebersold has created a large library of play-along recordings that are used extensively by instrumentalists. Many of these are just as useable by singers depending on key and range; but lately Jamey has created some volumes that are especially for vocalists, and he is mindful of male and female key differences. The ones that are especially good for singers are:

- Vol. 107 *Standards for Singer—It Had to Be You* (keys are for female singers)

- Vol. 113 *Embraceable You—Ballads for All Singers* (each tune has two play-a-long tracks, a low key and a high key)

- Vol. 117 *Cole Porter for Singers* (high key and low key for each tune)

- *Singin' with the Big Band*—11 Standards for Jazz Vocalists, published by Alfred

- There are many more vocal sing-alongs at jazzbooks.com

Jazz Vocal Books

- *Guide for Jazz/Scat Vocalists—A Survival Manual for Aspiring Jazz Singers* by Denis DiBlasio

- *Vocal Improvisation* by Michelle Weir

- *The Jazz Singer's Guidebook: A Course in Jazz Harmony and Scat Singing for the Serious Vocalist* by David Berkman

- *Jazz Singer's Handbook* by Michelle Weir

- *Chet Baker's Greatest Scat Solos* by Jim Bastian

- *Scat! Vocal Improvisation Techniques* by Bob Stoloff

- *Jazz Vocal Practice #1* by Jay Clayton

- *Jazz Vocal Practice #2* by Jay Clayton

- *The Complete Guide to Teaching Vocal Jazz* by Stephen Zegree

- *Hear It, and Sing It! Exploring Modal Jazz* by Judy Niemack

- *Hear It, and Sing It! Exploring the Blues* by Judy Niemack

Jazz Vocal Recordings

- Ella Fitzgerald, *Pure Ella, Ella Fitzgerald Sings the Duke Ellington Songbook, Ella Fitzgerald Sings the Cole Porter Song Book, Ella and Basie*

- Sarah Vaughn, *Ultimate Sarah Vaughn, Sarah Vaughn Sings George Gershwin, The Very Best of Sarah Vaughn*

- Dinah Washington, *Ultimate Dinah Washington, The Definitive Dinah Washington*

- Kurt Elling, *Dedicated to You*

- Diana Krall, F*rom this Moment, The Very Best of Diana Krall*

- Diane Reeves, *The Best of Diane Reeves, In the Moment*

- Tony Bennett, *Tony Bennett Celebrates 90, Sings the Ultimate American Songbook Volume 1*

- Frank Sinatra, *Nothing But the Best (remastered), Ultimate Sinatra*

- Billie Holiday, *The Essential Billie Holliday*

- Kitty Margolis, *Evolution*

- Dee Daniels, *Close Encounter of the Swingin' Kind*

- Dee Dee Bridgewater, *In Montreux (Live)*

- Stacey Kent, *Stacey Kent Collection*

- Al Jarreau, *The Very Best of Al Jarreau: An Excellent Adventure*

- Catherine Russell, *Harlem on My Mind*

- Kate McGarry, *Show Me*

Vocal Instructional DVD's

- *The Barry Harris Vocal Workshop*, Howard Rees, Jazz Workshop Productions

- *Vocalists: Practice Guide DVD*, published by Hal Leonard

- *Vocal Technique DVD*, published by Hal Leonard

Section 6

Thoughts on Administrative Issues:

Gives Meaning to Everything Else . . .

You're the administrator . . . .

Chapter 24   Behind the Scenes: Chart Selection and Programming for Concerts and Festivals

Choosing the right charts is half the battle and is one of the most important roles of the band director. Choosing the material that best fits the students and excites them and inspires them makes your job much easier. If the students love what they are working on, they will be motivated to practice and hold sectionals and prepare. You may first need some help with building your school library of jazz music. I would start by doing a lot of listening to big band recordings. Go after the stuff that turns you on.

Building a Jazz Music Library

The process of building a library can take a while depending on your budget for music. You may be able to lean on your present concert band library and use all the money for jazz acquisitions for a couple of years. Each year brings a new opportunity to add to your library.

It is imperative to first build a core of the classic swing big band tunes. These will normally come from the books of bands like: Count Basie, Buddy Rich, Duke Ellington, Stan Kenton, Woody Herman, Maynard Ferguson, Rob McConnell, Les Hooper, Thad Jones-Mel Lewis, and even some of the swing era tunes from bands like Glenn Miller, Tommy Dorsey, and Benny Goodman. I would add tunes of newer bands as well such as Gordon Goodwin, Bob Mintzer, Maria Schneider, Tom Kubis, etc. Then add to this swing core some straight-eighth tunes from Latin and rock genre's. It is also good to make sure there are tunes in 3/4, tunes that shuffle, and tunes that are ballads. Avoid too many pop tunes and other lightweight filler material. Students seems excited about these tunes at first, but quickly lose interest; and time on these tunes can distract the band from the real instructional needs at hand. Tunes with real substance will maintain student interest and help you reach educational objectives.

When I was in high school, it was very difficult to get good charts. Not much was published, and there was a lot of trading and sharing and dickering and under-the-table type stuff. The nature of the problem has completely changed, and now we have so much music available that we have to sort through a lot of junk to find the good stuff. I rarely buy music now unless I have heard it on a recording, and I know I like it. Sometimes we can order music on a trial basis; if not, I would be very careful. I also am more inclined to order music by composers/arrangers that I know I can trust. The following is my limited list of those people. They are not in any particular order.

- Tom Kubis
- Gordon Goodwin
- Sammy Nestico
- Mike Tomaro
- Bill Holman
- Lennie Niehaus

- Frank Mantooth
- Bob Curnow
- Matt Cattingub
- Don Sebesky
- Michael Abene
- John Clayton

- Les Hooper
- Mark Taylor
- Matt Harris
- David Berger
- Eric Richards
- Bob Mintzer
- Victor Lopez (can be dumbed down)
- Maria Schneider

- Dominic Spera
- Denis DiBlasio
- Frank Foster
- Thad Jones
- Oliver Nelson
- Johnny Richards
- John Fedchock
- Alan Baylock

This is not a comprehensive list, just some of the more prolific writers who you can trust to give you something worth playing. There are some obvious, deliberate omissions of people who are good writers, but who have been too willing to let schlock go out or who may write some things that are a bit far out for secondary school purposes. (Sorry to be so brutally honest.)

Here are some of the sources for music that I have felt good about, and these are ones I most often deal with and feel like returning to deal with again.

- Penders Music (800) 772-5918 www.penders.com

- Marina Music (800) 331-4528 www.marinamusic.com

- UNC Jazz Press (303) 351-1923 www.uncjazzpress.com

- Sierra Music (800) 255-6551 www.sierramusic.com

- J.W. Pepper (800) 345-629 www.jwpepper.com

- Alfred Music (800) 628-1528 www.alfred.com

- Hal Leonard Music (800) 637-2852 www.halleonard.com

- Kendor Music (716) 492-1254 www.kendormusic.com

- Stanton's Music (614) 224-4257 www.stantons.com

They are all willing to send out free catalogs and most of them have online ways of hearing the charts or will send out a demo CD on request.

The Art of Programming for Concerts

Here are a few of my ideas, which obviously reflect my personal biases, for programming concerts. I like to start with something that gets attention, but it also needs to be something that gets the band feeling comfortable and the audience feeling good, usually medium swing. I like to follow that up with something that is straight-eighth based. Then I usually move on to something more intense, so I can follow it up with a ballad for a change of pace. Then I'll often come back to something that swings really nice, and then end the first half with an up Latin or rock-type piece to bring it to the intermission. Then, the second half is similar thinking, but I want the end to come to an exciting climax. I would typically have a mellow tune third to the last (maybe another ballad or a gentle bossa). The second to the last tune would be more up, but something I can top with the last tune. I often program a drum solo in the last piece, because that usually helps to leave the crowd wanting an encore.

I try to make sure that at least some of the tunes are recognizable to the audience. I also, of course, try to have good variety in tempos, styles, moods, keys, etc. I look very closely at the flow of charts in terms of brass chops, especially the lead trumpet, but also the lead trombone. I also evaluate how the solo features flow; and I always redistribute solos so everyone that should play gets a chance, and solos for the same person are not all stacked together. If I am programming something that is going to be educational (either for the students or the audience or both), then I try to couch it in between things that are very accessible, so that the audience is willing to try something different or less accessible.

There are those who espouse the idea of putting the ballad second in the set so the program can build from there; but I feel the ballad should be a contrast to the intensity that has gone before, so I usually program it about fourth or fifth into the set. Then I can build the program back up to climax the set after that. There are also those who stick with the swing charts that are the back bone of the big band repertory; but I believe the concert flows better with contrasts into Latin, Rock, Funk, and Fusion styles and keeps the audience interested. I want to have something for everybody at different age levels. Some tunes seem to cut across generational lines such as *In the Mood* by Glenn Miller, or *Sing Sing Sing* of Benny Goodman fame, or any of the Stevie Wonder tunes. While I don't often program these tunes at a home concert, I do try to include one or more of them at a community outreach concert or a tour concert.

These planning ideas assume you are programming for a full concert; but at high school concerts, it is common for the jazz band to share the concert with one or two concert bands, possibly another jazz band, and even a choir or two or an orchestra. The jazz band may only play two or three tunes. In this case, the concert programming is similar to the festival set. If there is only time for two tunes, I would program a swing tune and a straight-eighth tune.

The Art of Programming for Festivals

Again, the following suggestions reflect my biases but are also based on extensive experience with festivals, both from the participant side and from the adjudicator side. High school and middle school festivals never leave time for the band to play more than three tunes. So, my first piece would be a nice swing tune that really shows how we have dealt with the issues of swing style. This also helps to get the band more comfortable at the beginning of the set. The second tune would, of course, be the ballad. This is really the only place the ballad can be placed for good flow. This can be either a swing (tripletized) ballad or a straight-eighth ballad (could even be a rock ballad), but it should feature one of your strongest soloists. If you choose a swing ballad, you may have more latitude in the choice of your first tune which could now be straight-eighth based. The third tune would normally be your straight-eighth tune such as a Latin burner or a sophisticated rock tune. Most rock tunes are probably not festival material, unless you've got one with enough sophistocation (ex. Gordon Goodwin's *Jazz Police* would fit the bill.) If you started with a Latin tune and did a swing ballad, you might end with a burning swing tune. Or you might end with the burning swing tune anyway and forget the straight-eighth tune in the set; although the students will always get into the straight-eighth tunes easier because this is what they hear all the time.

It is important to distribute solos as much as possible, but for a festival make sure you have strength in every solo. I have seen festival sets where all three tunes feature the same soloist—great for the soloist but doesn't reflect well on your program. Soloist choice may be different in a home concert, where it may be appropriate to give each student an opportunity to grow; but at a festival, soloists need to be strong. The more soloists that can do a good job, the better the rating. Remember that improvisation is the life blood of the music. Refer to Chapters 19-22 for help with grooming your soloists, and Chapter 23 for help if you have included a vocal feature.

It is also imperative to program music for the festival that has substance—no schlock, no cheese. I would not program *In the Mood* or other swing era (esp. white band) classics at a festival, unless it is a classic Duke Ellington or Count Basie piece. However, the students should learn classic swing era tunes on other occasions. For example, you could periodically include one or two on a concert, or do a dance each year where they get to learn a lot of this classic swing repertory. I would also not program anything of a pop nature. Remember, one of the categories on the judging sheet is the appropriateness of chart selection. This is the responsibility of the director. The level of the charts needs to be substantial (not overly easy), but not so difficult that band success is in jeopardy. The adjudicator should evaluate how well you pulled off what you chose to play. It is not impressive to get in over your head and do poorly. When choosing a challenging chart, be sure you have soloist(s) that can also handle the chart. If you choose to feature a vocalist at a festival, it needs to be first rate. The band will only sound as good as the singer on that piece. That is also true with the instrumental ballad (although the vocal could be the ballad selection—or not).

At university level festivals, there is often time for four tunes (depending on the length of tunes). If so, I would start with a nice medium swing chart, move to the ballad, do a straight-eighth tune, and end with an up-tempo, burning swing tune. This combination has paid off a number of times for my band.

It is critical in your festival programming to show off the strengths of your ensemble. So, if I have a great sax section, I will make sure I have a piece with a great sax soli. If I have a strong trombone soloist, I will make sure he has a solid feature. If the drummer is exceptional, I will create a drum solo (probably in the last piece). Show what your band can do, not what they can't do.

The director retains the responsibility for programming in these different scenarios, and the programming can make or break it.

Chapter 25   On the Front Line: Performance and Competition

There are a few issues worthy of discussion about the day of performance. This is what we are always preparing for! Some of the things that need attention are: microphone setup and technique, band setup and sound check, rehearsal and brass chops, lighting, mental-spiritual preparations, and directing the band in concert. Neglect of these issues can sabotage all the hard work from weeks of teaching and rehearsals. Some performances are also competitive, and how to handle competition needs our attention.

Microphones

Microphones are a necessary evil of performance. It would really be best for the big band to perform acoustically. This is what the old big bands did, and there are still situations today where it would be best just to perform without microphones. But trying to balance the acoustic piano and the soloists seems to always bring up the need for microphones even in the most acoustic situations. So, this is usually the simplest setup for either concerts or festivals—a mic on the piano and at least one or two mics for soloists. This is the safest setup anyway when we don't know the sound man or his understanding of what we are going for in the finished product. I'm sorry to say that not all my experiences with sound people have been positive; although I know some great ones that I really trust. When I can trust a sound man, I will do more extensive setups especially in larger halls. But I have little trust for the usual people running sound in high school auditoriums or gymnasiums. In that circumstance, the simplest setup is the best.

There are a few things to know about microphones that can really help your performance to be successful. Microphones are built with different pickup patterns. Most of us have had more experience with PA (public address) microphones at a podium or a pulpit. These mics have wide patterns and pick up fairly equally whether the sound source is directly on axis or coming from either side. Stage microphones have a tight pattern and are made to block out sounds from the sides and the rear. Proximity matters, and the best pick up is straight down the bore. Therefore, the director can do a lot at a performance to ensure that each soloist is on mic. I would teach the students to get up there early (leave out some of the ensemble part) and adjust the mic so they are aimed directly at it (but not too close, don't have to swallow it). But when the student doesn't get this done adequately, the band director should be right there to adjust it. I have seen countless festival performances where the soloist could not be heard; and a little simple attention to where the microphone was aimed would have made all the difference, but soloist and director seemed oblivious to the problem. Unfortunately, I have also seen the sound man destroy the performance by running the solo mic or the piano mic ridiculously loud. This is sometimes a conceptual problem and other times a problem of neglect. If I were the soloist that stood up to a microphone that was obviously too loud, I would back a distance away from it or step completely off mic.

Another issue that I observe frequently is when the band director brings the mic in front of the sax section for an in-place saxophone solo, and then leaves it there after the soloist has finished. The mic is still hot and is going to skew the balance of the whole band and especially the sax section. This would not be necessary if the sound man is alert and turns the mic down, but I have found that this is too much to expect. I always take control by turning the mic around backwards towards the audience as soon as the need for it is past, then my band sound cannot be damaged by a careless sound person. This is even the case when the solo mics are positioned over in front of the rhythm section, and there are no soloists using them at the moment. If they are left loud, the drums and cymbals (depending on proximity) may bleed through the sound system and take over the whole band. So, I always turn those around backwards, as well, until the soloists need them.

When I am in a larger venue or outside and have sound people that I trust, I like to tight mic the whole ensemble. This means there is a mic on every individual in the band, and it can be very exciting when handled well. In a normal hall, I rarely feel the need to do this for the purpose of making the band louder but rather for clarity and enhanced balance; although in a really large venue (or outside), it can be for power as well. This tight mic setup would give far too much destructive power to a sound man that does not have a concept of how to make this work so that it still sounds acoustic, and I would never consider it if I don't have the best sound people possible. This also gives us better recordings of our performances; and if the band is actually doing a recording session, then the tight mic approach will be necessary (in most cases). I typically bring my own sound man when I possibly can.s

An aware band director who does some mic training with students (and maybe with a teachable sound man) and who takes steps to control the microphone situation, can make a much better musical product. Take control!

Setup

The setup in the rehearsal room may be flat or all on the same level, unless your band room has terraced steps. But in the performance, we do want a terraced setup. The way I would accomplish this is to have a brass riser that is usually 16 feet wide, 12 feet deep, and 16" high. Then I can seat the saxes on the floor level with the trombones seated on the riser behind them and the trumpets standing on the same riser behind the trombones. This gives a nice terraced look, but it is even more important for sonic reasons. If the trombone section is seated on the floor level, their sound will be eaten up as they blow into the back of the saxes. If I ever do have to set up with everyone on the same level (happens sometimes on an overseas tour); I will space the saxes and ask the trombones to aim their bells right between the saxophone players, so we can get the sound out to the audience. The trumpets can still stand behind the trombones. Much better is when the trombones are sitting 16" higher than the saxophones. It is NOT enough to have an 8" boost, 16" is ideal. (Unfortunately, it is rare for those who set up at a festival to understand this, and we are almost always dealing with only an 8" lift which is not adequate.) I have seen band directors try to solve the level setup problem (and even the 8" lift problem) by having the trombone section stand, but this causes the same problem for the trumpets who are now getting buried behind the trombones unless they are standing on a high enough riser. I want to be able to see all of the brass players' bells in the free and clear. Of course, this requires a reminder for the students to hold their bells up and not let their sound get buried behind other players or eaten up by the floor.

I normally keep the rhythm section on the floor level, but it is possible to put the drummer on a raised platform. If I do that, I would put the bass up there, too, so they remain in hearing proximity and maintain good eye contact.

Please refer to Appendix A for a diagram of the above setup ideas.

Soundcheck

During the rehearsal/sound check, I always have three goals in mind. First, is to review the charts with the band. I will start each tune for tempo and review any problematic passages and finish any preparations still needed. But my second goal is to make sure I don't burn out the brass chops. Often, I will just have the band sing certain sections to preserve mouth endurance or blow it with the airstream (but no instrument). Sometimes, it is enough just to talk it down. I would much rather have the brass at the concert than in the rehearsal.

The other goal is to get the sound right and the band comfortable with the new environment. If the sound setup is complex, this may include checking mics for each section and checking monitors. If it is a simple setup, I still need to make sure the piano is at the right level, and the solo mics are comfortable for both the soloists and the audience and the monitors are good if there are any. Each soloist needs to have a chance to feel out playing with the mic. I need to go out into the hall and hear what kind of balances we have. I usually find myself at the mixing board helping the sound engineer and teaching concept. Don't just leave all of this to chance. If I do have a vocal soloist, it is imperative to have a monitor and to give the singer and the sound man a chance to deal with the sound in advance of the concert.

In a real production, lighting may also become a pre-concert rehearsal issue. I may need to spend a little time with the lighting person to help create my vision of the lighting. I always produce a concert tech page that outlines the tunes, the soloists, any other sound issues to watch for (ex: woodwind doubles or switch from acoustic to electric bass), and the lighting changes that may help the flow of the mood of the tunes. This attention is even more imperative if there will be any video recording of the concert.

Mental-Spiritual Concert Preparations

Another thing that tends to undermine all of the hard work that you and your students have put into preparing for the concert is stage fright. Students get nervous, and a lot of hard work goes out the window. I always discuss this with my students and try to set a tone where we can be relaxed, but focused. At the risk of being too blunt, let me suggest that what we call stage fright is simply being too centered on oneself. We start to entertain thoughts like, "Gee, I hope they're impressed with me." "Oh, I hope they didn't notice I just made a mistake right there." "I hope they don't feel badly about me now." "I wonder….., I, I, me, I, me……." We have to realize that it is not about me. It's about the music and sharing it with others in a way that uplifts them. A little mental preparation to remind ourselves what this is really about can help us enormously with relaxation. I believe with jazz great, Kirk Whalum, who said it first at an international conference of jazz musicians, that God gave us our talents; and our job is to hone them and give them back in service to His other children. Our talents were not given to us for selfish reasons, but to serve and bless others. (Sorry, Miles!) If we can get an other-centered orientation going instead of a self-centered orientation, we don't get so nervous. Self-centeredness and trying too hard to impress are our enemies.

I have found that just discussing other-centeredness together before the concert really helps get everyone on the same page. What is our real purpose tonight? Is it to play a perfect concert? If so, we have just set ourselves up for failure because it never happens on this planet. Is it to impress people with how great we are? This is not a worthy objective or motive and will fall short. But if we are set up in an other-centered way, can we make a few mistakes in the concert and still touch hearts and lift people? Yes! Now we are set up to succeed. A victory on this front, before the concert, can pay big dividends on the stage. Let's get into singing our hearts out on this great music we love so we can bless others! Let's play with pure joy in the music, not fear! Physiologists tell us that there is no difference in the nervous system between courage and fear. The body dumps an extra measure of adrenalin into the blood stream for either. So what makes the difference? Our mental outlook. This is a different attitude, and for years I have consistently tried to have this victory over self before my performances. After a while, this attitude of service just becomes a natural approach to life, and it becomes easier and quicker to get to that point of victory over self. Here are a couple of letters that I received after concerts that illustrate the power of what we do.

Letter 1

April 9th 2010

Dear Dr. Smith,

I am a producer/assistant for the KBYU radio station, and I attended the performance this week.

I wanted to write and say that is was a superb performance! The Malaguena the band played was remarkable! I felt like a jaguar that 1) pursued an animal 2) captured the animal 3) devoured the animal—delicious!

Also, I brought my Russian friend from Siberia to the performance. She is 50 years old and has had many troubles throughout her life in Russia and in her new life in America. On Tuesday, she had a particularly bad day because of an upsetting phone call from Siberia. I'll admit I was worried about bringing her to the performance because she was so upset/sad, and I figured the music would feel too much like a party. However, she had already planned on coming; so she came, and she had a WONDERFUL TIME! She loved it!!! She was smiling and happy by the end. All the stress of her factory job, her family and financial troubles, melted away.

I spoke to her the next day and she said, "Last night I got in bed and just fell asleep. I didn't have any bad dreams, I didn't worry. I went to bed." She attributed all of this to having attended the concert and the music.

I enjoyed the performance immensely. But I am very grateful for the effect of this music on my friend. Thank you again!!

Signed, Anonymous

Letter #2

April 28, 2016

Dear Dr. Smith:

This note of appreciation for you and Synthesis [the BYU Jazz Big Band] is long overdue, but I was thinking about you today and thought: "better late than never."

I usually listen to jazz because it's thrilling and energizing. The surprises in good jazz music make me laugh out loud. But your Christmas concert on Dec. 2 was much bigger than that; it had spiritual importance for me.

I've had a very easy and very happy life, but I admit that November was one of the hardest months I've had... I felt a spiritual darkness that I have rarely felt. But at the end of your Christmas concert I realized that not only had I forgotten about my frustrations for a moment, I had smiled ear-to-ear for 2 hours. My face ached from smiling for so long. I realize now that that night helped me to spiritually turn myself around a bit. You know how sometimes physicians need to help you manage pain so that your body is able to begin healing? I felt like your concert helped me feel and see clearly, and that in turn helped me to start feeling better.

I know that YOU understand the power of what you do. That night, I heard you play "What Child Is This," and it's obvious that you get the pastoral power of music. I hope that you are able to help your student musicians appreciate their ability to bring wholeness to others with their talents. A smokin' solo is not just great fun; sometimes it can heal.

Thanks for your continued service to the community through your teaching and your music. Thanks also to your great musicians for their dedication to their art. I have been blessed by your many hours of work.

Sincerely,

Signed, Anonymous

Competitive Performance

I have always felt that the sports mentality in music is antithetic to what we are trying to accomplish with our students; and the festival I run is not in a competitive framework and is oriented toward an educational, inspirational experience. But in real life, we do face competition, and it is not all bad to have to compete at times. Either way, you will find yourself in a competitive situation from time to time. When this is the case, it will matter how you set up the situation in the students' minds. I had a tough situation a few years ago that illustrates this point.

I was asked to travel to Idaho to adjudicate a high school jazz festival and to be a guest soloist with the host band on the evening concert. It wasn't until I arrived that I found out that I was the sole adjudicator, and the festival was competitive in a couple of different categories. The first category finished in the morning, and a winner was announced before lunch. One of the bands had come with the attitude that they had already won. When I didn't hear it that way, major repercussions broke out. In a few minutes, I found myself in the festival director's office with him and the assistant festival director and the band director of the band that thought they should have won with his assistant band director and two representatives from the parents' band booster association. I was asked to defend my decision. This was horribly uncomfortable for me with a tension in the room that I shall not forget. After all dispersed, I headed to the cafeteria for lunch.

On the way, I ran into the band director coming the other way. If looks could kill, I would have been dead on the spot. He came up to me right in my face shaking his finger as he accused me of destroying his students and his band program. He said many of his students were so devastated that they were going to quit playing and would not return to his band the next year. I had been pretty cool up to this point, but this is when I lost it. I came right back in his face and told him in no uncertain terms that I was not going to accept the blame for that. I told him that if what he said about his students was true, then he was going to wear that. I said emphatically, "If you set this up that way in your kids' minds, then you destroyed your own program. That is not music education; that is egotistical stupidity on your part!" (Yes, letters came later to my dean and department chair.)

In the old days of when I first took over my jazz program, I would ask the students, "Why are we going to this competitive festival?" I got answers like, "Kick butt!" "Take State" (so to speak). "No, No, No! That is NOT why we are going! Why are we really going?" Then I helped the band realize better motives. We go first to compete with ourselves, our past. We are pushing ourselves to grow and excel our past selves. We are going to help ourselves realize our own potential. We are going to receive helpful comments from qualified adjudicators. Second, we are going to hear other bands and to learn from them and be inspired by them. Third, we are going to attend great, educational clinics. We are also going to hear great guest artists and to be inspired by them. "Do we have to win, to accomplish these objectives?" Absolutely not! Set up with these motives, we are winners either way. If we happen to actually win, that is just frosting on the cake; and if we don't win, we are still winners. Our time and efforts have been well-spent. When we have this attitude, the pressure comes down in large measure. We can relax and play our best.

So, whether we are preparing for a concert performance, or a festival performance, or a competitive performance, it will help the students settle down and give their best performance if we spend time with them creating right attitudes and a positive mental-spiritual outlook. Help them overcome themselves and their nerves. If we neglect that or fail to deal well with any of the physical setup issues, we will compromise all that we have worked for in so many hours of rehearsal. This again is the responsibility of the conscientious jazz educator.

Directing the Band in Concert

When teaching in Kentucky, the choir teacher came to one of my jazz concerts. I ran into him the next day, and he told me he had been at the concert. Then he said, "I just have one question for you. What are you doing up there?" I said, "Dancing, having fun! My work was done in the rehearsal." It's true that a jazz big band conductor doesn't exist in the real world, only in academic settings, and some directors will start the chart and walk off the stage. I don't want the band to depend on me to do their work (such as counting rests, etc.), and I need to be free from conducting to help with a solo mic placement adjustment or a mic adjustment for a doubling change or a page that drops on the floor or an amp problem or to remind the brass to hold up their bells; but I do try to be involved and be part of making music with the band.

When we direct the band, we only occasionally need to actually conduct—fermatas, cut-off's, tempo changes, etc. The majority of the time I am just snapping fingers (or hitting time on my leg) on 2 and 4 in a swing chart or 1 and 3 on Latin, straight-eighth, and fast swing tunes. I think the audience appreciates it when I look involved, so I usually do some conducting on ensemble tutti passages like the shout chorus; and I think it helps the band by providing confirmation for ensemble members who are not positive they know where they are. I also conduct through most of a ballad. I mainly need to direct traffic on the stage—counting off the correct tempo, signaling the ends of open solo sections or vamps, bringing in backgrounds, helping the band through the roadmap, and the like. Arm up to the square (like a right turn hand signal but with a fist) signifies changes are coming. Usually less is more when it comes to conducting, and I never want to get in the way of the rhythm section playing good time. A baton is never necessary and looks out of place on a jazz stage.

I often feel like I am mostly a cheer leader for the band to help them keep focused and to bring out their energy and personal investment. I think it helps if I am relaxed but energetic and smiling and visibly enjoying the music we ase making—invested in the music myself. I also need to be the liason to the audience to announce tunes, acknowledge soloists during or after the piece, acknowledge special guests in the audience, thank sound and lighting people, etc. I try to keep talk in between tunes brief, and sometimes I don't talk at all, rather segue. Sometimes, I need to talk longer to give the bass player a chance to switch from acoustic to electric bass or to help the saxes switch to woodwind doubles. At the end of the concert, I have the band stand up (and usually bow) and again interface with the audience.

Chapter 26   Conclusion and Summary

Well, dear jazz pedagogue, we have come to the end for now. My hope is that if you are a band director without previous jazz experience, you feel a lot more qualified to take on your school jazz band. It is not your fault that your college music education program failed to prepare you for all the requirements of your job. But it will be your fault if you now fail to qualify yourself and cheat your students of the education they deserve. This book has given you a lot of ideas of what you can do on your own to improve yourself and to help your students.

If you have had previous jazz experience, my hope is that you have found a lot of ideas in these pages to strengthen your jazz teaching and your ability to improve on your weaknesses.

What can you do from here to continue learning and improving yourself?

First, there are countless resources outlined in this book for continued growth. Go back and listen to more of the recordings that are referenced. Go back and refer to more of the books that are referenced. Go back and go through more of the play-along resources that are referenced.

Second, attend jazz clinics and demonstrations at your state music educators' conferences. Get involved at the national level as well. The Jazz Education Network is the jazz organization that you should join. (https://www.jazzednet.org/) The JazzEd Magazine that comes with your membership is a worthwhile resource, and attending the national conferences is amazing and well worth the time and money.

Third, there are other jazz pedagogy texts for the teacher that may be helpful in various ways.

- *The Jazz Ensemble Director's Manual*, by Rick Lawn, pub. by Barnhouse—This is quite accurate information by a well-respected player and teacher.

- *Jazz Pedagogy: The Jazz Educator's Handbook and Resource Guide*, by J. Richard Dunscomb and Dr. Willie L. Hill, Jr., published by Alfred—This book tries to be the most complete guide published and comes with a DVD of demonstrations. Some information may be of questionable accuracy particularly in the Jazz Concept Section. (my view)

- *The Jazz Educator's Handbook*, by Jeff Jarvis and Doug Beach, published by Kendor. This book claims to be the "most comprehensive, how-to handbook for jazz educators ever published. This is clearly not true, but there are a lot of helpful ideas for the educator.

- *Teaching Music Through Performance in Jazz, Vol. 1*, by Richard Miles and Ronald Carter, published by GIA Publications. Helpful ideas for working with over 65 common jazz charts (contributions by many great jazz educators—one of the articles is mine).

- *Teaching Music Through Performance in Jazz, Vol.1 CDs*, by Ron Carter and the Northern Illinois University Jazz Ensemble, published by GIA Publications. Two CD set featuring recorded examples of 28 significant jazz charts for the developing and intermediate jazz bands.

- *A New Method for a Tighter Big Band*, by Mats Holmquist, published by Jamey Aebersold Jazz. Lots of valuable ideas!

- *Anyone Can Improvise!* DVD by Jamey Aebersold, published by Jamey Aebersold Jazz. Great!

- *Rhythm Section Workshop for Jazz Directors*, by Shelly Berg, Lou Fischer, Fred Hamilton, and Steve Houghton, published by Alfred. Can be purchased as a complete set or individual books for piano, guitar, bass, drums, and director's teacher training kit, and CD and DVD. Can help you fix rhythm section issues.

- *Jazz Pedagogy*, by David Baker, published by Alfred. Particular aimed at operating a college jazz degree program, but there are useful ideas for all.

- *The Teaching of Jazz*, by Jerry Coker, published by Advance Music. Also, aimed at college jazz teaching, but valuable ideas for all.

- *The Jazzer's Cookbook: Creative Recipes for Players and Teachers*, edited by Mary Jo Papich, published by Meredith Music Publications. Essays on a wide variety of topics by many of the most important jazz educators in this country. (I was privileged to write one of them.)

Fourth, there are several book series that are designed for use in rehearsals with the whole ensemble. These can be useful for training a band.

- *Chop-Monster Series*, Levels 1 and 2, by Shelly Berg, published by Alfred (21 books, score, CD. Jazz language tutor and improvisation method within the ensemble.

- *Essential Elements for Jazz Ensemble*, by Mike Steinel, published by Hal Leonard. Designed to teach jazz basics to students with 1 or 2 years playing experience, but with no prior experience playing jazz. Teaches the basics of swing style in a step-by-step approach using well-known songs.

- *Jazz Conception*, by Jim Snidero, published by Advance Music. Also in Easy and Intermediate versions. Aimed at developing improvisation but can be used by the entire ensemble (separate books are published for all instruments but are coordinated).

Fifth, perhaps your greatest resource is Jamey Aebersold's website (www.jazzbooks.com). This is the most complete resource for materials for jazz pedagogy, improvisation, rhythm section developmental materials, jazz ear training, jazz theory, jazz videos or DVD's, jazz play-alongs, and even real jazz recordings for listening. Every book mentioned above is available from Jamey.

Sixth, don't forget about A-ccompany for help with training your band, (see Chapter 14) as well as Tutti (also Chapter 14). These are incredible tools for the band director and the students!!

Seventh, use funds from the band kitty or parents' band booster organization to bring in expert guest clinicians. This is a big help for the students but maybe an even bigger help for the band director. I have seen guests come, and the band director spends his time in the office. What a mistake! The conscientious band director will be watching carefully and taking notes, maybe even asking questions.

Eighth, take advantage of summer training opportunities such as summer jazz workshops and the like. You could actually participate in one of Jamey Aebersold's Summer Jazz Workshops.. Essentially Ellington is providing some first-class training opportunities for educators with amazing clinicians. (see jazz.org or jazz.org/ee) In some cases, the school may be willing to help with some expenses related to professional development. (This may also apply to professional memberships or conference attendance such as JEN—Jazz Education Network.)

Last but not least, it is possible to find tutorials and help for nearly any question these days simply by researching on the internet. It is amazing what you can run into online. Don't forget to "ask Siri" or "Alexa" or "Google Assistant".

We have, in this volume, worked to build upon your previous music education training as we have worked through teaching the basics of tone production, intonation, balance and blend, section playing, swing style articulation and rhythm and application to other styles, rhythm section functions and development, improvisational development and working with your soloists including your ballad soloist and vocal soloist, taking care of the business of chart selection and programming, and finally concert and festival performance issues. YOU can create an excellent jazz ensemble that excels in all four of our areas—basic instrumental playing skills, stylistic understanding, a functioning rhythm section, and great soloists!

Never at any time has there been so much help for a band director to become proficient in jazz. Remember Bob and Janis from Chapter 1? If they can do it, we can all do it—including YOU. Have a great trip, and don't forget to enjoy the journey. This is fun and very rewarding!!

Section 7

Appendices:
Don't Have These Removed!

This will help, not hurt . . .

Appendix A Big Band Setup

Physical Setup of the Big Band

The physical setup, or seating arrangement, of the ensemble can have a profound influence on the performance in terms of balance and precision. Where students are sitting in relation to each other affects how well they hear each other and play together.

The block formation is the setup I would recommend for middle and high school jazz bands:

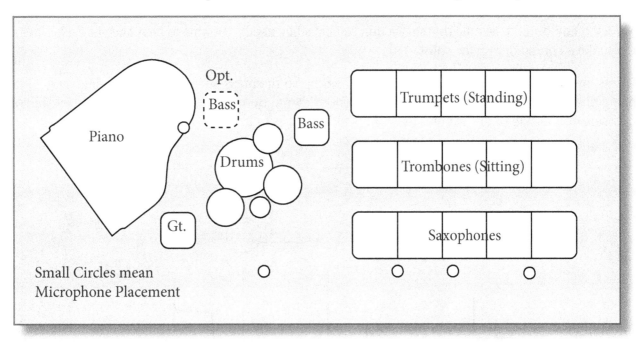

When using this block set up, there are different options for the seating order of each section:

    Trumpets: 2-1-3-4 OR 5-2-1-3-4 OR 3-2-1-4-5 OR 5-4-1-2-3 OR 4-2-1-3-

    Trombones: 2-1-3-4 OR 3-2-1-4-5 OR 5-4-1-2-3 OR 4-2-1-3-5

    Saxophones: T1-A2-A1-T2-B OR B-T2-A1-A2-T1 (if bones are 5-4-1-2-3)

The first two seating orders, in each case, are my personal preferences.

The mic's shown in the block setup diagram above would be for a smaller-type set up. Or the setup can go even simpler, just mic'ing the piano and soloists.

If you have sound people you can trust, the mic setup can go anywhere from this small setup all the way to tight mic'ing the entire ensemble (a separate microphone for each player).

A Few Thoughts to Keep in Mind

• The ensemble should not be spread out too far.

• The rhythm section needs to be as close as possible to the ensemble and to each other.

• The bass player can be positioned behind the drummer's hi-hat as pictured, or he can be between the piano and drums.

• The guitarist should at the front where good aural and visual communication is possible with the pianist.

• Lead players should always be in the center of their sections (not on the end).

• The bass trombone and the baritone sax need to be on the same side of the ensemble.

• Soloists should stand near the rhythm section because they need to be able to hear and see each other and work like a combo during the solos.

• Risers are recommended when using the block set up so the brass sound reaches the audience without being blocked or absorbed by the players in front of them. Some directors also put the drums and bass on risers, to the side of the trombones.

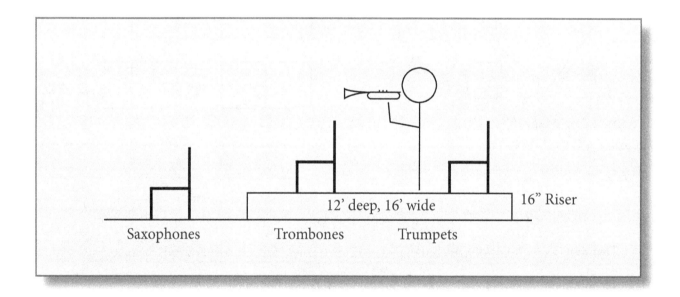

Saxophones   Trombones   Trumpets

12' deep, 16' wide   16" Riser

• Note that the height of the brass riser should be 16" to get brass bells above the saxes. The terraced effect, which is good for both visual and sonic reasons, is achieved when the trombones sit and the trumpets stand on the same height riser. (Festivals usually haven't figured this out for some reason, and they provide an 8" riser for trombones. This is inadequate, so I would get the trombones to aim their bells between the saxophones in that case.)

• If I don't know and trust the person running the sound system, I would keep it simple as in the block formation setup. And I keep the saxophone mics facing toward the audience until I need them for solos or doubles like flutes and clarinets. If you have a sound man you can trust, then you may decide to use a more complex sound reinforcement design.

Appendix B   Equipment Recommendations for the Wind Players in the Jazz Band

Here are a few recommendations to help with gear selection for the horn players in the band.

Saxophone

The saxophone is a woodwind instrument in the concert band but a brass instrument in the jazz band. Part of making that change is the mouthpiece. Jazz mouthpieces can be very expensive, and it may be impractical for all the students to own their own jazz mouthpiece. Some schools own a set of jazz mouthpieces that can be checked out by those who win those chairs. It is imperative that there is not a mix of jazz and classical mouthpieces in your section. Some jazz mouthpieces in common use would include:

Mouthpieces

- Alto—Jody Jazz Jet 7, Jody Jazz DV 7, Beechler L6S, Meyer 6-8 with medium facing and either small or medium chamber, MacSax (Eric Falcon)—especially the Bob Shepperd Series

- Tenor—Jody Jazz Jet 7-8, Jody Jazz DV 8, Jody Jazz Chicago 8, Yanigasawa metal 7-8, Otto Link 7-8, Dukoff 7 or 8 metal, MacSax (Eric Falcon)—especially the Bob Shepperd Series

- Baritone—Jody Jazz Jet 8 or 8*, Jody Jazz DV 8 or 8*, Yanigasawa 7 or 8 metal, Rousseau JDX6 or 7, MacSax (Eric Falcon)

- Soprano—Jody Jazz DV 6*, Otto Link 6-8* Hard Rubber, Rousseau 6r-8r, Jody Jazz hard rubber 6-8, MacSax (Eric Falcon)

Ligatures

For all: The Rovner Light model works well and is readily available and relatively inexpensive. The D'Addario H ligatures also work well and are relatively inexpensive. The Vandoren optimum ligatures also work well and are more expensive. Silverstein ligatures are terrific, but very expensive.

Reeds

For all: The D'Addario Rico Select Jazz Reeds work very well. The Vandoren, Rico Reserve, and other standard reeds can also work well. The Select Jazz Reeds seem to require the least work to make them work and keep them working these days.

Instruments

There are many instruments out there these days. I used to have to say, "Well, there is the Selmer, and then there is....uh......uh.......well, not much else." The landscape has really changed. Selmer is still making good instruments, but now there is Yamaha, Keilwerth, Yanagisawa, Eastman, and others. But for my money, the Cannonball Saxophone is unsurpassed! If I were recommending a saxophone to a student, I would recommend trying first the Cannonball Stone Series or Vintage Instruments. If that does not seem happy, I would suggest next trying the Yamaha Custom 875EX or the Eastman 52nd Street line.

Trumpet

Mouthpieces

Jazz trumpet mouthpieces in common use are The Bobby Shew Jazz Mouthpiece (section and solo) and the Bobby Shew Lead Trumpet Mouthpiece made by Yamaha; Joe Marcinkiewicz jazz mouthpieces—particularly the Jeff Tyzik, Bobby Shew, Roger Ingram, and Eric Miyashiro models; Warburton 5SV with KT Backbore or other small backbores (4, 5, 6); Bob Reeves 41M, 42M, or 43M with #2 smaller backbore; the GR Wayne Bergeron Mouthpiece either Studio or Studio M model; some Bach mouthpieces are also still in use such as the Bach 3C Megatone (section or solo), Bach 17C1 (also not a lead mouthpiece).

It's very important for your lead trumpet player to have a mouthpiece that is specifically designed for playing high. Most of the mouthpieces listed above are good for that unless otherwise noted. If you want to keep on the end of your tongue one lead mouthpiece recommendation, it would probably be safe to say the Yamaha Bobby Shew Lead model.

Instruments

Some trumpets are specifically well-fitted to jazz. These would include the Yamaha 8310Z Bobby Shew Model or the 8340EM, the Cannonball Lynx (especially good for lead) and the 42 Artist Series; the Schilke B5 and S42; the Benge Burbank; the Bach Stradivarius 37, and the Jupiter Roger Ingram 1600i.

With a number of trumpet players I know, there is a lot of excitement about how easy it is to play the relatively newer Cannonball trumpets.

Trumpet players also need to double on flugelhorn at times. It is common for the school to own flugelhorns that can be checked out. Most common are: Yamaha 631, 731, or the Bobby Shew or Wayne Bergeron Models; Couesnon; Schilke; Benge #3, #1 bells; Bach Stradivarius; or the Jupiter Flugelhorn.

Trombone

Mouthpieces

- Tenor Trombone—the best all-around mouthpieces include the Yamaha 46, 47 or 48 (48 better for section work) and the Bach 6.5AL—has good core to sound and can work for lead. Other lead mouthpieces (easier to play high) include: Bach 11C or 12C, King 21M, and the Yamaha 46C2.

- Bass Trombone—Common are the Bach 1¼G, 1½G, or 2G; also the Schilke 59 and the Griego .75 mouthpieces.

Instruments

- Tenor Trombone—the tenor trombones in a jazz band should be small bore horns when possible. The most common small-bore horns in use for jazz band are the King 2B, Conn 6H, and the Yamaha 697Z or 891Z. The best balance and blend is achieved when all the tenor trombones play small-bore horns. The orchestral trombones are larger bores. This may not always be practical, but we can sstill work towards it. Some schools own small-bore horns that can be checked out for jazz band students.

- Bass Trombone—the most commonly used bass trombones include those made by Yamaha, Edwards, and Conn. The important thing here is that the instrument have two triggers (or valves). The single trigger instruments cannot easily play a low B or C which are often written.

Appendix C Ideas for Applying the Concepts of This Book to Private Jazz Teaching

If you are a private jazz teacher, you can certainly make your own applications of many parts of this book, but I will offer a few thoughts from my experience.

Is it Different? Principles Are the Same

I would first point out that we are teaching the same things whether in the classroom with a group or in a one-on-one private lesson. Many of the teaching strategies I use in the classroom are those I have developed while experimenting in private lessons. On the other hand, I use many of the same pedagogical approaches I have developed in ensemble rehearsals when I am teaching privately. While the content of this book is especially aimed at the school jazz band director (whether junior high school, senior high school, or college), much of the content can be applied with equal effectiveness by the private studio teacher.

One of the greatest mayors ever to serve in our country was once asked how he did such a great job governing the people of his city. He responded, "I teach them true principles, and they govern themselves." That is my philosophy in both the classroom and the private studio. I teach the same principles either way, and the students can govern themselves accordingly in their private practice and in the ensemble rehearsal.

What are the basic principles that we must be sure we are teaching? I think they fall into a few general categories.

Playing the Instrument

We must teach the principles of basic sound production, articulation, and technique. This includes teaching concepts and techniques for playing in tune and would include techniques for producing vibrato and other idiomatic effects. There are many helpful ideas that can aid the private studio teacher in Chapters 2, 3, and 4 for wind instruments and Chapters 14, 16, and 17 for rhythm section instruments. I believe development in this area is enhanced and accelerated by working on the instrument classically.

Playing the Style

We must teach the rhythmic aspects and the articulation associated with various styles. There is a lot of help for these issues in Chapters 7, 8, 9, 10, and 11 for all instruments. Chapter 14 outlines many resources that can be very valuable in private lessons for rhythm section players.

Playing the Solos

I find that a lot of my private lesson time is spent working on improvisation. The principles for developing as soloists are the same for all the instruments, and there are a lot of helpful ideas given in Chapters 19, 20, 21, 22, and 23. Additional specific help for rhythm section soloists is given in Chapter 18.

We Must Do the Whole Job

When I take over a student from a previous teacher, I seem to find typically that one or more of the above pedagogical areas has been slighted or left undone. I may get a student who has done well with listening and imitation but has left out stylistic articulation. Or another student has worked a lot on technique but has done little about tone or intonation. Another student has worked on the instrument classically but has done little with improvisation, or has worked on jazz concepts but has done no classical study on his instrument. We need to set up a curriculum in the private studio that covers all of the bases and leaves out none. Some have done nothing about expected doubles for that instrument.

One of the challenges I have found with this is that during the school year the student will frequently come in with a need for his school band. For example, a student comes to the lesson and announces that his school jazz band concert is next week, and he is concerned about a couple of solos that he would like help with. Another week it is something else. It is easy to get into what I call a "band-aid curriculum". The student comes in each week, and I put a band aid on whatever is hurting that week. I think it is a good idea to help the student with the solo they will be playing because they have an immediate opportunity to apply in context the things they have just learned. That is powerful, so I don't begrudge doing it; but I think we do have to be careful to keep a more organized curriculum going as much as possible.

Classical Work

I have had a few experiences that have convinced me that I must not let any of my students slide through without working on classical playing. It is in classical work that we come face to face with the rigors and discipline of really controlling the instrument. This control, of course, also helps their jazz playing. I have noticed that the focus of the lesson shifts depending on the material being worked on in the lessons. If I am working with a student on improvisation, the lesson focus seems to go towards the chord progression and guide tones and improvisational ideas and approaches. If I am working with a student on a classical piece, the focus immediately shifts to tone, vibrato, intonation, soundness of technique and the like. By the time I have worked on both styles with a student, they become a much stronger musician all around.

In the earlier days, I would allow a high school student to work on only jazz with me. Then they would come to the university and get into my band. I would be pulling my hair out in the rehearsal with simple issues of intonation and high note tone production that we would have dealt with had we spent time on the horn classically. I should add that it doesn't have to be this way; it just tends to be this way. In other words, while working on jazz with a student, I could make sure to notice and offer help more with tone issues and intonation and similar issues; and that is what I try to do better now. I still don't think, however, that we will get everything done without the classical work. I certainly recognize that my students are not going to make a living playing the classical saxophone, but they will be more complete musicians and better saxophonists if they have had to deal with the instrument classically.

Organizing to Do it All

Of course, there is just not enough time to do everything every week in an hour lesson (and certainly not in a half hour lesson, which is something I never do). So it seems we have to go through various seasons in the lessons. Sometimes we are in a jazz season where that is our focus for a time—example would be getting ready for all-state jazz auditions. Other times we are in a classical season for a few weeks or two or three months—example would be getting ready for solo/ensemble festival. We may take a season of working on etudes or transcribed solos to really perfect stylistic articulation and then switch to a season of working on tunes for improvisational development. This seems to work. The thing that matters is that all the critical things we need to teach get a season. With some students, I have alternated weeks on classical and jazz. And the seasons continually rotate in what Jerome Bruner called the "spiral curriculum". We keep circling through the various topics, but the circle is spiraling upwards. Each time we revisit a topic, we are at a higher level.

Whether you are teaching in a classroom or in your private studio, do the job!! Don't leave things to chance or leave them undone. Earn your pay honestly. When students work with you, they are getting better, and they are very competitive with students from other schools and other studios. Few things are more rewarding!

Appendix D   Applications to Vocal Jazz Pedagogy

Vocal jazz teachers, both private and ensemble coaches, will find tremendous application of the principles in this book to their work. Chapter 1 certainly applies to all aspiring teachers, and I believe the measuring standards for excellence set forth there are the same for vocal jazz ensembles: 1) great vocal production and section/ensemble singing skills, 2) solid rhythm and articulation appropriate to the style, 3) strong rhythm section playing, and 4) excellent soloists.

In Section 2 (Chapters 2-6) there is information specifically about instrumental issues of tone production, doubling, and so forth that are not directly applicable to the singer; but some of the information is valuable to singers. For example, ideas for dealing with issues of intonation, balance and blend, and section work will be helpful.

The information and approaches in Section 3 (Chapters 7-13) are clearly of equal application to singers and instrumentalists. Singers need to worry about time feel and rhythmic accuracy and swinging. Articulation is just as important to singers, and I am often dismayed when I adjudicate vocal jazz groups that no thought has been given to articulation when deciding how to pronounce the words. For example, if a syncopated quarter note should be articulated short to swing properly, then the word that goes with that rhythm should have a short pronunciation. It appears that many coaches are oblivious to this issue. The percussiveness of attacks should also be the same. The information on applications to different styles in Chapters 10 and 11 is also equally valuable to vocalists, as are the rehearsal techniques outlined in Chapter 12.

Section 4 (Chapters 14-18) deals with rhythm section issues. Since the vocal jazz ensemble normally has a rhythm section, these approaches are equally valid for working with the players accompanying a vocal group—including the ideas for the drummer setting up figures and delineating form, and the bass and drums working together, and the guitar and piano coordinating their comping.

The approaches to dealing with improvisation and soloists in Section 5 (Chapters 19-23) should be no different in my mind for serious vocal soloists. It is true that a vocal soloist with understanding of theory or any of the left brain concepts is rare, but it should not be that way. When I have heard strong scat soloists while adjudicating and I inquire, they are almost invariably instrumentalists who could do the same on their instrument. I have personally had private jazz vocal students, who I have had work on the chord study (arpeggiating chords) and singing scales and patterns, and singing guide tones, who started being able to scat in the changes with strong jazz vocabulary. This is an obvious and glaring omission in most vocal jazz programs. Years ago, I had a name jazz singer as a guest artist with my big band. During the concert, she surprised me when she decided to engage me in a scat battle. I'm sorry to say I buried her, and it is clearly because I had worked on the needed skills instrumentally. I believe Section 5 is especially valuable to jazz singers, and Chapter 23 gives some good ideas for the developing vocal soloist with the big band including help with scat syllables (which are often corny and misguided).

The ideas in Section 6 on aspects of running a program in the school, developing literature, approaching competition, programming, and stage fright are certainly applicable to all. No, this is not intended to be the end-all guide for jazz vocal teaching, and no, I have not made direct applications to vocal pedagogy in my text; but I think a conscientious teacher will find tremendous value in this book by making their own applications of all the principles and approaches to the vocal studio and the vocal ensemble program.

Movement in Performance

Let me just add a word about movement in performance. When I first started adjudicating vocal jazz ensemble performances, I had to make some decisions about how I felt about the "choreography" and extra-musical movement in many of these performances. This is often a trademark of this type of ensemble. For what it is worth, I personally find little value in Broadway-type synchronized movement. It is often excessive and distracting from the music. I don't have a problem with some movement, but I think it should grow naturally out of the music and probably does not need to be coordinated or synchronized within the group.

Broadway Swing

And that reminds me of another pet peeve I have about the approach of many jazz vocal teachers. So much of what I hear is what I would call Broadway Swing. The problem with Broadway Swing is that it doesn't swing, and often the vibrato is more classical (or at least Broadway) than it is jazz. I find myself coaching singers with my ensemble away from these aspects of the Broadway they seem all too familiar with—not that I have a problem with Broadway. I have spent many hours of my life in pit orchestras and have recorded scores of musicals that are being used all over the country. But the Broadway approach is not usually a true jazz approach, and that is what I believe we should be using in the school jazz programs.

After all is said and done, I find myself often saying to my instrumentalists, "This should be done like a singer would do it. It should not sound like you are pushing buttons and tonguing." On the other hand, I find myself saying to my singers, "Handle this more like a horn player would do it."

Appendix E   Tuning the Saxophone Section

[This is an article I wrote many years ago for the NAJE publication, *Jazz Educators Journal*, which has not existed for many years now. (The parent organization went defunct.) Over the years, I have had many band directors from around the country tell me the article has been very helpful, and they use it regularly as a handout. So I repeat it here in case it can be of value to you in your work.]

Help! Why Can't the Saxophone Section Play in Tune?

Probably at least five or six times per year I get a phone call from a band director in distress ready to pull his hair out over the intonation in the saxophone section. Some years ago, I was adjudicating at a local jazz festival. After four bands, the fifth band took the stage and began to tune. Realizing the saxophone tuning was quite grim and knowing I was a saxophonist, the band director, who was not a wind player, called loudly to the back of the hall, "Ray, what do I do with these saxes?" I have a feeling there are many directors across the country who have the same question, and they deserve a good answer.

The usual quick-fix answer is to pull out the mouthpiece, since intermediate players almost always have a problem with sharpness. It is a common thing to see paper wrapped around the cork to keep the mouthpiece from falling off the neckpiece. But pulling the mouthpiece will attack only the symptom, not the root of the problem. The real answer is a much longer-range proposition that will probably even involve pushing in the mouthpiece instead of pulling it.

The Root of the Problem

Undoubtedly, the most frequent problem I have observed in young saxophonists is playing at the wrong basic pitch level on the mouthpiece alone. It is possible when blowing only the mouthpiece to play well over an octave of pitches. Indeed, full scales and arpeggios can be played on the mouthpiece. This makes a wonderful exercise for the development of flexibility but raises the question of where one should stabilize his blowing for normal tone production. The correct answer is critical to the development of intonation. Dr. Eugene Rousseau, world-renowned saxophonist, suggests the following pitches for the respective instruments.[1]

These are concert pitches to be achieved at a fortissimo level. I have found these pitches to be accurate guides, although I have found some jazz players play even slightly lower. This seems especially true for the tenor, which can tend to be closer to an F# at times.

I have done considerable mouthpiece-pitch testing over the years—both formal[2] and informal. Students always tend to play anywhere from a half-step to a major third too high on the mouthpiece. This triggers what I call the Saxophone Syndrome.

The Saxophone Syndrome

To illustrate the syndrome, let's take an example of an alto saxophone player who plays too high in the mouthpiece pitch, say around a B. His notes will be above the center of the tone and he will have to pull the mouthpiece out considerably from where it belongs to get his high notes down to the level of the band. This exaggerated pulling of the mouthpiece will distort the basic internal proportions of the instrument causing the low notes to go flat and the normal response patterns to be interrupted. The tone will still not be centered and some notes will be affected more than others. Consequently, the intervalic relationships of the instrument will lose their integrity, and the effect will be like being on a slippery slide of pitch every time the fingering is changed. When everyone in the saxophone section is having this problem, it becomes nearly impossible to match pitches consistently.

A Solution

Embouchure

Getting young saxophonists to bring the mouthpiece pitch down is a challenge, but this is the key to achieving a lasting solution for pitch problems. Obtaining the right mouthpiece pitch is a blending of several factors—correct saxophone embouchure, air stream type, oral cavity, and air stream direction. When I first tried to make the change from clarinet to saxophone, my well-meaning band director said, "Use the upper register clarinet fingerings for both registers of the saxophone and play with a sloppy embouchure." This was the only guidance I had for some years. The saxophone embouchure is not a sloppy embouchure, but it is very different from the clarinet. When I teach the clarinet embouchure, I compare it to a tug-of-war between the smile muscles (EE) and the pucker muscles (OO). The tug-of-war must be held in equilibrium; and if either side wins, you lose. But on the saxophone, the OO wins the tug-of-war. The embouchure should be round, giving solid support all around the mouthpiece. This may be compared to the closure of a drawstring purse or duffel bag. When the strings are pulled, the closure is even from all sides simultaneously. To form the saxophone embouchure, I would have the student follow these steps.

1. Curl the lower lip slightly over the teeth (no more than the red part of the lip should be curled into the mouth).[3]

2. Insert the mouthpiece into the mouth placing the top teeth solidly on the mouthpiece.

3. Effect the drawstring (round) closure.

The flat or pointed chin associated with the clarinet is not important and should be avoided.

Air Stream Type

The type of air stream used in saxophone playing also differs from the clarinet. The clarinet uses a pinpointed, concentrated, cool air stream analogous to the air stream used when blowing on hot soup to cool it. The saxophone responds better to a wider, less-concentrated, warmer air stream more similar to the air stream used for fogging one's glasses for cleaning purposes.

If a saxophonist plays with a clarinet-influenced embouchure and air stream, the reed will be encouraged to vibrate too fast and the mouthpiece pitch will be too high.

As with all wind instruments, the saxophone requires an open, relaxed throat; but the exact feel of the oral cavity and throat will be affected by the air stream direction. Air stream direction is another major difference between clarinet and saxophone tone production. The clarinet tone quality depends on blowing at the top of the mouthpiece pitch range (a concert C) which leads to a feeling that one is blowing up. The saxophone tone quality depends on blowing about a third below the top of the mouthpiece pitch range which creates a feeling inside the mouth of blowing down. Eugene Rousseau uses these terms when discussing how to get the mouthpiece pitch down to the suggested concert pitch.

If the pitch on the mouthpiece alone is higher than [the suggested pitches given earlier], direct the air stream down, remembering always to keep the embouchure solid. If the pitch on the mouthpiece alone is too low, direct the air stream up. In either case, never loosen the embouchure, which should remain solid at all times, while the air does its job properly.[4]

This ability to change pitch downward without loosening the embouchure is an essential coordination for achieving correct mouthpiece pitch level and for adjusting pitch for specific notes on the saxophone.

The following exercise was given to me by Eugene Rousseau several years ago. It is a little tricky to teach, but if the student can get the feel of it, control over tone and pitch will be greatly enhanced.

The entire line is fingered like high D while the lower pitches in parentheses are played by directing the air stream down with the embouchure remaining solid.

This exercise opens the door to dealing with the most difficult notes to play in tune on the saxophone. Because of octave key hole placement compromises made in the construction of the saxophone, certain notes are difficult problems on any saxophone—student or professional. Most band directors will recognize these traditional "sore thumb" notes: fourth line D and D#, fourth space E, A and B just above the staff . When one tries to lip down on these very sharp notes, the tone spreads and leaves much to be desired. But when the embouchure is kept solidly focused and the air stream is directed down, the centers of these notes can be found resulting in a pleasing tone and good intonation.

When the student is finally able to control all the factors so he can blow consistently at the correct mouthpiece pitch level, then the mouthpiece can be pushed back in on the cork to a position more consistent with where the instrument is made to play. At this point tones begin to center, the upper and lower registers line up so that octaves are in tune, and intervals tend to be in tune without having to "search" for each note. Now we've got a fighting chance of working together in the saxophone section.

An Approach

Stabilizing Mouthpiece Pitch

Let me now suggest an approach for applying the mouthpiece pitch concept and add two other significant companion concepts. After teaching the basic technique for embouchure, breath support, air stream type, and oral cavity, I would set up a regular routine for stabilizing the correct mouthpiece pitch. This routine must involve testing the pitch daily and then repeatedly attacking and holding the correct pitch for 2-5 minutes. Normally, the first test of mouthpiece pitch each day will be too high. The correct pitch can be sounded and students can be asked to match it. This could be incorporated briefly into the time allotted for the band warm-up. When students learn the procedure, they can be encouraged (assigned) to spend more time with it on their own. As the exercise is consistently applied, the first pitch test of each day will get closer to the correct pitch until finally the student is able, through feel and muscle-memory, to play the correct pitch upon request at any time without reference to a pitch standard. This is what is meant by stabilizing the pitch at that level.

Listening to Good Tone

Along with the mouthpiece routine, it is imperative that the student be involved intensively in listening to the great models for his instrument—Bird, Cannonball, Trane, Rollins, Mulligan, etc. It is even more valuable if this listening also grows into transcribing. These listening and transcribing experiences "program" into the student a concept of tone that ultimately must be there to allow the sum of the parts to reach an acceptable end product.

Centering the Tone

Another important concept that I would cover simultaneously is the centering of the tone. Centering tone quality and arriving at the correct pitch for a note are on the same continuum and ideally occur at the same moment. It is possible to manipulate a note into pitch without finding the tone center, but it is not likely that one will find the tone center without finding the pitch at the same time. The easiest way I have found to communicate the idea of centering to young students is the analogy of the radio. Every station received by a radio has an exact setting on the tuner. A station will come through clearly and sound best when the tuner reaches the exact position for that station. If the tuner is only slightly too high or too low, static will result and clarity is lost. If the tuner is too far away, the station is lost altogether. Different notes on the instrument are like the different stations and need to be tuned-in with the right embouchure-air setting. If these settings are not precise or centered, poor tone, poor intonation, and sometimes squeaks and indefinite sounds result. [This was a great metaphor in 1987. Now with digital tuners doing most of the work, the metaphor is beginning to lose power, although I have found most of my young students still understand it and find value in it.]

An aural concept of centering or resonance can then be engendered by the instructor performing on his instrument several contrasting examples of centered and uncentered tones.

More difficult than helping the students grasp the concept of centering is the challenge of helping them move from the abstract concept to a concrete experience with centering on their instruments. Once they feel the sensation and hear the sound of a few centered notes, the students will be well on their way to improving their tone quality and intonation.

One method I have found useful for helping the students establish air control for centering tones involves playing a nursery rhyme tune or any short sequence of pitches on the instrument. After the students play the tune on their instruments, they should be instructed to sing the tune at the same pitch level. Then they should blow through the tune at the same pitch level using only the air stream. This is done by blowing air through the lips while pronouncing the syllable "HOO." This will result in a specific half-whistled pitch which can be controlled to blow the exact pitches of the tune. It is important that this blowing step be done at a healthy, loud energy level. The student should then immediately play the tune on their instruments again with no delay. If this is done properly, the result will be astonishing. The tones will sound much better-centered and bigger and will feel much freer and easier to the students. The students will have experienced a concrete referent for the concept of centering. This little formula—play it, sing it, blow it (with the air stream), and play it again—can be applied on an on-going basis to other tunes, excerpts, etc.[5] I frequently use this method with my whole big band, and the results are always akin to magic.

Conclusion

Teaching these concepts and techniques takes a little more effort and follow through than yelling, "Tune that up, saxes!" But the conscientious educator will see the need for getting at the real root of the problem. Students who master blowing at the correct pitch level and strive for centered tones based on the tonal memory developed from listening hours are in a position to make real strides in intonation. When the whole section is in this position, then traditional approaches to working on intonation in the sectional will yield exceptional results.

(I will demonstrate these concepts in the videos for the book.)

Footnotes

1. Eugene Rousseau, *Saxophone High Tones* (Bloomington, Indiana: Etoile Music, 1987), p.7.

2. Charles R. Smith, "A Comparative Study of Blowing Pressure and Air Flow Rate in Clarinet and Saxophone Performance" (Doctoral Document, Indiana University, 1982), pp. 67-69.

3. Another school of embouchure would suggest turning the lower lip out slightly. Either way there should be no heavy biting, and the feeling of the lower lip cushion should be a "fat lip" feel.

4. Rousseau, p. 7.

5. K. Newell Dayley, *Developmental Exercises for the Breath, Tongue, and Embouchure* (Provo, Utah: Brigham Young University, 1970), pp. 5-6.

Appendix F   Helps for Intonation Work

The following three pages are intonation pages written by my good friend, Greg Yasinitsky, professor at Washington State University in Pulman. Greg is a fine saxophonist, composer/arranger, and a wonderful teacher. He has for years been the force behind the award-winning WSU Jazz Ensemble. He has been gracious to give permission to share these intonation excercises with you.

When we are tuning the jazz band, we encounter complex and high-tension chords that are different than most of the chords we have to tune in the concert symphonic band. The students come into our ensembles not knowing how to hear their position in these chords. It takes some practice to know how to play in tune in these types of chords.

Tuning Chords #3 is geared to junior high school/middle school level.

Tuning Chords #2 is geared to high school level.

Tuning Chords #1 is geared to the college level.

Of course, you can use any level that is suited to your band; and if you have a very strong high school band, I would recommend also using the college level sheet. In fact, it would probably be wise to use all three—start with the most basic and work up to the more advanced. You may make copies freely as needed for use in your rehearsals.

It may be necessary to take apart some of these chords in the rehearsal and just hear the saxes, then the trombones, then the saxes and trombones together, then only the trumpets together, and finally everyone together. It may also really help to have the 5th (or 4th) players of each section tune, then the thirds of each section, then the seconds of each section, and then the leads of each section.

It will be important to try to eliminate clutter in the sounds of the chords (caused by intonation problems). Work until there is a clear ring to the chords; and, in fact, you should hear a small ring (or resonance) in the room when you cut off the band if the chord is in tune.

This can be a great part of your band warmup!

(All Tuning Chord pages used by permission, Yazz Music.)

TUNING CHORDS #1

Greg Yasinitsky

Transposed Score

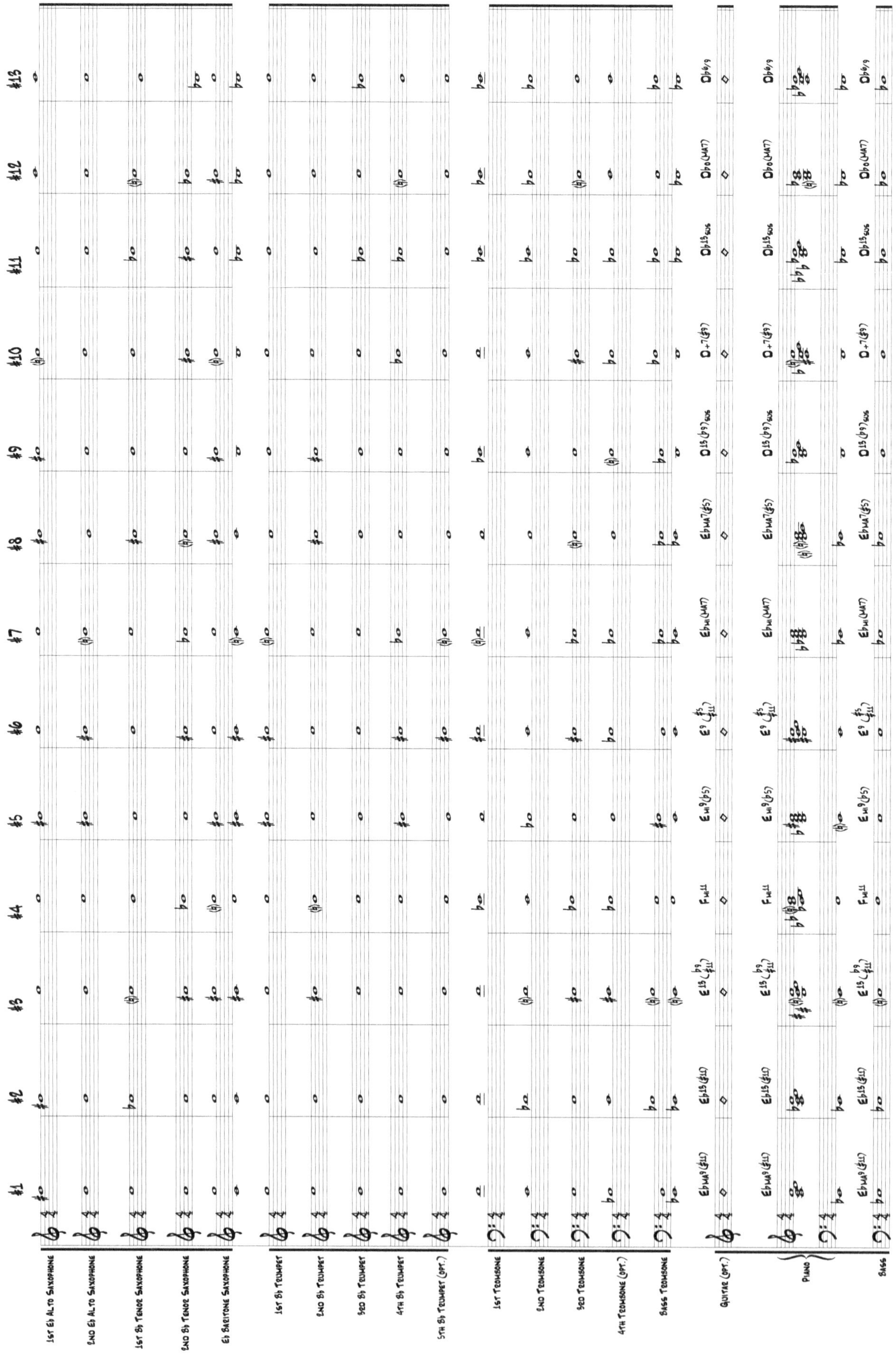

Transposed Score

TUNING CHORDS #2

Greg Yasinitsky

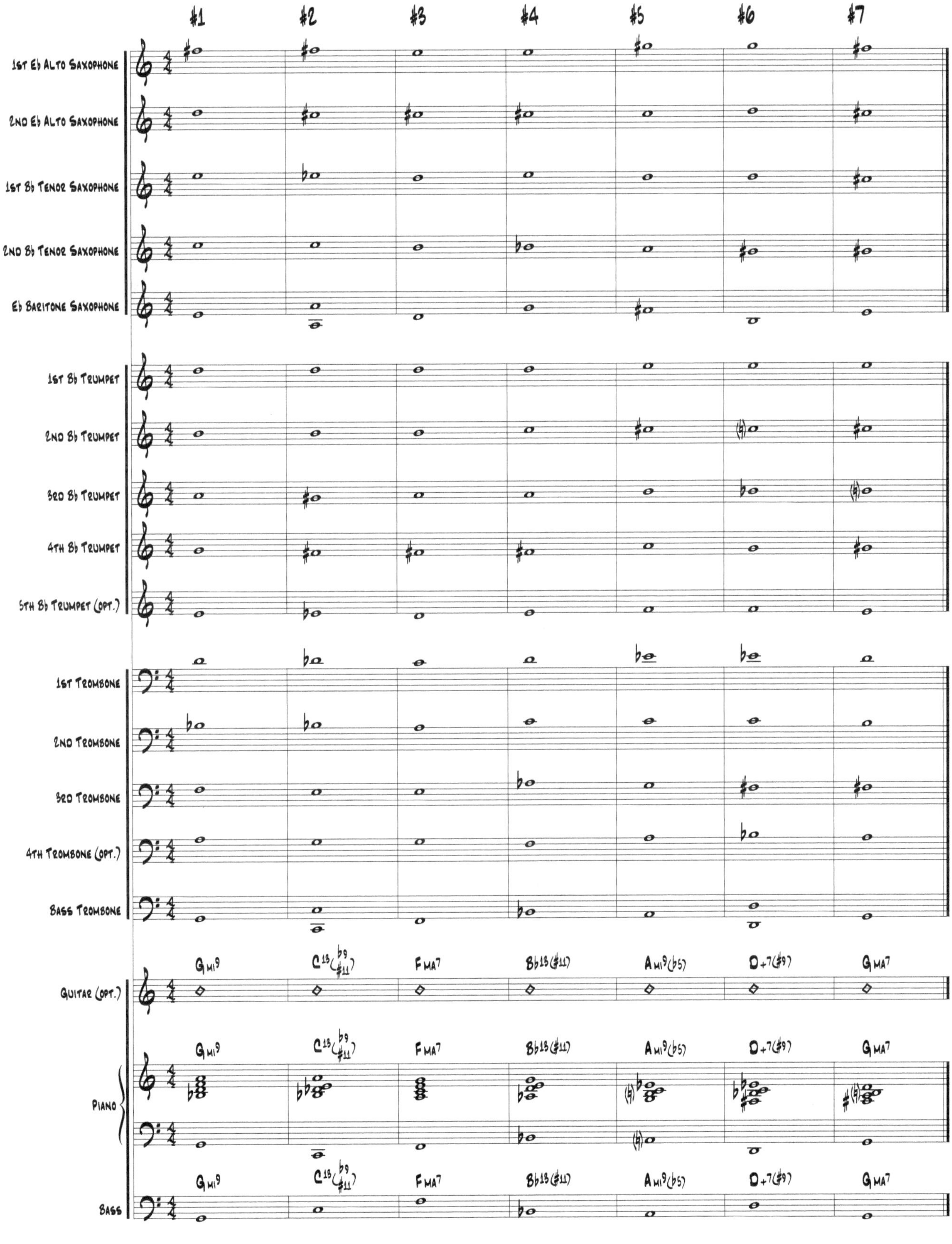

Greg Yasinitsky

TUNING CHORDS #3

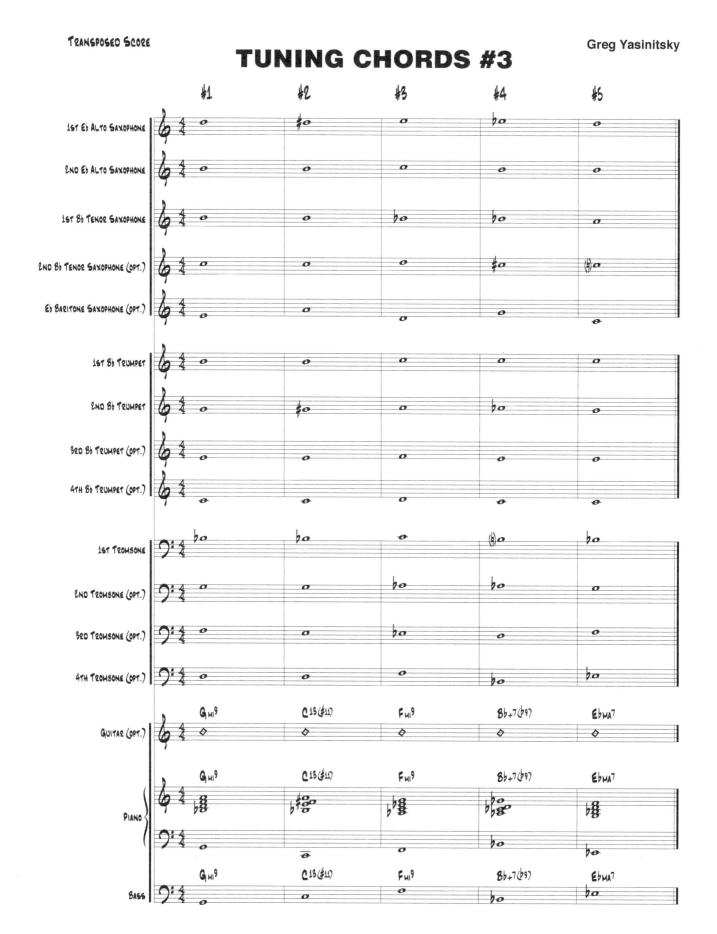

Appendix F Helps for Intonation Work | Page 234

Printed in the USA
CPSIA information can be obtained
at www.ICGtesting.com
LVHW081041201223
766919LV00006B/116